# The Life and Times of General China

# The Life and Times of General China

## Mau Mau and the End of Empire in Kenya

Edited by Myles Osborne

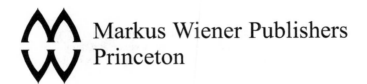

Markus Wiener Publishers
Princeton

Cover design by Noah Wiener
*Cover image, center:* General China in 1954.

For information, write to: Markus Wiener Publishers
231 Nassau Street, Princeton, NJ 08542
www.markuswiener.com

**Library of Congress Cataloging-in-Publication Data**

The life and times of General China : Mau Mau and the end of empire in Kenya / edited by Myles Osborne.
    pages cm
  Chapter 1 is an abridged version of Waruhiu Itote's "Mau Mau" General, originally published in 1967 by East African Publishing House.
  Includes bibliographical references.
  ISBN 978-1-55876-596-2 (hardcover : alk. paper)
  ISBN 978-1-55876-597-9 (pbk. : alk. paper)
  1. Itote, Waruhiu, 1922-1993. 2. Itote, Waruhiu, 1922-1993—Trials, litigation, etc.—Sources. 3. Mau Mau—Biography. 4. Kenya—History—Mau Mau Emergency, 1952-1960—Personal narratives, Kenyan. 5. Kenya—History—Mau Mau Emergency, 1952-1960—Sources. 6. Insurgency—Kenya. 7. Decolonization—Kenya.
I. Itote, Waruhiu, 1922-1993, author. II. Osborne, Myles, editor of compilation, author. III. Itote, Waruhiu, 1922-1993. "Mau Mau" general. Selections. Contains (work):
  DT433.576.I86L54 2015
  967.6203--dc23

2014034695

*For John Nottingham*

# Contents

# Acknowledgments

This book's initial kernel of inspiration came on a chilly Nairobi afternoon in August 2005. I had just finished reading the interrogation of "General China"—birth name Waruhiu Itote—in the long, dusty reading room of the Kenya National Archives. China was one of the central and most controversial figures in the Mau Mau uprising, and the transcript of his interrogation made for fascinating reading. This was largely because it seemed to gel little with what I knew about China from his memoir— *"Mau Mau" General*—or several other sources.

These discrepancies were still on my mind when I arrived at John Nottingham's office, a five-minute walk away from the archives on Kimathi Street. Nottingham is one of Kenya's most unique characters. A former district officer who served in central Kenya during the Mau Mau "Emergency," Nottingham renounced his British citizenship when Kenya gained its independence in 1963. After a long career in publishing and various other businesses, he most recently spearheaded a legal case brought by the Kenya Human Rights Commission and the Mau Mau War Veterans' Association against the British Government. The suit claimed that Mau Mau fighters were the victims of systematic abuses in British detention camps in central Kenya during the 1950s. In mid-2013, they won the case, and almost £20 million in compensation for more than 5,000 Mau Mau veterans.

The fact that Nottingham and I came to discuss China at all was perhaps surprising, given that he and I were both passionate cricket fans, and England was in the midst of a titanic battle against Australia for the "Ashes" (a five-match series that England ultimately won for the first time since 1987). But when we finally changed topic, I found him as erudite on China as he was on cricket or, for that matter, anything to do with Kenya's history. Moreover, Nottingham shared with me a series of firsthand reminiscences about China. Nottingham's wife, Muthoni, was one of China's cousins, and China gave her thirty-nine goats on her wedding day. The conversation convinced me that a book-length work focused on China would prove both captivating and invaluable for explaining the complexities of colonial history.

John Nottingham was the inspiration for this book, and he provided encouragement and assistance from the start. In countless meetings in downtown Nairobi—and more recently at Village Market in Gigiri—he shared his views and thoughts on China, as well as other projects about Kenya in which I was involved. He has always proved tremendously generous, with his time and more: for it was Nottingham who first published *"Mau Mau" General* in 1967 and provided permission for the reprinting of an abridged version here. I am delighted that this book will soon appear in Kenyan bookstores through his Transafrica press.

John Lonsdale kindly agreed to write the Foreword to this collection; it will inspire scholars and students to read its contents with a more discerning eye. John also offered comments on the Introduction and on the essay entitled *The Historiography of Mau Mau*, and clarified some of the more obscure abbreviations and phrases used by British officers in the 1950s. In addition, David Anderson and Tom Spear provided prompt and invaluable feedback on the Introduction, as well as on the volume's overall organization.

I am also grateful to the staff of the Kenya National Archives for assisting me in procuring documents relevant to China's life and times, as well as for graciously allowing the reprinting of his interrogation and trial here. The staff at the National Archives of the United Kingdom in Kew—and at Rhodes House Library at the University of Oxford—were similarly helpful, in particular Lucy McCann at the latter. Lucy helped me gain permission to reproduce China's letter to the chief mechanical engineer of the East African Railways and Harbours. In addition, Cambridge University Press kindly allowed the reprinting of the map of Kenya that precedes the Introduction. Finally, Markus Wiener, Janet Stern, and Cheryl Mirkin provided sage guidance and careful editorial assistance, transforming this book from manuscript to final product.

The friends and colleagues mentioned above, however, bear no responsibility for any errors, omissions, or misinterpretations that appear in the text that follows.

*Boulder, Colorado*

# Note on Primary Sources

All primary sources in this collection have been reproduced with minimal editing, in an effort to preserve the original presentation and sense of the pieces. The majority of these documents were written in English in Kenya during the early 1950s and 1960s, and thus some spellings—and the capitalizations of certain words—differ from modern American and British standards. Inconsistencies in abbreviations, word usage, dating, and so forth also appear throughout the sources. The only alterations that have been made are minor changes to aid readability: these include changes in punctuation and syntax (particularly related to quotations), formatting, dating (to avoid confusion between American and British date ordering), and the correction of clearly unintended misspellings in the original sources (for example, substituting "when" for "whne").

Unusual terms and abbreviations are explained the first time that they appear in each section of the text, permitting readers to comprehend discrete sections without knowledge of those that precede it.

# Foreword

BY JOHN LONSDALE

Primary historical sources—such as General China's autobiography or the records of his interrogation and trial—were once compared to "the little children of long ago [who would] not speak until they [were] spoken to, and [would] not talk to strangers."[1] So said Christopher Cheney, professor of medieval English church history at the University of Cambridge, nearly half a century ago.

Sources are the historian's lifeblood; they also lend excitement and purpose to any class discussion of history and its methods. They should be approached with care. Cheney's records, penned and copied by hand in an era long before print and still more distant from the computer, were not autobiographies written with a possibly hostile public or potentially profitable market in mind. They were legal documents that granted and defined property rights, proclaimed legal privileges and duties, or transcribed agreements between church and state. They were technically complex, intended to be understood only by a small circle of experts who had a direct interest in whatever partisan statement of fact, argument, or judgment they recorded and who knew, intimately, the polemical context in which the documents were produced—whom they argued against, what weaknesses they did not reveal, and the debates they were intended to win.

That is why they will "speak" intelligibly only to those historians who, centuries later, immerse themselves in the relevant period, becoming as instinctively expert in grasping their self-interested purpose as those, now long dead, to whom the documents were first addressed. Only when they are no longer "strangers" to the period, its political factions and social cliques or classes, its conventional and subversive ideas, may scholars know the key questions to ask. These must make our records "speak" so intimately that we are even able to read their silences between the lines, the hiding places of those key issues, those inner meanings that were left unspoken. The true scholar should know his or her historical records and their context, well enough to know both what they were bound to say in their own interest and what they were careful *not* to say; and what one would naturally expect to be their omissions, half-truths, exaggerations, and lies—even when their authors believed that they were telling the truth. We must think that we know them well enough to be surprised when they do not speak as expected, and to ask why not. Our sources take sides, they are never neutral—one of the first truths historians have to learn.

That is all the more true of autobiography. Historians of more modern times, whose sources include written autobiography or oral reminiscence, must add to Cheney's dictum the warning that modern records are less like the little children of long ago and more like those of today. They often speak before they are spoken to; and they learn at a distressingly early age how to lie or at least how to spin a self-justifying tale, edited with a view to avoiding whatever punishment parents—or posterity— might otherwise inflict on them.

It follows that we should expect historical actors to be all the more anxious to write their life's story when they have played controversial roles in turbulent times and feel the need to explain themselves. They will write because they have scores to settle, decisions to justify, victories to claim, defeats to forget or blame on others, all in order to sway the verdict of history and its historians, you and me. We must be still more skeptical than Cheney, although he will have met similar problems himself. An incident from my own past makes that point. In the early 1970s, Cambridge's history examiners were inclined to reject African oral traditions as legitimate sources of evidence. They objected that the researcher (one of my doctoral students) might have invented them. But another distinguished medievalist, Walter Ullmann, won the day for African history by asking what the problem was. Were oral African sources and their provenance any more difficult to test than the Latin church records he himself had used, most of them forgeries?

We are all ignorant strangers when we first meet historical actors. We have little idea what precise questions will encourage or oblige them to speak in ways that we can trust or know how to test. To become their crit-

ical friend—knowing them well enough to ask embarrassing questions—
we need to compare as many different sources as we can. Why, we should
ask, do they tell us (if they do) different stories about the same people or
events? Why is the information we learn from one source neglected, over-
stated, or denied in another? What does this or that discrepancy tell us
about the different contexts in which our informants found themselves,
about the different audiences they tried to persuade or deceive, about their
different rhetorical conventions (a trial transcript is not a newspaper
report) or about their changing self-interest? If, on the other hand, the
information or opinion we find in one of our sources is corroborated in
one or more others, in what senses does that make it "true"?

That is why Myles Osborne's collection of documents is so useful and
important in introducing students to General China and the cause for
which he fought. No period in Kenya's history was more controversial
than the "Mau Mau Emergency" of the 1950s—and few periods in the
history of Africa or of the British Empire. It was a struggle in which many
died or were brutalized, for a cause that is still debated both in Kenya and
in Britain. Was it nationalist or "tribal," noble or bestial, did it force the
British to grant independence or, to the contrary, did it make it more difficult for all Kenyans to enjoy, in solidarity, that inevitable and in any
case accelerating end of empire? How far do our sources help us to make
up our minds over such fundamental issues of historical interpretation?
All that controversy makes Mau Mau a stiff test for historians. Violent
conflict creates prejudiced views at the time and partisan memories there-
after. Whoever played a part in Kenya's "Emergency," on one side or
another, had supporters to please and enemies to condemn; had had to
make appallingly difficult decisions and face awful risks; and had had to
perform often dreadful and bloody deeds. They had taken part in key
arguments over strategy or tactics; and they might, therefore, want to
cover up indecision, weakness, even betrayal, or cast the blame on others.
(Why, for example, does China's memoir scarcely mention his lengthy
interrogation by Henderson?)

Few scholars, church mice by comparison with guerrilla leaders or
colonial governors, ever have to face such decisive moments, often
involving the issue of life and death (think hard about that) when we are
seated in our archive or library, in a seminar room or in front of a com-

puter screen. Nonetheless we bear a comparably heavy responsibility. We are professionally obliged to do justice to people who faced the sort of test we ourselves hope to avoid, for fear that we might fail (we cannot know in advance). Our scholarship can begin to measure up to the seriousness of what and whom we study only if we question every variation we detect in the different sources that, at different times and with different self-interested authors, purport to describe the same event, the same argumentative debate, or the same historical actors. All of that requires hard intellectual labor. We owe the past no less, a test we have to pass.

Dr. Osborne has collected and edited a set of very different sources that tell us strikingly contradictory things about Waruhiu Itote—a "complete fanatic," according to Police Superintendent Ian Henderson, his interrogator; "perfectly normal, cheerful and rational" to another policeman, Thomas McBrierley, at his trial; a "kind and obedient" employee in China's own letter to his former boss, but a tough leader of strictly disciplined men in his autobiography; and finally, in John Nottingham's eulogy at his funeral many years later, a hero who had "fundamentally changed" Kenya's history. Same man, different perspectives—what do these contrasts tell us about Waruhiu Itote, about those who appraised his character, about the contexts in which they formed their judgments and the changing audiences whom they intended to inform or persuade? We need to know something about Henderson, McBrierley, China's former boss, and John Nottingham before we can begin to decide what we think about China.[2]

Such questions are only the most obvious ones to ask, at the start of any inquiry. Dr. Osborne has set out many more, as aids to critical analysis and class discussion. There is no need to repeat them here.

But there is a further point to be made. Underlying all other questions is the question of provenance: who wrote our source, at whose request or demand, in response to what contextual need? Who may have tampered with it since? How and why has it been made available for study? Who translated it (where it was translated), and how far did the named author retain control of the message? Some answers may never be known. We cannot now know, for example, how well Henderson, one of Kenya's few white Kikuyu speakers, understood China during his interrogation; nor how well the interpreter did his job at the trial, translating Kikuyu or

Swahili into English for the judge, or English into one or another African language for the court's three African assessors. We can only guess at how far Waruhiu Itote's position in Kenya's National Youth Service later affected his portrayal of Kenyatta's connections with "Mau Mau." Itote was writing in a particular context, at a crisis in Kenya's politics of memory, in the mid-1960s, a few years after independence, when Kenyatta, his nation's president and the personal patron to whom he owed so much, was bitterly criticized for his alleged neglect of impoverished Mau Mau veterans (And why does China write of "Mau Mau" only in quotation marks?)

Indeed, to conclude what is intended only to be a stimulus to discussion, not a comprehensive answer to all the questions of interpretation that confront us here, one has to face a bitter but humbling truth, that there will always be some things about the past that we will never know. The thought that with more work they might be known spurs us on; and our own changing context (the importance of which we forget at our peril) will always raise fresh questions. Nonetheless, the fundamental unknowingness of the past, served up to us by self-regarding, adversarial sources, sometimes of uncertain provenance, should always make historians both slow to come to judgment and admit to what we do not know.

The dead deserve our respect before our judgment. We must, especially, respect the great gulf that yawns between their knowledge and ours. They will have thought some things so obvious that they did not bother to tell us, who are then left in the dark about vital matters that are no longer obvious to us. On the other hand, we think we know much more than they did. They did not know what would come next, what would result from their actions, but we have the benefit of hindsight. We think we know better. That is our greatest methodological snare, the trap of anachronistic judgment. We simply must not judge our actors by the standards of today and by what we suppose to be the consequences of their decisions or actions, but by what we think we understand both of their ethical culture and their motives and intentions at the time. The only historical law that most historians acknowledge is the law of unintended outcomes. One of General China's lessons for us is his own distrust of prophecy as a guide to action.

But there are some issues on which we can form at least provisional judgments. This brings us back to the all-important questions of provenance. Among these in China's case is the issue of translation. It ought to occupy the central, rather muddy, ground in any discussion of his interrogation, his trial, and, indeed, his memoir. China's English was never very good. He thanked David Koff, a Stanford-trained political scientist and radical young journalist, for his help in preparing the manuscript, *"Mau Mau" General*. This, one may reasonably guess, will have entailed some polishing of China's prose, with what effect on meaning we cannot entirely know. A parallel text in both Kikuyu and English nonetheless suggests some cause for concern.

At the end of Chapter 7, China calls his base camp *Thingira wa Iregi*, "the cottage of our ancestors." This English translation suggests a thatched cottage with roses around the door, home to a gentle old couple leaning on their sticks, an image of rustic calm. Nothing could be more misleading—probably unintentionally, through a misunderstanding between China and Koff, but how do we know? A *thingira* was a mud-and-thatch hut reserved exclusively for men, where youths learned, often under insults, the tough lessons of how to become men of determination and self-mastery. The *iregi* were a particular group of ancestors, the "refusers." They were that generation of Kikuyu warriors who either, in a mythical past, revolted against a tyrant Kikuyu king or, more probably, in the nineteenth century, defended Kikuyuland against attack from Masai and other neighbors. "Rebellious boys' dorm" might have been a better translation—a topic perhaps for class discussion?

This illustration means not that historical judgment is impossible, but that we need to put in hard work before we dare to reach our own interpretation. We have to take the time to learn to become our sources' critical friends, not content to remain their ignorant strangers. We have to learn their particular ways of speaking. We will never enter fully into the many argumentative minds of the past, but it is our duty to the dead to keep on trying and to tell our readers when we cannot be entirely certain.

*Trinity College, University of Cambridge*

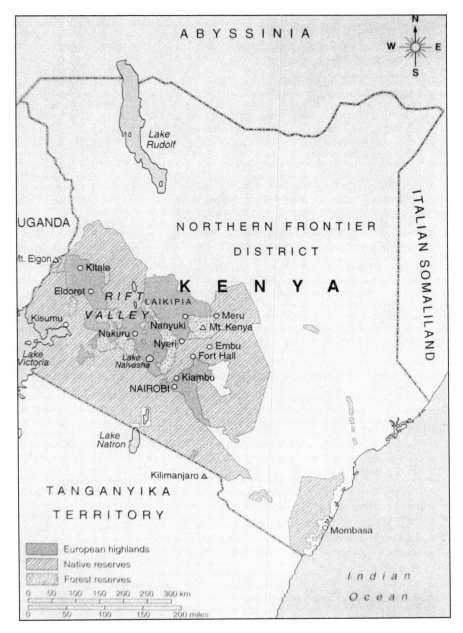

Map of Kenya, 1952.
This map first appeared in Huw Bennett, *Fighting the Mau Mau:
The British Army and Counter-Insurgency in the Kenya Emergency*
(Cambridge: Cambridge University Press, 2013), 10.
I am grateful to Cambridge University Press for allowing its reprinting here.

# Introduction

BY MYLES OSBORNE

*"Few men have the chance to fundamentally change the history of their country and fewer still take it."*[1]

Almost no topic in the history of sub-Saharan Africa has provoked more controversy, scholarship, and public fascination than the Mau Mau war, the guerrilla conflict that consumed Kenya during the 1950s. Sporting dreadlocks and frequently armed with homemade guns, Mau Mau fought against overwhelming odds to combat British forces and their "loyalist" African allies in and around the forests of central Kenya. Although Mau Mau did not "win" the war in any traditional sense, its broader impact far outweighed the military struggle: it was constantly raised and fought over in the British Parliament, inspired Malcolm X in the United States, and was lauded throughout the developing world as representing the struggle for freedom of oppressed peoples everywhere.

The Mau Mau forces were led by three men: Dedan Kimathi, Stanley Mathenge, and Waruhiu Itote, who was known in the forests as "General China." Itote was a short, wiry man, with bright eyes that reflected a charismatic personality, bolstered by an intelligent, analytical mind and an extraordinary memory. Itote was thirty years old when Mau Mau began in earnest, and was perhaps the most fascinating—and indeed the most controversial—figure in the organization's leadership. Itote was one of the first fighters to enter the forests in August 1952, and he led his men in a series of battles with significant success before his capture on January

1

15, 1954. What followed spurred a legacy that is debated even today.

During his interrogation, Itote provided a wealth of information on the composition of Mau Mau forces, their weapons and tactics, as well as details about troop locations. The information gave the government an enormous advantage in the prosecution of the war and played a significant role in turning the tide in the government's favor. After his interrogation, Itote faced trial. After three days in court, he was found guilty on two charges: consorting with "terrorists" and possession of ammunition. Each charge carried the death penalty. Yet unlike practically every other high-ranking Mau Mau leader, Itote escaped the war with his life: he agreed to work with the colonial government to negotiate Mau Mau's surrender, in exchange for the commutation of his death sentence. Itote stated that he was carrying out the wishes of the Mau Mau leadership by discussing surrender, which he claimed was debated in the forests before his capture. Yet Kimathi, at least, considered him a "collaborator" and a traitor.[2]

Reproduced here is an abridged version of Itote's memoir, *"Mau Mau" General*, which quickly became the "official" version of the Mau Mau struggle soon after its publication in 1967. The full texts of Itote's interrogation and trial appear next, and they provide a very different perspective. These two colonial files are reproduced from the Kenya National Archives with minimal editorial alteration. These texts are supplemented with a letter Itote wrote from the forests to the chief mechanical engineer of the East African Railways and Harbours in 1953; the eulogy delivered at Itote's funeral in 1993 by John Nottingham, a former district officer stationed in central Kenya during the 1950s; and a short historiographical essay that provides a point of entry into the voluminous literature on Mau Mau.

On one level, the texts permit the reader to unpack the personality, character, and motivations of Itote, arguably Mau Mau's most significant forest leader, and a man who continued to play an important role in independent Kenya after the British withdrawal. They reveal much about the promulgation of the Mau Mau war, and the experiences of those fighting on both sides. But more broadly, they speak to the experience of decolonization in Africa, and the challenges and complexities of building and maintaining support for nationalist movements, especially where intra- and interethnic challenges existed. They also explore the workings of the police and judicial systems that formed the structural foundation over which British imperial rule was molded.

## Colonialism and Mau Mau

Like Kimathi, Mathenge, and Itote, the majority of participants in Mau Mau were members of the Kikuyu ethnic group. Living in central Kenya, the Kikuyu were—and are today—Kenya's largest ethnic community.[3] Mau Mau began some three-quarters of a century after the famous prophet Cege wa Kibiru predicted the impending arrival of a group of "peculiar strangers" who would cause a "bleak time" for his people.[4]

Though a variety of explorers, missionaries, and hunters visited East Africa during the nineteenth century, it was a group of railway surveyors who brought the mantle of British control in 1888. They were employees of the Imperial British East Africa Company (IBEAC), and they were tasked with discovering the best route for a railway line that would connect Lake Victoria with the coast at Mombasa. The IBEAC bore a royal charter that gave it formal Crown assent to establish a system of government, a police force, and the other typical trappings of a state.

The IBEAC arrived at the height of the "Scramble for Africa," a roughly twenty-year period at the end of the nineteenth century during which European powers carved up 90 percent of Africa's landmass among themselves, forming colonial territories. Britain and France were the most prolific in this process, but Germany, Portugal, Spain, Italy, and the Belgian King Leopold II all rushed to grab "a slice of this magnificent African cake."[6] The European powers were motivated by a variety of geopolitical and economic concerns, but all were quick to justify their actions by claiming to act for the benefit of Africans. All framed their conquests as "civilizing missions" of sorts (although the notion received its most coherent ideological expression from the French).[7]

All the European powers had one major problem in common: how to pay for the administration of their new colonies. In Mozambique, Portugal sold tranches of land and labor to private companies, which then administered the new territories, covering their costs from taxes imposed on Africans, as well as the profits they could extract. King Leopold, on the other hand, established a repressive, personal fiefdom, in which Congolese were forced to harvest rubber to supply the burgeoning automobile and bicycle industries of Europe. Britain experimented with a variety of systems—the IBEAC, after all, was a private company—but in 1895 the British Crown itself took formal control of what it called the East Africa Protectorate (and the "Colony and Protectorate of Kenya—or simply "Kenya"—after 1920), and turned the problem over to its first governor, Sir Charles Eliot.

Eliot initially believed that Indian settlers might provide the solution to Kenya's financial difficulties. A good number of Indians were already in East Africa by 1900: some were "coolies" who had arrived several years earlier to work on the railway, and others were established businessmen. Thus Eliot officially approved Indian settlement in 1901, and, the following year, Indian farmers received "land grants, free seed distribution, and agricultural loans" in the Highlands, the protectorate's best agricultural land.[8]

But Eliot's policy was anathema to a small group of active and vocal European settlers (characteristics that would define their kind for the following sixty years). Despite the fact that fewer than 100 Europeans lived in the protectorate in 1900, they possessed great influence. They railed against the threat of Indian competition in agriculture and business. In 1902, they founded the Society to Promote European Immigration, which explicitly rejected the possibilities of Indian immigration. The settlers forced Eliot to turn entirely against Indian capital, and he instead decided to back a European settlement plan.

By 1906, almost 2,000 white settlers had moved to the protectorate, including several hundred farmers from South Africa. These settlers were complemented by the presence of a series of large syndicates from Britain, with high levels of financial backing. All interested groups received large amounts of land in first 21- and then 99-year leases in the Highlands (soon known as the "White Highlands") at low or no cost. This "alienated land" was ideal for European settlement, because it was the most agriculturally productive land in the protectorate, and it was situated close to the railway line. This land became the major source of conflict between Africans and Europeans for the remainder of the colonial period.

In areas such as Uganda, Nyasaland (modern-day Malawi), or Nigeria, the impact of colonial rule on African lives was relatively minor once initial conquests ("pacification," in British terms) had taken place. The colonial presence was usually limited to a small staff of administrators, with their only real task to collect a fairly minimal amount of tax. Inspired by Frederick Lugard's ideas about "indirect rule," British officials set about governing through existing political structures where possible, as it seemed simpler and cheaper.[9] This stood in contrast to the French system, which featured an extensive and complex web of European staff posted throughout the rural part of France's colonies.

But Kenya, Southern Rhodesia (modern-day Zimbabwe), and the French colony of Algeria were different from all the others: they became colonies of settlement. This added a layer of tremendous complexity to the colonial experience, and particularly the process of disengagement from the colonies that took place during the 1950s, 1960s, and 1970s. Many European settlers were genuine pioneers and had worked hard to establish themselves on what they viewed as *their* land: they would not relinquish it without a fight.

In these colonies, the system of European settlement became deeply entrenched between the two world wars (1918-39). In Kenya, more Europeans arrived (taking the settler population to 20,984 in 1938), and the government system became more heavily warped to benefit settler farmers to the detriment of African producers.[10] This was not the way that Eliot's plan was supposed to work out, and had come to pass for several reasons. First, initial offers of land at minimal cost resulted in a great amount of speculation. Well-capitalized companies and individuals bought up tens (and in some cases, hundreds) of thousands of acres of land but had little incentive to develop it. Development was essential to stimulate the industry and production the colony required. Second, the small-scale settlers had few financial resources and seemed unable to turn a profit from agriculture. They therefore came to depend almost entirely on the colonial state to assist them in becoming productive.[11]

Kenya's settlers had never paid income tax, and during the interwar period the colonial government showered them with additional assistance. It provided them with low-cost loans; gave them access to veterinary care and fertilizers for their farms; and ensured that their products received favorable conditions for export. Marketing boards were perhaps the most notorious examples of these settler-only benefits. African producers were forced to sell products like maize or cattle to the boards at low, fixed prices. The products were then sold at a vast profit on the international market, and the profits plowed back into the European farming sector. One of the greatest bones of contention was that Africans were not permitted to grow the valuable cash crop, coffee.

Some revisionist thinkers about empire today are quick to label colonialism a universally negative experience for Africans. But a certain class of Africans across the continent profited rather handsomely from it. They were the ones who had received education—usually through mission schools—during the early part of the twentieth century. Many had purchased land, grabbing title deeds once they realized their utility. Others had established themselves as clerks or farmers, and still more went into business. But they wanted more.

In Kenya, more educated Africans—in particular—protested the racialist legal system that stopped them from entering "white" hotels or living in the colony as the equals of Europeans. One of their greatest grievances was the *kipande* system that forced city residents and migrant laborers to carry passes (as in apartheid South Africa). A *kipande* had a person's employment details recorded on it, and the owner had to keep the document "up to date" or risk arrest. Disgruntled employers commonly kept or destroyed their employees' passes, opening them to the swift hand of the law. The *kipande* was among the most hated symbols of the colonial system, and frequently the source of protests.

Bubbling discontent was quickly quieted when the Second World War broke out in 1939. Britain's leaders initially hoped that the war might little involve Africa, but within months of its declaration, recruiting officers were hustling throughout the colonies to find troops. More than half a million Africans served during the war, with much of the actual fighting carried out by the Royal West African Frontier Force and the King's African Rifles (KAR) from East Africa.[12] African soldiers performed sterling service, in areas ranging from Abyssinia (Ethiopia) to Madagascar, and including a bout of extraordinarily difficult fighting in jungle conditions in Burma.[13]

African intellectuals expected serious discussions about independence—or self-government at the very least—to begin immediately following the war's end. The Atlantic Charter, after all—a document signed by British Prime Minister Winston Churchill and American President Franklin Roosevelt in 1941—promised the "right of all peoples to choose the form of government under which they will live."[14] Africans had fought side by side with Indian and American troops during the war, and been exposed to the sorts of differences in pay and overall treatment they received. In 1947, India received its independence: surely the African colonies were next? Optimism was quickly dampened, though, as thousands more white settlers poured into Kenya and Southern Rhodesia, and Churchill intimated that he had little intention of giving up Britain's African colonies.

Nonetheless, the war catalyzed a revolution in social and political life in Kenya and other parts of Africa. By 1945, roads connected practically all parts of rural Kenya to Nairobi, and buses rumbled along them in ever-increasing numbers. Every marketplace had several radios wailing in the background. The African press exploded into life, with forty different newspapers appearing between 1945 and 1952.[15] At the heart of this transformation sat the newly formed Kenya African Union (KAU). Claiming a membership of 15,000 in 1948, it rose from the vestiges of the Kikuyu Central Association and had links to an active network of trade unionists.[16] The "land issue" was the cornerstone of KAU's agenda. The union claimed that land "alienated" to Europeans earlier in the century belonged in African hands, and demanded its return to the "rightful" owners.

This land in the "White Highlands" was the inspiration for tremendous outpourings of discontent during the 1940s. In the years following the war, British officials took a far more interventionist approach to African land use, and tried to reorganize systems of agriculture among the Kikuyu peasantry, to reduce overcrowding and increase production. They had little success, except in provoking anger among farmers. A cadre of politicians, including Jomo Kenyatta (who would later become Kenya's first president) and trade-unionist Fred Kubai, fanned the flames of frustration, giving speeches and publishing letters and treatises drawing attention to the injustice of this "stolen" land.

Their speeches found a receptive audience in the increasingly large class of Kikuyu "squatters." Squatters were farmers who had lost access to their own land over the previous decades. They had taken up tools on

European-owned farms, providing labor and sometimes rent payments in exchange for a place to live, grow some crops, and raise livestock. Although this system of labor provision had worked adequately at times—acting as a "safety valve" for the crowded reserves[17]—after 1945 it was in crisis. Settlers "made up the rules as they went along" when it came to labor regulations, and required that squatters sign restrictive and demanding labor contracts, evicting them if they refused.[18] Many settlers, in any case, had little need for squatter labor after 1945: they had prospered during the war years as they produced goods vital for the war effort (greatly assisted by wartime regulations that benefited them). The profits had permitted many to increase the mechanization of agriculture on their farms, removing the need for high numbers of workers.[19]

Thus squatters experienced a tremendous sense of uncertainty, aware that their access to land was insecure, and subject to the whims of their employers. Many, indeed, were forced off the land and had nowhere to go: the reserves were already crowded to bursting point, and Nairobi's dirty slums were obviously unattractive. According to Kikuyu custom, each man was meant to possess at least some amount of land. Many of the younger generation had no prospect of achieving this, and Kikuyu society came under tremendous stress as long-established systems of gender relations and generational authority collapsed.[20] Although these former squatters and landless peasants were angered by the European domination of land resources in central Kenya, they were equally angered by those middle- and upper-class Kikuyu who had proved adept in consolidating smaller parcels of peasant land into their own burgeoning land portfolios. These disadvantaged peasants comprised the largest proportion of Mau Mau's membership.

The origins of the term "Mau Mau" are shrouded in mystery.[21] The appellation was used originally by its enemies, and Mau Mau themselves never referred to the movement in such terms at the time. Mau Mau "crystallized" in 1952, as a conglomerate of a series of groups with grievances in Kikuyuland that had developed since the 1940s.[22] First in secret and later more openly, Mau Mau leaders administered oaths to their followers, binding them together in the fight for the removal of Europeans from the colony, and in the hope of a resurgent, ordered, and stable Kikuyu society.

The colonial administration in Kenya was slow to address these developments, in part because Governor Sir Philip Mitchell was ill and determined to avoid trouble before his impending retirement. From the start of 1952, Mau Mau fighters made their presence known: they attacked settler cattle and started killing Kikuyu they considered "loyal" to the government. The murder of Senior Chief Waruhiu wa Kung'u—a staunch government ally—inspired Mitchell's newly arrived successor Evelyn Baring to declare a "State of Emergency" on October 20.[23] British soldiers rounded up a number of pre-selected "ringleaders" including Kenyatta, and the conflict began in earnest.

The war had great relevance in other colonies, and even more broadly. In Africa, Mau Mau was frequently an inspiration to intellectuals and political parties with nationalist aspirations. The latter had appeared all over the continent during the 1950s, pressing for greater recognition, rights, and then independence. The Gold Coast (modern-day Ghana) was at the vanguard of this movement, under the leadership of Kwame Nkrumah and his Convention People's Party, and it achieved independence in 1957. But although Nkrumah called for Kenyatta's release and courted the young Luo trade unionist Tom Mboya, he seemed to maintain his distance from Mau Mau itself.[24] Beyond the continent's shores, a range of actors from Soviet propagandists[25] to American civil rights activists[26] had strong interests in the conflict, and observed carefully as the fighting raged in the forests between 1952 and 1954.

Kenya's "Emergency" lasted until December 1959, although the bulk of the fighting was over four years earlier when Mau Mau was finally defeated militarily. As the Emergency ended, it was clear that the European colonial era was close to its culmination. Harold Macmillan, the British prime minister, famously gave a speech in Cape Town in February 1960 in which he alluded to the "Wind of Change" that was sweeping the continent. The "change" took place in Britain and France's sub-Saharan colonies during the 1960s (with the exception of Ghana and Guinea). Kenya received its independence in 1963, and all the other British colonies on the continent by 1968, with the exception of Southern Rhodesia. In the French case, the majority of colonies became independent in 1960, although they remained more closely bound to France economically, politically, and socially. The Portuguese withdrawal was more drawn out, with decolonization taking place during the mid-1970s.

The process of decolonization occurred mostly without conflict; yet it featured a predictable range of detentions and bannings of African politicians and their parties. But in the British, French, and Portuguese cases, there was one distinctly common factor: colonies of settlement produced bloody wars of independence. From Kenya (and Southern Rhodesia) to Algeria to Angola, these more brittle and entrenched systems of colonial rule led to many thousands of deaths: in Kenya, official estimates stated that over 11,000 Africans died. The number was certainly higher, although scholars disagree over precisely *how* high (see *The Historiography of Mau Mau* below).

The Mau Mau conflict represents the complexities of colonial rule perhaps better than any other moment in African history. Mau Mau was no simple black versus white war (fewer than 100 Europeans died during the event), and it was closer to an intra-Kikuyu civil war in many regards. Men and women of different generations fought for a range of motives, including access to land, changes to the systems of social ordering, and gender and generational issues.[27] Moreover, the legacy of the Mau Mau struggle has been hotly contested: some have viewed it not as a civil war, but a nationalist struggle,[28] and others as a peasant protest.[29] Whether Mau Mau hastened or slowed Kenya's progress to independence has also been debated.

Mau Mau's legacy is still contested today, and few episodes in African history can have such salience in the present: in 2013, Mau Mau veterans won a ruling in a British court that led to the British Government's taking responsibility for atrocities carried out in Kenya during the 1950s. The case has inspired numerous debates about the legacies of British colonial rule and the nature of Mau Mau itself. Itote's autobiography, published in 1967, is in large part responsible for establishing the narrative of Mau Mau as an organized, nationalist, guerrilla war against the British. Thus unpacking Itote's motivations and potential biases in the creation of his story is of the utmost importance.

# Waruhiu Itote

Waruhiu Itote was born in 1922 in Kaheti, a village in South Tetu Division, which formed part of Nyeri District in the northern part of Kikuyuland. Contrary to the wishes of his father, who believed that "education was all nonsense," Itote received schooling, first at the Church of Scotland Mission at Kiangurue and later at Mihuti School. The mission school, in particular, had a great impact on him, for, as he later wrote in his memoir, "I ... became a keen Christian." Yet he soon dropped out of school to work on a farm in Kiambu—far to the south of his home—before departing for Nairobi following a disagreement with his employer. A year later he returned home, and he enrolled again in two different mission schools, before his inability to pay the fees meant that he had to leave again. He journeyed back to Nairobi, where he worked grinding flour for Unga Ltd. for eighteen shillings per month. After several failed attempts in business, Itote decided to enroll in the KAR, the largely African, colonial military, where he joined the fight against the Axis powers in the Second World War.[30]

Itote enlisted on January 2, 1942, at Langata Camp and began his three months' training. His first formal posting was to the 36th battalion of the KAR ("36 KAR"), stationed at Moshi in northern Tanganyika (then a British-controlled territory, and today Tanzania). His unit was then transferred to Ceylon (modern-day Sri Lanka), where he and his fellow soldiers received jungle training for their imminent deployment to Burma. The Japanese had occupied the self-governing British colony of Burma in 1942, and the KAR joined the Allied effort to drive them out. The 11th (East Africa) Division formed a part of the forces commanded by Vice Admiral Lord Louis Mountbatten in the new South-East Asia Command. There, Itote and his compatriots experienced some of the most difficult fighting conditions in the Second World War. Disease was ever-present in the swampy terrain, and the Allies fought hurriedly because they had to liberate Rangoon before the onset of the monsoon rains. As in the First World War, Britain's leaders had assumed that they would require little assistance from African soldiers; yet again, African manpower proved invaluable.[31]

Itote famously credits his experiences during the Second World War as causing him to question the institution of colonial rule. He opens his memoir *"Mau Mau" General* by explaining, "The first time I ever thought of myself as a Kenyan was in 1943, in the Kalewa trenches on the Burma Front." Itote found himself in conversation with a British soldier who expressed surprise that Africans were fighting in support of the British Empire, "instead of fighting to free yourselves." After the British soldier was killed, Itote had a similar discussion with an African-American soldier called Stephenson, who told him about the color bar in the United States, as well as the Haitian Revolution, in which slaves overthrew their French colonial masters. Later, an Indian raised similar themes, telling Itote, "You should have demanded Independence as your minimum price for fighting." At the time, India was engaged in its own struggle for independence, which it achieved two years after the war's culmination.[32]

Fired by the desire for independence, Itote returned to Kenya. "We had to awaken and train a whole nation," he later wrote. He therefore refused a promotion in the army and instead asked for a discharge. He formed a charcoal-selling company, before joining the East African Railways and Harbours as a fireman. Itote now found himself constantly angered by the discrimination he faced all around. It came first from Indians in his charcoal business, who prevented him from storing wood where he pleased. Then it came on the railways, where African drivers were paid less than Indian or European drivers, irrespective of skill and experience.[33]

As a result of his dissatisfaction, Itote joined the *Anake a 40*, or "Forty Group," a gang whose members included many war veterans, and which had links to African political groups. During the war, British officers had promised former servicemen that their economic needs would be met in the postwar era; many had visions of owning businesses and buying lorries and taxis, but they found their hopes quickly dashed. In Forty Group, members undertook both crime and political activity, although which was more prominent is unclear.[34] What is certain is that the elite politics of the KAU were unattractive to these men, and they identified closely with the poor and landless. They supported peasant protest in Central Province during the late 1940s, and provided backing for the squatters at Olenguruone, many of whom were evicted from their land in 1948.[35]

In 1950, Itote joined Mau Mau—which he described as "the

Movement"—by taking an oath in Naivasha, a town in the Rift Valley of central Kenya, to the north-west of Nairobi. The oath existed in many different manifestations, but it typically included some stipulation that members pledge not to betray the movement, and to assist in driving Europeans from the colony.[36] The circumstances of oath-taking were frequently traumatic: it was common for Mau Mau to round up young men and women in their villages at night and to take them to the forest, where they were forced to take the oath if they did not volunteer. On one level, the severity of the oathing ceremonies was sometimes exaggerated by European or American authors, trying to depict Mau Mau as "primitive" and "bestial."[37] Yet several participants do recall beatings and terror during the process, and Joram Wamweya and H.K. Wachanga were forced to place their penises in pieces of meat as they repeated the words of the oath. Itote, however, recalled no such violence in his own oaths.[38]

In his memoir, Itote uses lofty rhetoric to describe the conflict's opening days: "We were fighting with the weapons of Truth, Love and Justice." He operated under the direction of the Nyeri Committee, a level below Mau Mau's Central Committee. Itote began organizing oathing ceremonies, as well as collecting guns and medical supplies. On August 16, 1952, he experienced one of the definitive moments of his career. Together with some of his compatriots, Itote drove to Gatundu in a beaten-up red car to meet Jomo Kenyatta. There, at Kenyatta's homestead, the future president offered words of encouragement for the upcoming struggle: "Some of you … will be imprisoned … some of you will be killed…. We must buy our freedom with our blood." Itote's account of this meeting strongly resembles the Last Supper, with Kenyatta appearing as a Christ-like figure, predicting his upcoming arrest to his loyal disciples. This was the last time Itote would see Kenyatta until their detention together two years later. The following month, Itote drove to Karatina with fellow members of Mau Mau and entered the forests.[39]

## General China

Outside the forests, the escalation of Mau Mau activity in late 1951 and the early months of 1952 was facilitated by a temporary break at the highest level of colonial administration. Governor Mitchell left the colony in June and had, noted one commentator, remained only "out of a sense of duty."[40] Three months followed during which Kenya was a ship without a rudder. On September 30, Mitchell's successor—Evelyn Baring—arrived, and was horrified at the state into which the colony had descended. Lawlessness was ever-increasing in Nairobi, and the assassination of people loyal to the government was common. Kenya's white settlers were up in arms, demanding action. Following Chief Waruhiu's assassination by Mau Mau—in broad daylight—Baring declared a State of Emergency and moved to round up the organization's purported leaders in Operation Jock Scott.

There is evidence that the leadership of Mau Mau knew of the government operation before it was carried out. In any case, more and more Kikuyu now entered the forests to join the movement and bolster the tiny band of Itote's followers. By now, however, Itote was known inside and outside the forests as "General China," a name he created, but spelled "Chaina" on his stationery.[41] The Mau Mau leadership assigned military ranks to its soldiers—typically described in quotation marks in European sources—and fighters chose "forest names" to prevent easy identification by the police and Special Branch.

The majority of Mau Mau fighters operated from the forests around Mount Kenya (known to the Kikuyu as Kirinyaga) and the Aberdares (Nyandarwa) mountains to the west. China headed the Mount Kenya forces, and Kimathi and Mathenge those in the Aberdares. They fought against a force that included British Army regulars, the Kenya Police, the Kenya Police Reserve, the Kenya Regiment (largely comprised of European settlers), the KAR, and the Home Guard, part of the loyalist segment of the Kikuyu population.

In his first months in the forests, China was involved largely in recruiting new members and performing oathing ceremonies. He and his men undertook these tasks boldly, moving between the forests and the reserves with a degree of freedom that later disappeared. They devoted much time to gathering food and supplies from sympathetic villagers. In early 1953, China began a series of attacks on settler farms in Nyeri and Nanyuki, which garnered significant British attention. These attacks were interspersed with an almost constant stream of assaults against Home

Guard positions and loyalist targets.[42] China was demonstrating to British military officials that they were up against a clever and organized forest leader. As he later summed up, "Scarcely a day would go by without excitement of some kind, whether in the form of a planned raid, an attack by security forces, a minor operation to obtain a gun or some ammunition, or just an unanticipated encounter with the enemy." China and his men faced death on a regular basis.[43]

In his memoir *The Swords of Kirinyaga*, Wachanga describes a battle in which China—along with Generals Tanganyika and Kaleba[44]—fought between Kiamachimbi and Ruiruiru near Tumutumu in late 1953. The location was dangerous: it was close to Karatina, the main KAR and police base in the area. China sent his clerk, Faranja—dressed in women's clothing to avoid detection—ahead of his main force to spy. Wachanga reports that China had 1,000 men at his disposal that day (although the number is certainly an exaggeration), armed with weapons ranging from rifles to grenades. According to Wachanga, the battle went on for several hours, and "[t]here was so much gunfire that the trees and green leaves caught fire." Despite the fact that the government called up reinforcements, including air strikes, Wachanga alleges that China's men killed 61 of the security forces, losing 21. The victors wrote a song to celebrate their achievement:

## Tumutumu Hill

1. You rulers listen to this song of Tumutumu Hill,
   So that you may know
   God Almighty is with us
   And He shall never leave us.

2. It was on a Wednesday,
   We were in a valley village.
   The warriors decided to ascend
   So as to have a look at the Gikuyu Country.

3. At about two o'clock,
   Faranja was sent down to the valley

Dressed like a woman
In order to gather information.

4.   He brought back useful information:
"Kirimukuyu is now surrounded,
In the valley there are four hundred boys
Which valley will be surrounded."

5.   Good luck came through one girl
Whose name was Kanguniu.
With her warning to us
She saved many of our lives.

6.   Then at about two o'clock
We praised God Almighty.
We climbed the hill
Expecting to see the end of our children.

7.   And just after two o'clock,
There was thundering on the mountain.
Bullets were raining down from every side,
God led us down the mountain.

8.   A great surprise came
When we reached Karimiu village.
All houses were ablaze and
The village was as one fire-flame.

9.   Gakuru gave away his life
Attempting to save his friends.
He "lit a fire" which started to burn,
And stopped the raining bullets.

10. We have many warriors—
Kagume, Mangecha, and Corpral [*sic*],
And the trumpet-blower
Faranja is the clerk.

11. When darkness fell
We began "thanksgiving" the Lord.
On our way to Rititi,
We looked for Gomery[45] and the rest.[46]

During this period, China transformed his band of followers into a well-organized, guerrilla army known as the Kenya Land and Freedom Army. He claimed that his army in the Mount Kenya forests—frequently described as the Hika Hika—comprised at least 7,500 men (and some few women), split among nine battalions. Part of this force was, however, held in reserve unless required.[47]

In his memoir, China is careful to depict daily life in the forests as highly organized and little different from any other formal army. This is likely a response to a bevy of European authors (and one American) writing in the late 1950s and early 1960s who depicted Mau Mau as a motley band of poorly organized, mindless terrorists.[48] On any day, China's troops could expect morning exercise, followed by tea and porridge; then drill, lectures on "bush-craft," hygiene, or cleanliness, and finally fighting instruction.[49] China also describes an elaborate system of defenses against possible incursions from the security forces: these ranged from "mock camps"—decoy camps to draw the attention of the enemy—to rings of sentries spread out in increasing distances from the camps to act as a progressive warning system.

Mau Mau fighters were subject to a series of strict regulations on conduct in China's army. China includes an appendix in *"Mau Mau" General* that details more than fifty rules of prescribed behavior, which were formalized in January 1954 for all Mau Mau soldiers. These included, for instance, a stipulation that "[n]o one may drink beer without permission of his company commander." Similarly, "[a] soldier may not abuse his comrades or commander." When it came to relations between men and women in the forests, China encouraged both groups to practice them faithfully: "No soldier has the right to fall in love with his comrade's girl-friend; a soldier who falls in love and keeps it a secret is liable to prosecution." Rank also played an important role: China stated that Mau Mau officers could not have relationships with women connected to rank-and-file troops, but instead with "women leaders." This strictness stood in contrast to forest life in the Aberdares, where Kimathi commonly captured women who brought food to the forests.[50] John Lonsdale—in reference to the Special Branch officer and later interrogator of China, Ian Henderson—writes, "Henderson may not have been far from the mark in referring to Kimathi's 'harem.'"[51]

China is clearly sensitive to the charge levied on Mau Mau by British authors that they were simply violent "terrorists" or crooks. He specifically contrasts his disciplined force with the *Komerera*, men who joined Mau Mau for the simple monetary advantages it could produce. These men entered the reserves and beat people up, often stealing their money, all the while claiming to be doing Mau Mau's work. Yet they had no principles and followed no appropriate ideology in the struggle. (It is worth noting, of course, that the existence of the *Komerera* allowed forest leaders such as China to explain away distasteful episodes carried out by Mau Mau.[52])

China is also careful to demonstrate that killings carried out by Mau Mau were justified. In his first days in the forest, China and his men killed a schoolteacher whom they believed was a British informant. In China's words, "We never took lives unnecessarily, but … there was no alternative but to kill [him].… If we released him, he would go to the nearest Police Station.… It was equally impossible to keep him prisoner indefinitely, moving him with us."[53]

A judicial body called the Executive Committee No. 4 determined appropriate conduct in the forests. This was one part of its remit: it also had the authority to determine overall war strategy. Executive Committee No. 4 was comprised of the twelve most prominent leaders of Mau Mau—six from the forests of Mount Kenya and six from the Aberdares—and they met roughly every two months in 1953. China was called before the committee in the Aberdares on November 17 that year—two months before his arrest—to answer charges that he had said that Mau Mau might lose the war. China claimed that he had made such a statement to warn that Mau Mau could lose the physical fight in the forests unless they took care. The charges were dismissed, "through the judicial authority of Dedan Kimathi," China noted. China continued to use the episode as an example of the type of formal process required to bring and address charges in the forests.[54]

The relationship between China and Kimathi was functional: Kimathi—a field marshal— outranked China, but the latter nevertheless had a practically unrestricted hand to do as he pleased in the Mount Kenya forests. The relationship between Kimathi and Mathenge, on the other hand, was extraordinarily fractious. The educated Kimathi, scribe always close at hand, clashed with the illiterate Mathenge. As historian David Anderson describes, their disagreement "has become the stuff of Mau Mau legend." Anderson suggests that the inability of Kimathi and Mathenge to work together, combined with China's capture in early 1954, meant that "Mau Mau's military potential would not be realized."[55] China's capture came on January 15, when his luck finally ran out.

## Capture and Interrogation

China had planned an operation to pick up weapons from a "secret store" in an abandoned house in Mathira Division, close to Kiawarigi. He was accompanied by General Tanganyika and likely by General Kaleba. But early in the morning, they were engaged by the police and KAR, together with forty of their men. At some point during the fighting—the precise timing is difficult to ascertain—China was shot once. The bullet was fired from a lower level, and passed through the lower right side of the front of his neck, exiting the left side just below the jaw, taking a piece of jawbone with it. Desmond Walker, who later examined China, stated in court that the bullet had "cut through tissues and laid bare the wind-pipe," nicking it in one place, noting that if China took deep breaths, air bubbles appeared.[56] China stated that he continued fighting for possibly another hour before collapsing. He recounts that two KAR soldiers helped him away from the scene of the battle, before leaving him to crawl into the KAR camp and surrender.[57]

The European officer in charge of the KAR post at Kiawarigi was Lieutenant Wallace Young, who knew China from his days working with the East African Railways and Harbours. Young took custody of China, as well as a notebook he had in his pocket (another notebook belonging to China was found later). China was transported several miles to the hospital in Karatina, where Walker operated on his wound, and then to Nyeri

Civil Hospital, and finally on to King George VI Hospital in Nairobi late that night.

The following morning, a man appeared who would enjoy a long and—at least from his own perspective—fruitful association with China. Assistant Superintendent Ian Henderson was the son of Jock Henderson, an early settler who had come to Kenya before the First World War to set up a business trading seeds.[58] The younger Henderson was raised in Nyeri among Kikuyu children and spoke the language with total fluency. He was known as "Kinyanjui" to the Kikuyu—an appellation of great respect, because it was the name of an influential and powerful southern Kikuyu leader with whom the earliest British traders and administrators had negotiated. Henderson was uniquely suited to carry out China's interrogation.

At this juncture it is important to pause to consider the context of the interrogation.[59] Could Henderson have used coercion to procure information from China? Certainly the latter was likely exhausted toward the end of an encounter that lasted sixty-eight hours, and the promise that "more can be extracted" with which the interview concludes is somewhat ominous.[60] Henderson is a controversial figure: British police investigated allegations that he carried out torture and other violations of human rights as a major general and head of the Security and Intelligence Service of Bahrain, where he worked from 1971 until 1998, following his deportation from Kenya after independence.[61] Amnesty International, among others, has stressed the need to prosecute Henderson.[62] That torture was used against Mau Mau detainees is emphatically demonstrated in Caroline Elkins's *Imperial Reckoning*.[63]

There is, however, little suggestion that Henderson tortured China, although the latter likely expected it. In his own account, China is silent on his interrogation; he makes no mention of it and indeed barely mentions Henderson's name. At a later point, however, when working directly with Henderson in surrender negotiations, China praises Henderson for his "courage." In only one Mau Mau account is any wrongdoing by Henderson hinted at. Paul Maina, in his laudatory mini-biography of China published in 1977, states that "General China was pressured by Henderson to talk and reveal the secrets." China helped Maina extensively in the writing of this book; yet even here, no torture is mentioned.

Henderson appears in at least two of the other Mau Mau memoirs: Wambui Otieno mistakenly refers to him as "Anderson" but maintains, "he was very kind to me."[64] In Wachanga's account, the author describes Henderson as "cruel" and "vicious," but his hatred appears to be related to the fact that Henderson caused the deaths of many Mau Mau in the forests. Again, there is no mention of torture, although Wachanga appears to do all he can to attack Henderson.[65]

As the interrogation began, China seemed resigned to die. He had good reason: the courts hanged 1,090 men and women for Mau Mau offenses during the 1950s, and a Mau Mau general had little chance at trial.[66] Henderson described China as a "complete fanatic," and a "martyr to the cause." "His sole wish was to expound his political testament . . . and then walk to the gallows without trial," Henderson noted. The transcript of the interrogation reveals that at no point did China offer information in the belief that he could save his own life. In contrast, it exposes a confident, bullish man. The general believed that Mau Mau was winning the war. He recognized that it had suffered reverses, especially in late 1953, but he was adamant that neither he nor Mau Mau had entertained "thought of surrender" (in contrast to his later statements). He accepted that Mau Mau could likely not drive the Europeans from Kenya, but he believed that the war would force the British to provide rights to Africans that they had not previously enjoyed. Yet as China began talking, it became clear that he was wont to impart more information than he perhaps intended.

China described an organization that was far more extensive than officials had believed. He was insistent that the forces in and around the Mount Kenya forests numbered 7,500, and suggested that Mau Mau had spread beyond the Kikuyu, Embu, and Meru to the Kamba.[67] China's forces were divided like the British regiment to which he had belonged a decade earlier. The smallest unit of organization was the *batuni* (comprising between 10 and 50 men). Several *batunis* joined together to form a section (50 to 160 men). Several sections made up a company (160 to 350 men), and the largest unit was the battalion (350 and more men)—of which there were nine in the Mount Kenya forests. The Mount Kenya Committee (and within it, the Executive Committee—not to be confused with Executive Committee No. 4) was in charge of overall war policy. The committee comprised eighteen senior men from Nyeri, Embu, and

Meru. Until his capture, the committee was chaired by China, with Captain Faranja (China's clerk) as secretary, giving a total of twenty men.

The level of detail China provided in his interrogation was quite extraordinary, leading Henderson to announce himself highly impressed by China's memory. (Henderson made several attempts to catch China out on matters of fact or detail, but each attempt proved unsuccessful.) To take the Hika Hika Battalion as an example: China named the six companies it contained, their commanding officers, and several other details, including the numbers of weapons they possessed and their areas of operation. One of the companies, the Rumuri Company, had six sections, which he named, with their commanding officers. One of Rumuri Company's six sections—the Kuhanga Section—had two *batunis*, and in these *batunis* China named eight "prominent members."

The level of detail that appears in the interrogation raises the question as to how much information China could possibly have provided verbally to Henderson, and how much was culled from China's two captured notebooks, and possibly other sources. The text of China's interrogation is no word-for-word recounting, but an organized summary of all information gathered from him, combined with other known facts. At several points, Henderson refers to documents that established or confirmed certain facts relating to the war, but it is unclear what these documents were. One hint is perhaps found in China's account: he berates himself for having failed to jettison one of his notebooks before his capture, recalling his "dismay" at this "regrettable oversight."[68]

It is also difficult to believe that China verbally volunteered the entirety of the information presented in Henderson's typescript, because at certain moments he is careful to conceal things from his interviewer. At one point China describes one of the six companies of the Hika Hika Battalion called the 375 I.W. Sarema company, commanded by Colonel Njune, which had 600 men. Known as the "suicide company," 375 I.W. Sarema was charged with carrying out attacks where loss of life was likely. As a result, it was the only company allowed to smoke *bhang* (cannabis) or to keep any money it procured during its operations. In January 1954, the company had been inactive for eight months, yet China refused to explain why, nor what its future plans entailed. China also refused to reveal the strength of General Kassam's Embu Battalion.

Henderson thought it likely that Mau Mau had planned a campaign against those loyal to the government for early 1954, but he could procure little information on the subject.

China's interrogation also revealed that the leaders of each Mau Mau battalion—and indeed smaller units—had a great degree of freedom in decision-making. This was in large part the result of difficulties communicating across long distances in tricky terrain, and in gathering high-ranking commanders to discuss tactics for promulgating the war. This was a problem shared by lower-ranking officers, as well as leaders such as China and Kimathi. Although the two men met on January 4—just eleven days before China's capture—this was a "rare" meeting. The town of Nyeri stood between the Aberdares and Mount Kenya forests, and moving safely between the two areas—a crossing of perhaps five miles at its narrowest point—certainly entailed great risk.

As for his relationship with Kimathi, China was unenthusiastic. In Henderson's words, China did "not consider ... [him] a good leader." China stated that Kimathi had lost much of the "prestige" he once possessed. But China grudgingly admitted that, because Kimathi was the first man to head the forest fighters, he could not be removed. China's relationship with Kimathi had been stretched at times over the previous eighteen months. For example, they had once disagreed over homemade guns. China's team had manufactured two prototypes and had sent them to Kimathi. The latter forwarded them to the reserves, much to China's anger, as this new innovation might easily be discovered by the colonial government. China also disagreed with Kimathi's stipulation that only leaders of Mau Mau could collect funds from the reserves. In addition—as noted above—in November 1953 China had had to appear before Kimathi's Executive Committee No. 4 in the Aberdares.[69]

From the interrogation transcript it is clear that China was deeply concerned with maintaining good relations with Mau Mau's "passive wing," as well as Kikuyu villagers living in the reserves and outside the forests. Delineating between the two groups is somewhat arbitrary: there was no formal "membership" in the passive wing, and both groups provided essential support for Mau Mau by risking their lives to bring food, supplies, and even ammunition to the forest fighters. Based on his discussions with China, Henderson concluded that "virtually 80%" of Kikuyu in the areas involved in the war were part of the "passive wing." China, after all, boasted that Mau Mau enjoyed vast support in the reserves: he told Henderson that a gang of 200 Mau Mau could travel from Ndia to Tumutumu—a distance of approximately four miles—in "broad day-light" without anyone turning them in. Despite the fact that fighters did not grow food in the forests, China told Henderson that "[procuring] [f]ood … presents absolutely no problem." Fighters received the majori-ty of their food from people living in the reserves, and they could even enter shops to get more. They received so much food that they could afford to prohibit the consumption of venison among the fighters.

One of China's main aims in the war was to gain the good feeling of the reserve inhabitants by contrasting his force with the security forces and the Home Guard. Kikuyu outside the forests suffered at the hands of these two groups. The Home Guard, in particular, was notorious for phys-ical abuse and corruption in the villages. China gave an example: when Mau Mau heard that the security forces had killed a woman's child, they gave that woman twenty shillings to show that Mau Mau was "doing good." China implemented strict regulations in order to prevent Mau Mau abuses of the local population, which were highly effective. His troops were not allowed to prevent children from attending school; rape or abuse local women; kidnap innocent women from the reserves; or take money from people in the reserves without permission.[70]

On one level, China's actions were logistical tactics of war. Yet, taken together with his other writings, they seem to suggest a desire to give Kikuyu society the best possible chance to re-form successfully after the end of the fighting. Reconciliation would be impossible if a lack of trust and respect existed between Mau Mau and the majority of those living in the reserves (as occurred in actuality). This perhaps explains China's point that "no large-scale attacks are carried out in reserved areas unless the 'Muhiriga' i.e. The 'Clan of the area in question' supports the action." This desire to listen to the words of traditional clan elders emphasized their long-standing role in ordering a Kikuyu society that was in the midst of trauma and fracture.

Finally, China's interrogation revealed an extensive network of Mau Mau intelligence services. In the reserves, a group called the "Special Police" collected information, which they then passed on to the closest

Mau Mau force. China also claimed that Mau Mau had informants in many branches of government, including the army, the police, and the prisons system. The Mount Kenya forces possessed four wireless sets, monitored by English-speaking Mau Mau, who gleaned information from news bulletins and occasionally from police radio broadcasts. China demonstrated an awareness of British propaganda and stated that his forces countered these efforts by mounting their own types of propaganda.

By the time the interrogation was over, Henderson was convinced that he had stumbled across a gold mine of intelligence. He quickly produced a 44-page summary of the interview, and officials made 124 copies to send to posts throughout the colony. One went to the governor's secretary, one to the chief secretary, and one to the attorney general. A total of 45 went to army headquarters for dispersal to the armed forces. Police inspectors and assistant superintendents, the Special Branch, and district commissioners working anywhere near Central Province received copies, as did people in the upper echelons of the Nairobi administration. British officials now understood precisely how Mau Mau operated, and in such detail as they could never have dreamed.

## Trial and "Surrender"

The exercise of the law in British colonial Africa was never a plain matter of keeping order. It was also the bedrock on which the colonizers' claims to authority, control, and "proper governance" was laid. In Kenya's reserves, the standard of judgment was based on "customary law." Customary law was derived from supposed "tribal" regulations that administrators had codified following extensive consultations with elders and senior members of each particular ethnic group.[71] Where customary law was inapplicable—in Nairobi, for instance, or in any case where a defendant was accused of committing a capital crime—English Common Law was the basis for legal judgment. This standard was expanded during Mau Mau, when the government established a system of Emergency Courts to try those accused of Mau Mau-related crimes.

China appeared before Judge MacDuff at the Supreme Court of Kenya at Nyeri on February 1, 1954. He was assigned Saeed Cockar, a young

Indian lawyer, to serve as his defense counsel. The prosecution was carried out by Anthony Somerhough—the colony's deputy public prosecutor—who had represented the government in the trial of Jomo Kenyatta at Kapenguria the previous year. Initially, China was charged with four offenses: murder, consorting with "terrorists," possession of ammunition, and possession of firearms. Each of the four charges warranted capital punishment, based on special Emergency Regulations passed in 1952.[72]

But days before the trial began, doubts surfaced regarding the possibility of a successful prosecution for murder. The charge itself concerned a policeman stationed at Kiawarigi, who was killed in the attack on January 15. Several *askaris* (soldiers) had initially provided evidence that they had seen China during the battle, but then retracted their comments. In addition, it appeared that various entries relating to the engagement—recorded at the post—had been forged or altered, possibly by *askaris* wishing to claim the £500 bounty on China's head.[73] Ultimately, two of the four charges were dropped, so China faced the remainder: consorting with armed men and possession of ammunition. He pleaded "not guilty" to both.[74]

China's trial lasted for three days. The prosecution called fourteen witnesses, including five Africans (two tribal policemen, one private in the KAR, one medical assistant, and one Home Guard), one "Hindu" (a medical officer at Nairobi Prison), and eight Europeans (one medical professional, one former missionary and translation expert, and six drawn from the KAR, the police, and the Criminal Investigation Department (CID). The defense called just two witnesses; one was China.

On the first charge of "consorting," Cockar contended that prosecution witnesses had failed to conclusively prove that China was with the group of "gangsters" involved in the skirmish. On January 15, the majority of the engagement took place over the course of approximately one hour, and involved various rounds of firing at distances of several hundred yards. While witnesses claimed that they saw figures "stagger" and could identify some colors and types of clothing, it was difficult to identify the accused from such a distance. Thus, contended Cockar, it was impossible to say that China was part of the gang, and therefore he could not be charged with consorting with terrorists.

On the second charge—possession of ammunition—the testimony of

Wachera Kimaro, a tribal policeman stationed in Karatina, and Cyril Collins, chief inspector of the CID in Nyeri, stood to convict the accused. Kimaro stated that he had found two rounds of ammunition in China's trouser pocket when he searched him at Nyeri Civil Hospital after his capture. He did this at the order—and in front—of Collins, who supported the account. Collins explained that China had confirmed that the ammunition belonged to him ("This is mine"), but Judge MacDuff deemed this statement inadmissible. China, when he took the stand, claimed that the ammunition was planted before he arrived at the hospital. Cockar said that, at the very least, there was "reasonable doubt" about how the ammunition came to be in China's possession. He asked: "Would [a person in Accused's [China's] position walk into [a] military camp with ammunition on him [?]"

Cockar and China's defense was thorough, and included a further safeguard in case MacDuff found China guilty on either of the two charges. They claimed that China was in the process of surrendering to colonial forces when he was shot. This, they explained, was why China was in the vicinity of Kiawarigi at the time. The colonial administration had offered surrender terms to Mau Mau fighters in August 1953, which seemed to promise amnesty for crimes committed, provided that murder was not one of them. Because the Crown had decided not to file for murder against China, he might receive amnesty for the two charges if he was able to prove that he was in the process of surrendering. But MacDuff would not entertain the possibility: he did not believe that China was in fact surrendering, nor that the terms applied to the case. In any event, China had pleaded "not guilty" to the two charges rather than admitting them and asking for amnesty. Consequently, the three African assessors[75] found China guilty on the first count, and two found him guilty on the second. MacDuff then passed his judgment on February 3: "The Accused is sentenced to be hanged at the neck until he is dead."

The fact that China had claimed he was surrendering had a far wider impact than he probably realized. Two days after the sentencing, a flurry of top-secret telegrams began whizzing between Governor Baring and Oliver Lyttelton, the colonial secretary. Lyttelton was under pressure to explain to British parliamentarians why a man who had surrendered was about to be executed. It was highly likely to offend the British sense of right and wrong, and would surely require explanation. Lyttelton ordered that Baring postpone executing China until the two of them had discussed the situation.[76] Baring, however, was adamant that no mercy should be shown, as China's surrender claim was bogus. He was particularly worried about the effect such a commutation would have on the Kikuyu Guard, and Kikuyu "loyal" to the administration.[77] Kenya's director of intelligence and security, Richard Gribble, disagreed: "In the opinion of most Africans China undoubtedly surrendered, therefore in sentencing him to death Government has already broken its promises in connection with surrender."[78]

Baring did state, however, that he would "consider commutation" of China's sentence "were he to give information of sufficient value or were he to induce a sufficiently large number of terrorists to give up the fight." If that was to happen, he told Lyttelton, "I will let you know at once."[79] Baring was not being entirely forthright with the colonial secretary. Five days earlier, Gribble had interviewed China, and the following day submitted a report entitled "Future Possible Use of China." (It is likely that "using" China had been discussed since the day of his capture.) Gribble had noted that he believed the government could use China to procure mass surrenders of Mau Mau fighters still engaged in the war: with the high level of respect China commanded in the forests, he would surely be able to convince Mau Mau that the war was not worth continuing. Gribble did, however, note the moral quandary and potential military danger: "We are I think morally committed to sparing China's life because I do not think we can say 'succeed or hang' nor must we risk creating a modern martyred 'saint.'"[80]

The moment produced an extraordinary dilemma for Baring and the commander-in-chief, General Sir George Erskine. On one level, they had a chance to end Mau Mau with one blow. Yet they were also sparing the life of one of Mau Mau's most notorious leaders, who almost certainly had a significant amount of blood on his hands. For the month of February, secrecy was paramount, as officials began working with China. They postponed Operation Anvil, a vast "sweep" through Nairobi to catch suspected Mau Mau, to see what China's assistance might produce. On March 3, Baring publicly announced the previous weeks' dealings. The reaction was predictable: the Conservative Lyttelton won some plaudits in the House of Commons from his usual opponents, who praised this attempt to spare lives and end the war.[81] And the majority of Kenya's settlers were up in arms, horrified that China's life would be spared. Baring had steeled himself for this reaction, affirming to Lyttelton before his announcement that settler opinion "should be ignored." Lyttelton, indeed, viewed this reaction firsthand when he visited Kenya the following week. His conclusion—of which he informed the prime minister, Sir Winston Churchill—was that "Europeans with the low whiskey prices and high altitude pressures are both irresponsible and hysterical."[82]

*       *       *

China's work with the government had begun abruptly at 2 PM on February 14, 1954. He was taken from prison and bundled into a police van without warning. He was instructed to put on a policeman's uniform and to carry a tin box, which concealed the ball and chain attached to his ankle. "Constable Wambui" was then secretly flown to Nyeri, where a guard of KAR soldiers received him.[83] The following day, China began writing the first of twenty-six letters to Mau Mau leaders in the forests, under the watchful eye of Henderson. China's letters requested that fighters come to meet government representatives to discuss possible surrender terms. He wrote one to Kimathi, asking for his views on the surrender negotiations, but "insisting that we agree to attend the surrender conference."[84] Operation Wedgwood had begun.[85]

Henderson and China traveled into the forests together on several occasions to drop off or pick up letters from the forest fighters. Other letters were delivered via the extensive network of Mau Mau "friendlies." At certain points, Mau Mau leaders came out of the forests for discussions and were then returned unmolested by government soldiers. Each side made its demands: the government wanted Mau Mau to lay down its arms as a prelude to negotiation; Mau Mau wanted its leaders released. Representatives of each side finally agreed on a ceasefire: Mau Mau would remain in the forests and out of the reserves, while colonial forces would cease any bombardment of the forests.[86]

China's message seemed to resonate with a significant proportion of high-ranking Mau Mau. China's close associate, General Tanganyika, left the forest to take part in the surrender negotiations and became a conduit between the government and the forest fighters. Kimathi showed at least some desire to discuss terms with the government. Although he did not reply directly to China's letter, he wrote a missive to the government around this time, but with terms he knew that it could never accept:

> My soldiers will never leave these forests until the British Government accepts our demands:
>
> 1. disarms its forces unconditionally;
> 2. releases all the political prisoners;
> 3. recognizes our country's independence.
> These are our terms for negotiations.[87]

In another letter, sent to Baring, Erskine, and the premiers of Britain and the Soviet Union, Kimathi thanked Baring and Erskine for treating China well. He pointed out that although China was a "sensible man ... we will not be moved by his pleas unless he and the Government agree to the *Charter* issued last year by F.M. [Field Marshal] Dedan Kimathi."[88] The Charter was a list of seventy-nine articles—demands, in fact—which rejected practically any possibility of persons of European descent even living in Kenya.[89]

Many forest fighters feared two things: first, extended periods of detention and second, reprisals from the Home Guard in the detention camps. But despite various hurdles, the negotiations progressed. A large-scale surrender was arranged for April 10. By April 6, 1,000 Mau Mau had gathered in order to surrender, with more arriving each day. But the following day, a KAR battalion commanded by Brigadier Orr attacked them. As Anderson summarizes, "[S]ome thought Orr's action deliberate sabotage, others countered this by suggesting that Gatamuki's [the ranking Mau Mau leader there] intentions were to disrupt the surrender." After this incident, trust was broken: those in the forests were totally convinced that the entire process had been a ruse to try to kill them. Operation Wedgwood had failed, and Operation Anvil proceeded.[90]

# Detention

A little after noon on April 14, 1954, a small airplane landed at Todon-yang, near the shore of Lake Rudolf (now Lake Turkana), where two trucks' worth of tribal policemen were waiting to escort China to Lokitaung Prison. China was put in chains to avoid any possibility of his escaping, although the precaution was unnecessary in this lonely desert outpost that was more than 250 miles from a town of any size (Kitale). China's fellow detainees included—most prominently—six men the British claimed were the ringleaders of Mau Mau: Jomo Kenyatta, Bildad Kaggia, Fred Kubai, Kungu Karumba, Paul Ngei, and Achieng' Oneko. The "Kapenguria Six," as they were known, had been arrested in October 1952 during Operation Jock Scott (with the exception of Ngei). They had faced trial the following year and were sentenced to hard labor in northern Kenya.

China's arrival came none too soon for Kenyatta, who by 1954 had sunk into a deep depression and was physically ill. Since their arrival in April 1953, the other members of the Six had bullied Kenyatta. Leslie Whitehouse, the district commissioner of Turkana who was a frequent presence in the jail, referred to "hatred" existing between Kenyatta and the other prisoners. Ngei, in particular, violently disparaged Kenyatta's claims to have been an important person during his almost two decades living in Britain. The five were frustrated for several reasons: they believed that Kenyatta was excused difficult tasks due to his age, and they objected to the quality of his cooking (he was the chef for the group). In addition, all were more radical than Kenyatta. Certainly, Kenyatta was quick to associate himself with Mau Mau when politically expedient, but the poor, landless Kikuyu who largely comprised Mau Mau's membership had nothing in common with the elite, educated, and wealthy Kenyatta. Five of the Six even wrote a letter to the Luo politician Oginga Odinga, a member of the colony's Legislative Council, "denouncing Kenyatta as being on the side of government."[91]

Into this situation came China, who quickly became Kenyatta's only friend and confidant. Initially, the two men were housed in separate cells, but close to each other. They began exchanging information by singing loudly in Kikuyu, aware that the wardens would not understand them and would assume that they were simply singing for the sake of entertainment. China described to Kenyatta the events of the forest war; for though the detainees could access newspapers, they were heavily censored by prison authorities. It is clear that China idolized Kenyatta: "My spirits were soaring at the sight of him," he later described. When it came to describing his leg irons, China stated that he had eight links in each chain that bound his legs, as did the others. Kenyatta, however, had nine. "Even in chains, he was the greatest of us all," China recorded.[92]

The two men formed a close bond, and the conditions of their imprisonment improved. This was aided in large part by the arrival of Lieutenant Colonel de Robeck, an officer with whom China had served during the Second World War in Burma. De Robeck invited Kenyatta and China to his house on occasion and lent them books. The books provided the inspiration for China to suggest that Kenyatta teach him to read in English. Each day, for between twenty minutes and one hour, Kenyatta picked two English words and explained them to China. He did this "exhaustively," recorded China later, "their spelling, pronunciation, meaning, application, and use." In time, China was able to read the novels de Robeck had loaned him.[93]

It is likely that China saved Kenyatta's life by his very presence at Lokitaung. In one regard, he achieved this by becoming close to Kenyatta, helping to end his depression, and providing him with an ally. But China also acted as something of a bodyguard to the future president. In 1955, he overheard a plan hatched by the other prisoners to attack Kenyatta, which he reported to the prison authorities. And in 1958, he actually prevented a young prisoner named Kariuki Chotara from stabbing Kenyatta. (Chotara was considered by many to be *Komerera*—see above.) As Chotara moved to attack Kenyatta, he caught his trousers against a wooden table in the room. Kenyatta—now warned of the danger—struggled with his would-be assassin, while the other prisoners tried to restrain China from going to Kenyatta's aid. China was able to break free of their clutches and to secure Chotara's knife. The battle lines were well and truly drawn: when the five other members of the Six smuggled a letter out of prison to the editor of the *Observer* in London, alleging poor treatment, neither Kenyatta nor China signed it.[94]

China's account of his detention with Kenyatta differs from this story.

He seems motivated to describe how everyone loved Kenyatta, and he bolsters the senior man's credentials as a freedom fighter at every step. China states, for instance, that all the detainees were greatly concerned during a period in which Kenyatta was ill—which does not mesh with other evidence. China also makes no mention of Chotara's attack on the future president.[95] His description is closer to hagiography: China waxes wistfully about Kenyatta feeding his rations to hungry Turkana children outside the wire. He also describes how a small tin of soil sent to the future president by his eldest daughter, Margaret, was able to cure Kenyatta of a painful rash on his legs.[96]

In 1959, China was transferred to Mwea Camp, and then on to Hola, Marsabit, and finally Nairobi Prison. He was released on June 14, 1962. Friends from Nyeri picked him up in a rented vehicle and drove him to a house they had built for him. But China was soon on the move again. He traveled to Israel for military training, with Kenyatta's blessing, before returning to Kenya in the months before independence. Yet on the rainy night of December 12, 1963, as the Union Jack was lowered and the new Kenyan flag hoisted, China was absent. Kenyatta had sent him north to convince Generals Baimungi and Mwariama to exit the forests. They had remained there, convinced that Mau Mau's fight for freedom was not yet over.

## Beyond Mau Mau

Evaluating China's actions is fraught with difficulty. Was he a collabora-tor trying to save his own skin, or was he attempting to bring a peaceful end to the conflict and ultimately save Kikuyu lives? Certainly, China was in a difficult position in early 1954. He was living in the shadow of the gallows during February: Cockar had lodged an appeal on China's behalf following his conviction, but the Court of Appeal rejected it.[97] Working with the colonial government was a route to survival at least in the short term. It is clear that officials kept China in the dark about the possible commutation of his sentence, perhaps as a way to increase the likelihood of his cooperation. As late as February 27—and possibly later—China believed that he was in imminent danger of execution.[98]

The bevy of accounts written by foreign observers about Mau Mau that appeared during the late 1950s and early 1960s identify China as a plain collaborator interested only in saving his own life. William Baldwin, an American graduate of the University of Colorado who found himself fighting in Central Province, describes China in disparaging terms, explaining that he acted simply so that the government would "go easy on him."[99] Journalist Fred Majdalany also had little respect for China, nor did the author of a *Time* article in March 1954 who described China's actions as a simple exchange: the removal of his death sentence for cooperation.[100] Peter Hewitt of the Kenya Police called China a "traitor" and wrote, "China astonished us all when he relinquished the struggle and opted for the more secure ... life."[101] It is undeniable that China's actions around the time of his trial stood in stark contrast to many Mau Mau in the same situation: Anderson describes one trial in which twenty accused "[b]ehaved sullenly in court.... They refused to utter a word and stood mutely before the bench.... They were taken to death row ... [and] hanged, one after the other, at twenty-minute intervals."[102]

Kimathi's thoughts aligned with these European accounts. Kimathi spelled out his views in a letter to General Kago in March 1954:

> China has agreed to collaborate with our enemy, to work against the homeland, to save his neck. In this connection, he has told the enemy all he knows about the movement.... Furthermore, in order to prove his loyalty to his new friends, he has written to all Mount Kenya Front Commanders and the members of the Kenya Parliament urging them to call off the fighting and surrender to the British forces.... [When I read this] I was filled with indignation. If China thinks I will mortgage this great struggle to save his life, he must be crazy.... We have written to China and denounced him for his treacherous acts.[103]

Similarly, Karari Njama—Kimathi's secretary—is damning. Like Kimathi, he uses the term "collaboration" to describe China's interaction with the government. Njama states that the government used the information gained from China to launch a new offensive in early 1954. He blames China for giving up information "which resulted in a complete destruction of our communications and supplies, and detention of about 60,000 great supporters," and depicts him as selfish for saving his own life while sacrificing the wider movement.[104]

But these sorts of depictions dissipated as China became closely associated with the Kenya African National Union (KANU) government of Jomo Kenyatta after 1963. China started to climb the rungs of the government ladder, and his close personal connections with Kenyatta were well-known. When Kenyatta established his first government, he made China a "section commander" in the National Youth Service (NYS), and he continued to keep a watchful eye on his protégé. China won great success through his association with Kenyatta: he rose to become deputy director of the NYS, and he became a public figure of some import. Over time, this position provided a degree of insulation from common accusations voiced by the Kenyan public in the early 1960s: that China was a self-interested coward who had sacrificed the country's interests to save his own life.

And from Kenyatta's perspective, China was invaluable. The NYS came to constitute a sort of informal army of youth that protected the interests of KANU politicians. It also provided a way for Kenyatta to prevent disaffection from developing among young people that could lead to a sort of movement similar to Mau Mau.[105] Moreover, China possessed forest fighter credentials that Kenyatta could use to bolster his own efforts to associate himself with the physical struggle for land, freedom, and independence when politically expedient.[106] China gave Kenyatta legitimacy as one who had "fought for freedom": his memoir, indeed, explicitly connected Kenyatta to this struggle. As Anderson explains, "As a former forest fighter, Waruhiu Itote represented the heritage of the nationalist struggle for land and freedom.... He became a hero."[107]

The majority of memoirs written by Mau Mau fighters appeared from the mid-1960s onward, and not one depicts China in a negative light. China is absent in the accounts of Mohammed Mathu, Ngugi Kabiro, and Karigo Muchai.[108] Wachanga, Gucu Gikoyo, and Kiboi Muriithi mention China with varying degrees of brevity, but they offer no judgment on him nor his actions.[109] In Mathu's case at least, this seems deliberate: Mathu describes General Kaleba as "one of our best Nyeri fighters." Yet he ignores China—Kaleba's commanding officer, who was with China when he was captured. He simply states that Kaleba "was captured and killed on the basis of information given by an Athi River detainee.... Most of us ... refused to do anything to increase the suffering of our people."[110] Bildad Kaggia, writing in 1975, praises China as one of Mau Mau's "truly great soldiers," and Maina's *Six Mau Mau Generals*—written in close collaboration with China and published in 1977—of course offers high praise.[111]

Any attack on China's version of Mau Mau would have been not just an attack on China but, by extension, Kenyatta. And taking to task a close, personal friend of Kenyatta during the 1960s and 1970s was risky business. Several of those who opposed Kenyatta were murdered at the time (and many more detained), including left-wing political activist Pio Gama Pinto (in 1965), Luo politician Tom Mboya and Foreign Minister Chielo Argwings-Kodhek (both in 1969), and Kenyatta's former friend and later harshest critic, J.M. Kariuki (in 1975).[112] No connection to the president was proven, although whispers circulated about his role behind the scenes, especially when Mboya's assassin—Isaac Njenga Njoroge—referred darkly to the "big man" pulling the strings.[113]

In this context, the first of China's two books—*"Mau Mau" General*—came to dominate the narrative of Mau Mau. The memoir is clearly written and logically progresses from the days of China's childhood through to independent Kenya. Within a few years of its publication, it became the definitive guide to the movement, not least due to China's prominent position in Kenyan life. The memoir takes a nationalist tone, describing Mau Mau as a Kenya-wide struggle for freedom from colonial rule. *"Mau Mau" General* had an immediate impact on the Kenyan public and the scholarly community. Marshall Clough describes the account as possessing "quasi-authoritative status," and Robert Buijtenhuijs calls it a sort of "'official' history" of Mau Mau for a proportion of the Kikuyu.[114] Thus China's version of Mau Mau gained a level of authority. It ignored many of the difficult truths about the episode, and instead constructed it as a Kenyan struggle that dovetailed neatly with Kenyatta's nationalist narrative.[115]

*"Mau Mau" General* is also a narrative of China's experiences written to justify his actions in early 1954, and to reject assertions that he

betrayed Mau Mau. In the memoir, China presents the story of his capture as part of a planned battle against colonial forces; there is no pretense
that he was not associated with Mau Mau that day (as he described in his
trial). China is quick to defend his negotiations with the government: he
describes a series of meetings in the forests in 1953 in which surrender
negotiations were apparently discussed, but we have only his word about
this. He thus presents his dealings with British officials as a part of Mau
Mau strategy that would have been implemented in mid-1954, suggesting that he just brought the timing forward a few months. China also
claimed to have in his possession a letter from Kimathi, written on July
8, barely four months after the scathing missive above. The letter sup-
posedly stated:

> Dear General China.... The KAF Executive Committee met
> on July 8th.... We are thankful to you for keeping your prom-
> ise ... that even if you fell into hell you would not desert our
> cause.... We trust you, for you are with our leaders and can
> decide the way to be followed.... This Committee has confi-
> dence in you and gives you the honoured title of "Hero of the
> African Nation of Kenya."[116]

Kimathi was hanged in February 1957, and thus China's version cannot
be contradicted.

China also suggested that he had acted to *protect* his fellow fighters
during his trial. In this, he was responding in part to the criticism of
European authors, including Fred Majdalany, who asserted that China
had "the intelligence of an eleven year-old child" and that Henderson
(with his "far superior brain") had tricked the hapless China into giving
up information during his interrogation.[117] China entirely omits any
description of his interrogation with Henderson in the 300 pages of *"Mau
Mau" General*. But he claims that he portrayed himself as deliberately
stupid during the trial to conceal information from his inquisitors.[118]

Perhaps at one point in his memoir does China hint that he should
accept some blame for his actions in early 1954. He admits to having a
sense of "self-preservation," which led him "to want to try [his] utmost
to evade the death sentence" during his trial. And there is, perhaps, an

appeal for the reader to understand the position in which he found him-self: "Whether anyone tells the whole truth in a court which is trying him for life is doubtful; at least, I doubt it."[119]

But Mau Mau was never a simple battle of black against white, or Mau Mau versus "loyalists" and the colonial government. John Lonsdale has shown how it also reflected deep fissures in Kikuyu society related to gender relations, civic virtue, morality, generational order, and class. Mau Mau fighters worried about creating an ordered society in which all could attain land and maturity and achieve success for their families.[120] China's words and actions seem to hint at a concern about these sorts of issues.

Gribble's reports, in particular, seem to demonstrate China's genuine worry about what was happening to Kikuyu families. Gribble spent many days and nights speaking with China, and he concluded that China's actions "were in no way induced by offers, nor … thought of saving his own neck." Gribble noted that China paid no attention to his appeal. He came to the conclusion that China was horrified by the numbers of Kikuyu who were dying in the struggle. Gribble concluded that China would work with the government only if he believed that it was genuine about saving Kikuyu lives, and he would do nothing if he thought that the government was using him to round up and hang Mau Mau.[121]

It is certainly plausible that China came to believe that he could best serve Mau Mau and the Kikuyu by ending the slaughter in Central Province. The careful regulations he laid down about gender relation-ships and order in the forests seem to hint at this; moreover, China was adamant that women should not be harmed in the forests, even if they were deemed traitorous.[122] Dead women, after all, do not bear children for the next generation. China mandated that the government must "sincere-ly under[take] to consider 'the reasons why the men took to the forests.'" With the forest war over, Mau Mau's aims could perhaps be better addressed through public discussion and politics.[123]

China's personal conflict over the struggle is perhaps clearest in a let-ter he wrote to the chief mechanical engineer of the railways—likely Wallace Young—in 1953. The letter (reproduced here) is the only origi-nal piece of writing in existence from the time that bears China's name. The letter is no fanatical rant; rather, it reveals a man filled with insecu-rities, desperate to know whether his former employer remembers him well. Twice he asks, "How do you think about me?" and he reminds Young of the good service he gave to the railways. "From the time I left business of yours I got much troubles," he writes, "and the troubles let enter into the Forest [*sic*]." But the letter seems to contain a threat toward its end, raising the possibility that its chief purpose was extortion: China demands money from Young and warns that if the request is ignored, "I have to come there myself."[124] The letter perfectly sums up the contradictions, complexities, and ambiguities of China's motives and position.

\*     \*     \*

Unlike the majority of Mau Mau fighters, China won success in his career after independence. He used his position to advocate for the rights of freedom fighters, many of whom lost their land and livestock during Mau Mau, often to the loyalists who fought on the government side. China called for better treatment for these men and women, including from the government—perhaps surprisingly, given his role—and he attacked those who claimed to have fought for freedom but had done little.[125] He also turned his enormous energies to working with the NYS, which—although it certainly had a political role—assisted many youths in becoming productive members of society. China was utterly committed to the project, and he served for more than two decades in this fashion, only retiring in November 1984.

China's account of the Mau Mau struggle, published as *"Mau Mau" General*, is on one level difficult to reconcile with the typescript of his interrogation, and again with that of his trial. Yet perhaps thinking of China in another way helps to alleviate the confusion. China was no one-dimensional, Mau Mau fanatic. He was a man motivated by his personal interests both before and after independence; by his wishes as a Kikuyu man aching for the betterment of a society torn apart by conflict; and by his aims as a general of Mau Mau. The tensions between these three interests are clearly visible in his words and actions.

Waruhiu Itote, General China, died on April 27, 1993, but the most visible legacy of this conflicted man represents just one aspect of his life. The bullet that wounded him on January 15, 1954 was only removed by doctors in 1988, thirty-four years after it lodged in his neck.[126] It is exhibited for all to see in the Nairobi National Museum.

# "Mau Mau" General (Abridged)

## BY WARUHIU ITOTE

The text that follows is an abridged version of *"Mau Mau" General*, Itote's autobiography published in 1967. It is, unfortunately, difficult today to procure a copy of this text in the United States or Kenya. The material that follows is reproduced with the kind permission of John Nottingham, proprietor of Transafrica publishers of Nairobi (formerly the East African Publishing House).

The original version of *"Mau Mau" General* contains 38 chapters and 3 appendices. The abridged version is focused directly on Mau Mau itself, and omits Chapters 2-4, 9, 13-14, 16-17, 21, 26-27, 30-34, 36-37, and Appendix C. Short summaries of the omitted parts are interspersed in the relevant places throughout this abridged version, and, in many cases, the content of these chapters is discussed in the Introduction.

## Chapter 1
## Prologue

The first time I ever thought of myself as a Kenyan was in 1943, in the Kalewa trenches on the Burma Front. I'd spent several evenings talking to a British soldier, and thought we had become friends. But I was rather surprised one evening when, after we had been talking for a while, he said, "You know, sometimes I don't understand you Africans who are out here fighting. What do you think you are fighting for?"

I didn't have to reflect much on that question—we had all had it drilled into our heads many times.

"I'm fighting for the same thing as you are, of course," I told him.

"In a funny way," he said, "I think you're right—and I'm not sure that's such a good idea."

I asked him to explain this.

"Look," he began, "I'm fighting for England, to preserve my country, my culture, all those things which we Englishmen have built up over the centuries of our history as a nation; it's really my 'national independence' that I'm fighting to preserve. And, I suppose, all that goes with it, including the British Empire. Does it seem right to you, that you should be fighting for the same things as I?"

I did not know how to answer this, so I said, "I doubt it, I don't think so."

"You'd better not think so," he replied. "Naturally, we're all fighting to protect not only our own countries but the whole world against Fascism and dictatorship; we know that. But I can't see why you Africans should fight to protect the Empire instead of fighting to free yourselves. Years from now, maybe, your children will fight a war to preserve the national independence of your country, but before that it's up to you to see that they get an independence in the first place, so they can preserve it later!"

He turned away for a moment, and then turned back for a last word before leaving me alone.

"At least if I die in this war," he said softly, "I know it will be for my country. But if you're killed here, what will your country have gained?"

A week later he was killed, in Burma and far from home, but still a link in the defence and preservation of his own Britain. What he'd told me never left my mind. At first I could only ease the conflicts in my head by thinking of myself simply and purely as a mercenary, fighting for a foreign power which just happened to be our colonial ruler. But being a mercenary seemed cheap and second-rate, especially when there were more worthy causes much nearer my own home.

The following year I was at the Calcutta Rest Camp, where I met a tall and powerful Negro from the American South. An English-speaking Tanganyikan, Ali, was with me and the three of us started chatting.

"What's your real name?" I asked the Negro, when I read the name "Stephenson" on his American Army bush jacket.

"What do you mean, 'real name?' That's my name right here, 'Stephenson,'" he replied.

I explained that I meant his African name. Since he was a black man like the rest of us, he must have an African name somewhere in his background.

"If I had an African name," he said, "it must have been lost a long time ago, probably on the slave ship that brought one of my grandfathers to America."

"What about your tribe?" Ali asked him. "Can't you even remember that?"

Stephenson shook his head, looking round at the handful of other African soldiers who had gathered at the interesting sound of our conversation.

"You guys," he said very clearly, "are all looking at me as though I'm some freak, something strange, just because I don't have an African name. Well, I got this way because somewhere, a long time ago, some Arabs shipped my people to America, and after that we all grew up in a Christian country. But the same thing can happen to people when the Christians come to them—you don't have to be taken to England to lose not only your names but your whole way of life as well. You can lose it right out from under you in your own country! Right now you're being baptized as Christians generation after generation; one day you'll all wake up and think you *are* Christians. Won't this make it easy for the white men to keep on ruling you? Some of you will believe it when you're told that the white way of life, the white religions, everything white is the best thing for Africans to believe in and follow. Then who will be willing to fight for your freedom?"

He must have seen that his conversation was turning into a speech, and I thought for a moment he was going to break off out of embarrassment. But we were all somehow held by his words, and fortunately I think for all of us, he didn't stop. Instead he told us about the colour-bar in America, a fact, he said, which screamed at him in hotels, cinemas, buses and shops even though all Americans, from Roosevelt downwards, denied there was such a thing. America was a great nation, he said, but eaten away inside by racial discrimination; a nation of two standards and two faces, seemingly lacking the capacity to heal itself.

"We Negros in America are always being told that it is the land of freedom," he continued, "that we have nothing to worry about as long as we work hard. So we go along, suffering for decades. And you'll be misled in the same way after this war, I'm sure. The British or whoever rules your countries will tell you that nothing is wrong, that you should leave everything to them and not worry. I don't know how much you've suffered in the past, but I know you'll suffer in the future if you don't have your own freedom."

I was listening very closely to all this, for it had called up in me memories of that other strange conversation I had had in Burma.

"All I can say," Stephenson went on, "is that you shouldn't be misled by white Christians who tell you they are superior with their holy names and their holy way of life. Jerusalem isn't in heaven, you know, it's just in Palestine and people are fighting there with bombs and shells, dying in the so-called Holy Places."

This rather shocked me, for I had always believed Jerusalem to be in Heaven. "White Christians are fighting each other right now, so don't you worry when they tell you not to fight for your own freedom," Stephenson told us, almost with a shout. "But the whites who are fighting now will be heroes in their own countries forever and amen, while you Africans will be heroes for a day and then you'll be forgotten. If you want to be heroes, why don't you fight for your own countries?"

Stephenson's speech and the long talks I had with him over the next few days were like being in school again. He was fond of talking about history, and especially about wars and revolutions—his favorite example was Haiti, where black men had fought and won their freedom from Napoleon, despite claims that they could never succeed. Before we parted, Stephenson told me he liked my "guts" and that he would make arrangements for me to get to America, where I could find the education I would need to help my people. His promise was sincere, but the fortunes of war never brought us together again, and what was then a big part of my dreams never came true. Still, he had been a good teacher at an important moment in my life.

I was still in Calcutta when I lost my way in a subway and asked a passing Indian lady for directions. It turned out that her family had been in Tanganyika for many years and she herself spoke Swahili. She invited me to her home for a meal and I was only too glad to accept the chance of some conversation about Africa. Her husband was particularly interested in knowing what my fighting experiences had been, and what the war in Burma was like. We were taking tea when our conversation turned to political topics, in which, after my talks with Stephenson, I had begun to take a great interest. I was anxious to hear what somebody who knew Africa would have to say about our situation there.

"While you're here in India," the man was telling me, "you ought to pay attention to what we are doing, because you might learn something to help your own countries. We Indians are fighting for others in this war, but in return we've received a promise of Independence when it ends I have seen many Africans fighting alongside our men, but I haven't heard what demands you've made for the end of the war?"

I certainly didn't know of any myself, and said so. "So you mean," he asked, "when the British in Kenya came and told you to fight, you just got up without a word and went?" I had to admit that was more or less the case, except of course that we had been told our country was threatened with invasion by the Germans and Italians, whom we could only imagine to be the worst monsters on earth.

"You should have demanded Independence as your minimum price for fighting," he said.

"But," I interrupted, "Europeans have all the land and schooling, and the Africans have no factories or anything else to support themselves. How could we begin to run our own country right now?" My background on such topics was limited, and I could only feel a sense of wonder at the whole idea.

"If you must have them," the Indian replied, "you can keep all the Europeans you need after Independence—we will even be doing that for a while here in India. But at least you will have your say in what goes on, instead of being always at the mercy of foreigners. And it won't take long before you are running everything yourselves. If you remember, you were colonized in the first place because you had no education and no weapons to match the Europeans. Now some of you have got education, and some of you know how to use European weapons and can get them if necessary—is there anything else you have to wait for?"

Conversations like this continued throughout my stay in Calcutta. My new friends took a great interest in me, and often talked about the things we servicemen could do for ourselves once we were back in our home countries. Co-operatives were important, they told me, for a hundred ex-servicemen with gratuities could get rich much faster than one man alone, struggling against large organizations. Unity and trust seemed to my Indian friends to be the most important elements in any kind of social or political activity, and they transmitted to me a high regard for co-operation, as well as a deepening awareness that I personally wanted to play an active part in bringing Independence to my people.

## Omitted section: Chapters 2-4

In this section Itote recounts the years of his childhood. He then describes his experiences serving in the King's African Rifles (KAR) during the Second World War, emphasizing the importance of the military discipline and organization that he learned for his future role in Mau Mau. He then details the various jobs he held in Kenya following his return from war.

## Chapter 5
## I Join the Movement

The Railways at that time were riddled with racial discrimination. Just because of their colour, Asian and European drivers were paid far more than the African drivers who often had taught them all they knew. In one way or another, in 1947, I was as frustrated about our intolerable position as I had ever been.

An energetic young man called Mwangi Macharia started a society which he called *Anake a 40* or *Kiama Kia 40* ("The Forty Group"), and I joined this in that year. Although many of the members were ex-KAR, it was not exclusively for old soldiers. At first, the objectives were to fight, with all the means in our power, the government's plan to force our women to terrace their land in the reserves.[1] This scheme had caused great hardship and considerable social and family upheaval. It was administered very harshly by certain chiefs in the Fort Hall and Nyeri Districts who were anxious to please their District Commissioners with monthly reports of a record number of yards dug up.

I believe that even agriculturally this campaign was not necessarily the best thing, but it brought out into the open a clash that was to become ever more marked in succeeding years. On the one hand were the keen young ex-Army officers who formed the core of the British Kenya Administration and were District Commissioners and District Officers in the Central Province during the period between the end of the 1939-45 War and the declaration of the State of Emergency in Kenya on 20th October 1952; on the other hand were the young ex-Army Kikuyu NCOs [non-commissioned officers] whose whole outlook had been changed radically by their service overseas and who had survived death and much hardship in the cause of a country which now seemed determined to block and humiliate them at every opportunity.

The *Anake a 40* had several thousand members and achieved some notable successes, especially the so called Women's Riots in Fort Hall in 1949 and the comparative failure of the compulsory terracing plan. The group operated mainly in Nyeri and Fort Hall. It had no membership oath and eventually disappeared when the Movement of Unity had grown to significant proportions.

In 1946, I had joined the Kenya African Union (KAU). Although many of us had great hopes for this organization, past experience had taught us that it might well not be enough. Still, it was the only public and national political organization we had. I was also a member of the Transport and Allied Workers' Union whose chairman was John Mungai. At that time the trade unions had the most militant leaders and were the most active groups working for Independence in the city. Fred Kubai and Bildad Kaggia were especially outspoken and popular with the crowds.

I remember the tremendous enthusiasm generated among all of us in the city in May 1950 when Kubai said that he proposed to get Independence within three years. The older men thought this was wild talk and only calculated to make things more difficult. But we younger men, from the Army and from the new schools, saw it as a realistic and open possibility if only we could unite the country and if all our fellow-Africans could believe us when we told them what we had seen. When would they learn that the whole world was not like Kenya; indeed Kenya was one of the last outposts of feudalism, racialism and minority privilege and domination? When would they understand that things *could* be changed *and* within our lifetime?

The militant spirit among the younger men was fostered by the attitudes and actions of the European settlers at this time. They had produced a "Kenya Plan" which was nothing more nor less than a scheme for taking over the country and ruling it on South African apartheid lines. This pamphlet was widely circulated among our group and read out even to those who were illiterate. It had a profound effect on our thinking and on our plans.

Looking back it seems fantastic that we could ever have believed the Europeans could carry it out, but there was no "give and take" then, the line between the races was taut and brittle with hate and fear. We even suspected them of grander designs still, of linking a White East Africa with a White Central Africa all the way down to the torture chambers and horror farms of Malan's[2] South Africa. We had seen enough of these Boers [white South Africans of Dutch and French descent] in Kenya to know what that would mean. We had seen them flogging our women and children on the Plateau farms at Eldoret; we had seen their ruthless brutality in the Rift Valley Police Force and we wanted nothing of them, not their whiteness nor their apartheid, not their hypocrisy nor their condescension.

In late 1950 an old Army friend of mine, Kamau, asked me to visit him at Naivasha. We had been good friends and I was delighted at the chance of renewing our acquaintance. So one weekend I slipped away down the glorious Rift Valley to the small lakeside town with its groves of fever trees. I soon found the farm where Kamau worked and that evening we drank tea together with his family. After the meal he called me to the inner room and we began to talk about affairs in Kenya. Kamau and I found we were at one in thinking that something decisive must be done soon to show the Government that the people were growing angry. Kamau asked me to go with him to some other friends, also living on the farm, and I gladly went. It was thus in Naivasha that I took for the first time the oath of unity and dedication in the struggle for the freedom of my country.

When I returned to Nairobi my acceptance into the Movement was reported to the local Nyeri District Committee operating in the city. With hundreds of other young men I found myself swept into service. We had the formidable job of uniting a nation and peeling off the top coats of slavery and discrimination to the common undercoat of blackness that was all we had underneath. We were fighting with the weapons of Truth, Love and Justice a veritable arsenal of opponents, disguised as Christianity, Loyalty, Wealth and Power.

I was under the orders of the Nyeri Committee, many of whose members I came to know well. Somewhere floating above them was the awesome Central Committee responsible for the overall direction of operations. Their veil of secrecy was not penetrated during the Emergency and even today few people know many of those who served on it. They were humble men working for their people, not for their place in history. Soon after the Committee formation they gave orders for the stealing of guns and for the collection of funds to finance the revolution that might become necessary if the settlers' Kenya Plan was to be thwarted.

During the next two years I was a fireman on the Railways by day and a revolutionary by night. I rapidly became a trusted confidante of the Nyeri Committee and organized and guarded the oath ceremonies which were daily being stepped up. I also had the job of eliminating traitors to our Movement. Such people first had their case decided by the Committee, in their presence if they were members of the Movement, in their absence if they were Government servants. Appeals to the Central Committee were only allowed in most exceptional cases, indeed I do not remember any during my time, although I believe there were some afterwards. But this was not wholesale, indiscriminate murder as the British Government tried to say. Only a real two-faced traitor, and there is nothing worse in the world, would be sentenced to death. Our courts were much fairer than those of the Government with their summary justice, their framed evidence, their perjuring, bought witnesses. To take away a man's life is a very solemn act, something that requires deep thought and consideration of all the circumstances, in case there are any possible mitigating factors. We needed every African in the country alive, we did not wish to kill a single person unnecessarily. Only those were sentenced who had become a major threat to our security or whose brutalities to their fellow-men had become excessive.

# Chapter 6
# The Forest Fighters

In January 1952, a secret committee, called the "War Council" was formed. Members of the Council were nominated by each district from among those people willing to go and fight in the forest. Although there was close liaison between the Nairobi Branch KAU Central Committee and the War Council, the membership of the Council was strictly guarded by the Committee. And, even within the War Council, there was a further secret committee, composed of those who had no reluctance to use violence in furthering our aims. Some of our leaders and members in both the Committee and Council, especially the older ones, were opposed to bloodshed, while we of the secret committee knew that our people could never win their independence solely through peaceful means.

The secret committee gave instructions for the elimination of informers, and also encouraged its members to collect firearms. As an incentive, rewards were offered: Shs. [shillings] 200 for a .303, Shs. 100 for a pistol, Shs. 10 for a grenade, and other amounts, depending on the size of the weapon. A Bren gun [a light machine gun, often fired from a tripod], for example, fetched Shs. 500 and a Sten [submachine] gun, Shs. 250, while ammunition was worth 25 cents a bullet. In actual fact, few people received any rewards, and I for one received nothing although I collected many guns. Nevertheless, the incentive was necessary to make our younger people aware of the vital need for weapons.

We were so anxious at times to get arms that once, when we broke into a shop in River Road and stole twelve guns, we were so elated that we did not even bother with the nearby cashbox. Aside from arms, we also collected medical supplies, although without offering rewards. But we had a general rule, which was adhered to, that the families of young men who were arrested while taking a risk would be looked after, their children educated, and lawyers found for any subsequent legal proceedings against the arrested man.

In July 1952, while we were very much involved in these activities, we received information through our reliable sources that Kenyatta and other political figures were about to be arrested. The following month I had my last meeting with Mzee[3] before we entered the final struggle. On the 16th August, eight of us crowded into an old red car and drove out to Gatundu. It was a warm, sunny day and when we reached the farm, Mr. Kenyatta was walking in the garden, dressed in an old pair of trousers and an open-necked shirt. One of his fingers had been cut on a farming tool and was bandaged.

Despite the graveness of the time, he was calm and confident. Rather than talk in his house, we walked together to the river and stood watching it while we spoke. We had gone to him mainly for the advice on which of our men should be promoted to leadership positions, and what means we should use to select our leaders.

"Look, my sons," he said after we had put our problems to him, "you have come to me because you want to select some young people to work for our country. But you must realize that to be a leader is not an easy job, you don't become a leader simply because someone points at you and says, 'You will be a leader.' Those who are equipped to lead our people," he went on, "must know it in their own hearts. They themselves must be the first to recognize that they possess the qualities and determination that is needed."

He went on at length about the struggle which lay before us.

"The Europeans are not stupid," he said, "and if we wish to win our freedom we must not sleep—we must work day and night until we achieve our goal. Those of you who are leaders must not think of your own importance, but rather of how you can serve your country. One thing above all, which you must never forget, is that leaders are the servants of their people."

Kenyatta knew his own arrest was imminent, and he warned us of it. "Some of you, too, will be imprisoned, and some of you will be killed. But when these things happen, my sons, do not be afraid. Everything in this world has to be paid for—and we must buy our freedom with our blood."

Although most of us had had some kind of education, it was limited, and so we listened eagerly when Kenyatta told us of other countries where men had fought and died for freedom. Like my American Negro friend he, too, referred to Haiti as an example, and described the heroic struggle of the people against Napoleon, and how the great Tousseaud[4] led his people to freedom.

"They succeeded—but they suffered," he said. "We too, after suffering, will get what we want. But we must be courageous and determined, and have faith in our ultimate victory. When I first went to England in 1929," he told us, "I vowed to myself that Kenya would be free, and I have never lost sight of this goal. I shall go to prison, and perhaps I shall die. But if I die, remember that I shall never change; even then, my blood and my heart will remain with you, my people."

While we were at Gatundu, I blessed the circumstance which had made me join the army. Although at times I regretted having fought for our Colonial masters, on that day I was glad, for I was now going to use the knowledge they had given me, against them. Kenyatta, too, referred to this military knowledge.

"You learnt many things in the army, my son, and now you can lead our people.

"If you had died in Burma," he reminded me, "no one would have remembered you, for you were fighting for the British. But should you die tomorrow in our struggle, you will die for your own people and your name will live in our hearts."

He then charged us to carry out whatever tasks we would be assigned, and to maintain the utmost secrecy. We walked back to the house with him, and he offered us pineapples to eat before we returned to Nairobi. As I shook hands with him I knew it would be a long time before I saw him again; indeed, I wondered whether we would ever meet again. We were to do so, but not until many difficult days had passed, and not before I had lived for weeks in the shadow of the gallows. Yet during these hard years to come, the memory of this meeting with Kenyatta, and of the many serious things we discussed, stayed with me. Often, when I was discouraged or doubtful, I recalled Kenyatta's words, and above all, his confidence in our victory gave me strength.

A few days after this meeting with Kenyatta, the moment for which I had been waiting arrived. I received instructions from the Nyeri (Nairobi) Committee to report to Karatina, an important market town on the slopes of Mount Kenya. At Karatina I was to meet forty young men, untrained and unarmed, but inspired with patriotism and ready to fight. These men were to join me in the Mount Kenya Forest and to become the nucleus of an Army of Liberation. I was also told that Nairobi would send us money, guns, ammunition and medical supplies, while the District Committee would provide us with food, and would control the supply lines. It turned out that we had to find our own arms and ammunition.

Early on the morning of 18th August, 1952 I set out for Karatina in a taxi with two friends. I felt a sense of excitement as we sped along the wide road, and despite the new problems which faced me I was exhilarated. None of us talked much; each was occupied with his own thoughts. My mind wandered back to my army days in Burma, and then jumped to the lessons I had to teach our young recruits in the future, and the difficulties I would encounter through ignorance of the Mount Kenya forests. And, too, I recalled the inspiring words of Kenyatta, spoken only a short time before.

Our taxi suddenly slowed, and we found ourselves in a police road block. Although these were not uncommon at the time, it still seemed like a sign of ill-fortune that we should meet one on the very first day of our project. The car ahead of us was waved on after a thorough search, and we waited for the uniformed constable to approach us. It could have been dangerous, for I had in my pocket my most treasured possession, a pistol and twenty bullets, which I had purchased from a Somali for Shs. 200. The finding on me of one bullet alone would have justified my arrest. My companions, too, were armed, but with *simis*, deadly dual-bladed weapons that can sever a man's head with a single blow.

God must have been with us that morning, however, for we only had to show our poll-tax receipts (which were in order), and we were allowed to pass. Incredibly we were stopped again, outside Karatina, at a second road block, but again we passed through without difficulty. By midday we had reached Karatina, and a quarter of a mile before the town itself we left the taxi and were met by a local Committee member, who led us quickly into the bush.

# Chapter 7
# Oath Taking

We followed a small track by the river and then climbed above it to crouch behind a huge spreading tree; thus we remained well-hidden from any passersby. We waited while Achieng Mundia, from Karatina town, reported our safe arrival to the local KAU office. Unfortunately, he was spotted by a local headman, who immediately reported the presence of a stranger to the Police Station. Although we were not aware of this at first, even the idea of waiting made us nervous, for people knew that a secret movement had been launched and had been scared by the tales which Europeans told about it. Though the ordinary man in the country didn't know what the Movement was, what it wanted, or who belonged to it, he could still be frightened into betraying us unwittingly.

Before Mundia returned, another man, Mr. Chiira, came running to us and warned us to move quickly, for the police were about to search the area. He brought us meat wrapped in banana leaves and we ate it while we went along with him to a safer hiding place. By this time it was 3 o'clock, and we were beginning to think it was wiser to move on. While we waited in a house well away from the river, some women were sent out as scouts. They soon reported that our original refuge had indeed been searched, so we decided to move on to another house, a mile away. The owner, a friend of ours, had just arrived from Nairobi. After making us welcome, he asked us to administer the oath to his family.

I agreed to this, but one of my companions, Ngando objected.

"The police are hunting for us," he said, "this is not the time to administer oaths."

I disagreed, telling him, "The police are doing their job, and we must do ours."

We decided, however, to wait until the night before performing the ceremony and for security reasons we left the house to wait in the thick undergrowth some fifty yards away. A few minutes later the police arrived and searched the house thoroughly. We were near enough to see their features: there was a middle-aged ex-teacher chief with one eye, Eliud Mugo, an African Home Guard member, and a European police officer. We heard later that similar groups had scoured the entire area, under orders to stamp out the Movement before it got a foothold. But they were too late.

That night we held a massive oath-taking ceremony in which two hundred people, including the family of our friend, participated. Afterwards we explained what was expected of them: the British had taken our land, we said, and we had dedicated ourselves to the fight for our liberty—those who had taken the oath must now help us in every possible way. This continued as the basic theme of our ceremonies: the oath-giving, an explanation of our people's fate under British colonialism, and a clarification of the new obligations to which the oath bound its takers.

The following morning, tired after a short sleep, we set off across the country, keeping as much as possible to the groves of sugar canes and banana trees. The morning fog helped shroud our movements, and in the early hours, few people were about. We reached Kiangai market about noon, and since this was Achieng's home village we had no trouble finding shelter. After settling ourselves, one of our first tasks was to get a local tailor, one of our members, to make cotton gloves for us. Now that the fight had begun in earnest we couldn't afford to leave fingerprints on doors or weapons.

In the evening, members of the local committee called us and administered the second oath, the forest or *mbatuni* oath, to us. After four of us had taken this oath we were introduced to the forty young men who were from the core of our army. Their leader, Gaitho (later known as Major [then General] Mapiganyama) brought them in and formally placed them under my command. I was requested to teach them all that I knew about fighting, and particularly to show them the "jungle" methods used by the Japanese in Burma. Gaitho said that the local committee would help us with money, clothes and communications, but that it was up to us to find weapons.

In the darkness I saw the young men clustered round me, and it was probably then that I felt for the first time the enormity of the task we had undertaken. The lives of these men, and many others to come, were essentially in my hands; the training and the leadership which I would give them would determine the future of all of us. I chose nine of the men to act as section leaders, men whom I would train and who would then pass on their knowledge to the remaining thirty-one, and to subsequent recruits.

"You will be the leaders of the Mount Kenya Army," I told them, "and you must teach others what we are fighting for. There are no wages in this Army, and nothing can help us but our own skill, and the unity of people in the villages behind us. There cannot be unity unless we give the oath to these people, for that is the only way to be sure of them, and the only way we can know who is on our side and who we can trust with our lives."

We agreed to meet in the morning, and broke up for the night; for me, sleep took second place to the many thoughts which were with me in the darkness.

With my nine section leaders I left early the next morning to open our first headquarters. One man was left in charge of the thirty-one others, who were ordered to prepare themselves physically for the coming struggle.

"Imprisonment or death might be in store for all of us," I told them before we left, "but it is our duty to save our country, and no one can be spared who tries to prevent us from carrying out this task. Even if it is your brother or sister, it is better for him or her to die than for us to remain slaves."

Our first camp was located in a favourable spot, on top of a hill near the farm of an old man called Kariuki. The hill was topped by a flat plateau, and afforded a magnificent view of the surrounding countryside; its sides were free of bushes and trees and thus no one could approach us unseen. There were no roads leading to the hill, and although a few people came to this isolated spot on foot, we could never be taken by surprise. We could move freely among the cane and banana trees on the hill top. I explained to Kariuki what we were doing on his land, and he was pleased to play a part in the preliminary training of our forest fighters.

The first job was to administer the forest oath, so that the young men would understand the responsibilities of leadership. Each one was given a bracelet, made from the skin of a pure black goat—no other could be used. After this, it was a matter of giving them basic training: moulding them into one group, loyal to each other and to our cause; teaching them the background to our trouble, and the goals for which we fought; and teaching them the physical skills of war.

"The first step in any war," I told them, "is to know your enemy and to know his weapons. I shall teach you the tactics of the British so that we can know in advance what to expect from them, and how we can defeat them."

As we advanced further in the training, I learnt that none of my men had been in the army, and thus they knew nothing of the secondary organizations which supported the actual fighting men. We had to have our own Intelligence Department, I said, to match that of the British. We also had to make certain that our supply lines remained open. Although the enemy would have many wonderful weapons, airplanes and automatic guns, and a great deal of money as well with which to bribe people to betray us, we had a stronger weapon. Because we were fighting for our country, we would always have the advantage in propaganda to persuade the people to support us.

Yet all of us were conscious of the urgent need for weapons; there could be no substitute for firepower. I reassured the men that there was little to fear; we would have few difficulties in obtaining weapons. As an initial tactic, since we were not strong enough to organize a full scale raid on a police station or even a private house, we decided to ambush someone on the road and take his weapons.

"I know a man with a rifle," one of them said. "He's a watchman at a European's house near here. Let me go with one other man and the two of us will return with the rifle."

The man's enthusiasm and eagerness for action impressed me, and I let him go, with a companion, after warning them both to be cautious and keep their heads.

The next morning, Mitambo ([forest name] Batabatu) and his friend returned, tired but elated, with the precious rifle. They told us all a good story: Mitambo had approached the guard in the evening, and drawing out a packet of cigarettes, had asked for a match. He explained that he was in the neighbourhood searching for his wife, who had run away from home. Falling into the spirit of the tale, Mitambo had grown excited, and the guard himself became indignant at the idea of Mitambo's imaginary domestic quarrels. The "mythical" wife, Mitambo had said, went off and left a two-month-old baby, without milk, and he feared it would die unless she returned. Sympathetically the guard lit a match for him, and as he did so Mitambo struck him with a short but heavy club which he had concealed behind his back. The guard was not killed, but he fell to the ground, unconscious. Mitambo seized the rifle, took eleven bullets from his pocket and hurried back to his companion.

The outcome of this first effort pleased me considerably; if all our young men showed the same coolness and initiative, our future looked good. And, of course, we had our first weapon!

"In one day," I said, holding up the rifle, "we've got one gun. By being careful and thinking hard, we shall collect more. There's no need to buy them—we'll simply take them from the British and their stooges and use them against their former owners."

We continued with training throughout that day, and on the next morning I sent for the thirty-one others, who were still in the vicinity of Karatina township. Under cover of darkness we all moved together to Kihari, in the Hombe forest of Mount Kenya, about twelve miles from Karatina. We stopped at a place called *Karima ka Mburi* a quiet spot with one or two small farms and a hut which we ourselves occupied. I called the hut *Thingira wa Iregi*, "the cottage of our ancestors."

## Chapter 8
## Training Recruits in Forest Warfare

Our training thus began in earnest on 23rd August, 1952. The weather was perfect, cool at night, sunny but not too hot by day, and the rains were not due for another two months. Although the lack of weapons made certain parts of the training difficult, even one rifle sufficed to demonstrate many things—proper handling, loading, and cleaning, for example. We could not afford to use our tiny store of bullets for any shooting practice. However, after two days of hard drilling in the forest clearing, we went into action as a group for the first time.

We had learnt through our intelligence system that an African school teacher, an informer in the pay of the British, was coming to visit our farm to look for strangers. We expected him to arrive armed and by bicycle, and sent four of our men to ambush him along the way. As the teacher came pedalling past, the men jumped out from the bushes, pulled him from the bicycle and brought him, with his shotgun and 15 bullets, to our camp. I could see even before he spoke that he would not co-operate with us.

"Even if you kill me, I shall never surrender," he shouted at me, "because you are bad people, you are Mau Mau and you are spoiling the good name of Kenya."

We never took lives unnecessarily, but we knew, in this case, there was no alternative but to kill the informer. If we released him, he would go to the nearest Police Station and we would soon have every soldier and policeman within miles on our track. And it was equally impossible to keep him prisoner indefinitely, moving him with us under prolonged siege conditions. So he was killed, and his body buried in the forest in a grave which we dug carefully and later covered with turf and dead leaves, leaving no signs of disturbance.

Knowing that the British would come to check on the teacher's where-abouts sooner or later, we prepared to leave for the reserve. Even before we broke camp, a girl came to warn us that a band of KAR men would search the area the next day, as they suspected that something had befall-en their agent. They found nothing, of course, when they did come, but nevertheless they still suspected us. They vented their anger instead on a group of woodcutters staying in that part of the forest, sending them down to the "Reserve." When the news of this minor tragedy reached me I could not help feeling pleased as well as sorry, for now we would have the camp area entirely to ourselves.

On 26th August I received word that a large number of potential recruits had been mustered in Nyeri District and that I should go to meet them. I took Achieng Mundia, Ngando and Ngatia with me, and left instructions with my section commanders to continue training in the for-est. In particular, I ordered them to practise such things as crawling through dense bush with a rifle in their hands, hiding their tracks and fol-lowing those of other people. Mock battles should be staged, and a search made for potential camp-sites and storage places.

Leaving the men in the forest, we returned to our first Headquarters on the flat-topped hill. We had one major problem to deal with before we returned to the forest with the new recruits. About half a mile from the Headquarters at a junction of four roads, near Karura market, there was a Home Guard camp. The guards were detailed to search all cars and pedes-trians passing the crossroads. Their leader, Mbuthia Gachuiri, was a good man, a member of our Movement.

After reaching Headquarters, I arranged quietly to meet with Mbuthia.

He came up a bit later and I said to him, "We're going to surround your camp tonight, and administer the oath to your men. You, as their leader, must be the first to take it—although of course you've already taken it anyway. But if you take it then, your men will not argue, nor will they suspect that you're already with us."

Mbuthia agreed to our plans, and we arranged to make a "surprise" raid on his camp at 10 o'clock that night.

Administering oaths on this scale was sometimes risky, for there were always likely to be a few people in the group who, even after taking it, would report us to the police. On the whole, however, our people respected the oath, because we always explained its meaning to them and told them what we were doing and why. It was seldom that anyone disagreed with us once he understood the whole question.

Before the raid, I briefed sixty newcomers as to our plans. It was to be a non-violent manoeuvre, I told them, we wanted simply to recruit the Home Guards onto our side and this could be done only through giving them the oath. The value of gaining these guards was immense, for while appearing to work for the British they could, in fact, keep us informed and assist us in many ways. Only Achieng Mundia objected to the plan—in a group of thirty Home Guards, he argued, there were bound to be one or two traitors; if they reported us to the police our work throughout the area would be hampered. Since one finds in such large groups all kinds of people, some stupid, others clever, some trustworthy, others false, Achieng suggested we talk to each person separately, assessing him as an individual, before deciding whether to give him the oath or dispose of him.

"We cannot do that," I said, "the time for such cautious tactics has passed. You've learnt from me what it means to be a commander—if I say kill, you must kill. Now, today, I've ordered this plan to be carried out, and whatever the consequences, we must get on with it." And we did, although we still had only a shotgun and a rifle and, of course, my own ever-ready pistol. To make up for this deficiency we planned to surround the Home Guard camp in four groups of about fifteen people, with two groups on opposite sides sharing the two larger weapons. Upon surrounding the camp we would fire from both sides, thereby giving the guards the impression that many armed men had attacked from all directions. At the first sign of surrender, we would call out that we were armed and that unless they laid down their spears we would kill them.

The plan worked perfectly, and we soon had Mbuthia, the camp's leader, in our hands. As we had planned, he said publicly that he could not speak for all his men. He surprised me, however, by asking us to explain the meaning of the oath and of "Mau Mau" before the ceremony. We could not agree to this; the oath had to come first, and as time was short, I ordered them to sit down and stop talking. I told them that no one would be hurt as long as they co-operated. Mbuthia also asked them to co-operate, and after collecting their spears, we administered the oath in the usual way.

The following night, I moved with the new recruits to Thagara, another hill a mile from our Headquarters, an isolated but well-watered place. Before returning to our group in the forest we had to find someone to instruct us in forest lore, in the thousand and one details we would have to know to remain alive. Fortunately we found Ng'ang'a father of Bahati, and already an old man. This elder agreed to join us as a guide, and I sent some of my men with him to establish the first camp and to locate food caches.

They decided upon a spot about eight miles from Thagara, inside the forest; it was an excellent camp-site in every respect. Known among tribesmen as *Kieni kia Ngarari*, "a place of arguments," it had been the scene of a clash many years before between the Kikuyu and the Masai—through arguing, the Kikuyu had lost the fight! It was well up in the bamboo belt, yet there were also some large trees under which as many as thirty men could find dry shelter during a heavy rain-fall. There was a natural clearing, ideal for drill and exercise, completely surrounded by bamboo, a plant for which we had many uses.

After fixing the camp-site, Ng'ang'a called a number of elders together and in a short time we tried to memorize the knowledge which they had acquired in a lifetime on the slopes of Mount Kenya. It turned out to be an interesting meeting, for in addition to much practical advice, they also shared with us some beliefs based more on superstition than fact. They warned us emphatically not to fire towards the hills above the camp, lest we annoy the spirits which dwell there. Never cut bamboo with a knife without first sacrificing a goat, they said, or you will bring a hailstorm upon your heads. And, they said, if an animal is killed without the intention of eating it, heavy rain, thunder and lightening would follow. (This belief was soon put to the test, for one day a herd of cattle was brought from Meru for our fighters, and I decided to kill an animal so that rain would fall and obliterate the hoofprints of the cattle. I shot a buck and then killed a bird with a stick—but not a drop of rain fell.)

Another belief of the elders was that if you cut down a tree on Mount Kenya without first smearing bamboo trees with animal fat, heavy thunderstorms would occur. Most of the men came to believe this, and we always carried some fat in our pockets. But again I was forced to prove our fathers incorrect; after many days without rain I deliberately cut down a tree without performing the traditional ritual—as you can guess, the drought continued. Nevertheless, on this occasion to avoid the blame of the elders should damage be caused by the next heavy rains, I ordered my men to sacrifice a lamb to bring rain and pray to God for permission before cutting down any trees. I knew such sacrifices were pointless, but they were necessary to counter our breach of custom when we failed to smear the bamboo trees with animal fat. This incident had the effect of ending the custom, and the bother, of carrying animal fat around, and also enabled us to make freer use of the fire-building materials of the high forest.

As to the belief about not firing towards the sacred mountain, I too felt it had a measure of validity. To encourage us to follow tradition, the elders also said that if our enemies fought us while facing the mountain, none of our men would be injured. Much later, this warning was borne out, for we engaged a group of Government soldiers sent down from the Northern Frontier District and easily defeated them. Yet not long afterwards, facing the same way, we lost two men in a battle with security forces, and from then on we knew that the direction in which we stood had no effect on the outcome of the battle.

## Omitted section: Chapter 9

Chapter 9 describes Itote's activities in August and September 1952. He spent his time recruiting new members for Mau Mau—moving between the Kikuyu reserves and the forests—and evaded arrest on several occasions.

# Chapter 10
# "Emergency"

Throughout the period before the Emergency, and in its early stages, life at our camps had a routine and a purpose which we all contributed to and lived by. Over a period of time, through trial and error, through necessity and experience, we developed the practices and procedures required for normal life in what at first would appear to be a very hostile environment. We always adhered to schedules, and maintained a high standard of discipline. It is worthwhile sketching in some of the general quality of our lives—while it was not always the same in every camp, certain experiences and practices were fairly common.

When you live in the forest, for example, many of your senses, particularly those of smell and hearing, are heightened. We soon learnt to distinguish the ordinary—and the unnatural—sounds of the forest with ease, and spent the first half hour after our five o'clock rising as a "listening" period. We would sit in absolute silence, straining to catch every sound in the forest: the varying sound of wind in different trees, the call of birds, the noise of animals moving, the approach of rain. Above all, we trained ourselves to recognize the sound of danger, such as a man coming near, or a frightened animal, or a low-flying aircraft. Only after we were certain that there was no one in the vicinity of the camp who could take us by surprise did we get down to the day's business.

There were, of course, other and more permanent security measures. One guard system in particular was adopted by most of the larger camps, which were generally deep in the forest. First a series of "mock camps" was established, usually by a six-man detail which would build huts, dig holes and burn fires using damp wood, which caused voluminous smoke. The security forces would concentrate their bombing raids on these empty camps and send soldiers to search them, while we remained in safety many miles further up in the forest. The men employed to build these "mock camps" were trained to find ready exits at the first sign of trouble and they would always be well away from the area before an attack.

The human guard system for these larger camps was even more elaborate, for our lives depended on security. The first ring of defence was a chain of guards surrounding the entire camp-site, which was always chosen so that there was only one ordinary approach to it, and one secret exit. About a mile from the camp, on the approach route, four armed guards were stationed; two miles from the camp were another three guards, with similar posts at the four and six-mile marks. Thus we had a chain of security stretching almost to the forest's edge.

In the event of attack, two men in each group were detailed to resist, while the third would run to the next post, and so on, until the camp was alerted. Men from the two-mile post would move out to join those at four miles, to act as a further delay to any attackers. At times, the enemy was allowed to pass freely through the guard posts, only to be fired upon from behind by our men. Reinforcements from the camp would soon be on their way to the two- and four-mile posts, while others prepared to defend the camp itself; at the same time, documents and stores would be evacuated by the secret exit route to a pre-selected camp-site.

If the battle was a lengthy one, or if the security forces played a waiting game, we would dispatch a small group to the "reserve," where they would attack the nearest homeguard or security post. This frequently led to the recall of the attacking force to the "reserve." Our imagination, the swiftness and skill of our security patrol runners, and our careful judgment made it possible for us to resist for a long time a much larger number of well-trained and well-armed Government troops. Had we had their weapons alone, even without their numbers, we would have wiped them out completely.

Security, then, was well arranged, and this permitted the activities of the camp to proceed normally for the most part. After our early morning "listening" sessions we would have a vigorous physical training session, running and exercising. This was followed by a simple breakfast of porridge and tea; the kitchen was always out of bounds except for the few men assigned to cooking. We then had a short parade drill, and began lectures and instruction in forest-fighting skills.

The lectures covered a wide range of topics, ranging from principles of army discipline to basic "bush-craft." Cleanliness of the camp-site and personal hygiene were continually emphasized, not only because we had no doctors but also because carelessness literally could cost us our lives—a spent match dropped by accident could put the enemy on our track or reveal the location of a secret store. We learnt, too, to walk through the forest with great care, leaving no traces of footprints or broken twigs. If we were going to the reserve we would sometimes walk backwards across the murram [red, clay soil] roads, or at other times we would brush away our footprints.

Although these relatively simple tactics worked at first, we later found it necessary to develop more complex ones, especially when the security forces turned up a trump card—bloodhounds! We feared them not only because they might capture us, but also because they might discover the paths to our camps. Two techniques were generally used to evade the dogs: where possible, we would walk through rivers or streams; otherwise we would divide our group into couples, each pair of soldiers walking a different direction for a mile before rejoining the others. For the most part, this confused the bloodhounds enough to throw them off our trail.

We had codes and signals to distinguish each other from the enemy. A stranger would be greeted with the word *Itimu* ("spear"); if he was with us, he would reply *Ngo* ("shield"). The first man would reply *Ndemwa*, which refers to the marks which used to be made on a man's skin when he took the oath (this was eventually made illegal). Since there were seven of these scars, the correct response would be *Mugwanja* ("seven"). When we met strangers beyond talking distance, a series of signs was used. Our man would turn his rifle swiftly so that the butt faced the stranger, then swivel it round to the correct position. If the stranger responded similarly, all was well; if not, we might fight or flee.

Within the camp itself, food and shelter were carefully organized. At Barafu, for example, we built several houses of bamboo, a large one for soldiers, a smaller one for officers. My own place was about five hundred yards from the main camp, and I used a bell to signal the camp. I installed a heavy-duty lorry [truck] battery in my office so that I could have light when necessary.

As for food, we went so far as to finance two men in the "Reserve" to operate a bakery for our supply—one of the men is, in fact, still in business though he has somewhat more conventional customers now. These men set up bakeries at strategic points and conducted what appeared to be a normal trade with the local people, yet every day or two we would send men down to collect the sacks of bread prepared especially for our soldiers. Other food was supplied by trusted women in the "Reserves," who sent us sheep, goats, and vegetables, usually through a transfer system with soldiers at the forest's edge. As the fighting grew fiercer, however, these relatively comfortable arrangements deteriorated and many of us grew thin and accustomed to small and sporadic meals. We became more and more self-sufficient, and honey was one of our life-savers—we learnt how to locate it and to smoke out the bees, and we gained much strength and nourishment from it.

# Chapter 11
# Life in the Forest

Wildlife was a constant source of danger, unlike the infrequent though bothersome raids by Government forces. At first we found it difficult to sleep, since we were all unused to the roars and cries of animals in the darkness. Some of them, not surprisingly, caused great fear among us, especially leopards and elephants, which often wandered into our camps and prowled round the walls of our houses. We had some close calls with them, but in my eighteen months in the forest none of my own group was seriously hurt or killed by wild animals.

On one occasion, I was with a few men when we were caught by darkness, far from camp. We settled down by a fire and decided to sleep where we were, for we had blankets with us. In the middle of the night I was awakened by a sharp knock on the foot, and looked up to see, in the dying glow of the fire, a large leopard hitting my foot with her tail. A cub had just scuttled away at the sudden movement I made on waking, and the mother, angered and perhaps frightened herself, sprang towards me. The lessons of the Mount Kenya elders saved me then, for they had taught us that a sack or blanket is the best protection against leopards, as they cannot easily withdraw their claws once they are caught in the material. I ripped off my blanket and held it forward shouting for help; in a moment, as the animal thrashed in the folds of the cloth, we had killed it.

From the outset of our activities in the forest, it was forbidden to shoot animals: we could not afford the ammunition, nor the risk of giving ourselves away. And, in any case, we soon learnt how to trap such food-sup-plying game as elephants, buffaloes and small antelopes. Elephants were also helpful, as their tracks would guide us swiftly across valleys and hills, and often to the most direct route to streams. In the higher reaches of the forest we followed antelope trails. An elephant, too, cost us a rifle one day when he surprised me and a companion, a Masai, in the forest. The Masai stumbled, dropped his rifle, and bolted round a nearby tree beside me; the elephant went away, but not before trampling the rifle to pieces.

Aside from the meat of trapped animals, we also obtained food from our own gardens, which we had to plant as it became more difficult to reach the "Reserves," and as the supplies which were hidden for us before the Emergency began to dwindle. At that time great hunters' pits were filled with maize, beans, potatoes, peas, flour, and other storable vegeta-bles; carefully covered and camouflaged, these pits kept us going for a long time. But when these supplies began to run out, we planted onions, and arrowroot, which grew well on the banks of the rivers and in the marshy swamps high in the mountains. We learnt what we could about herbs, both for nutritional and medicinal purposes.

Since we had few medicines, and no doctors, we abided by the rule that prevention is better than cure. We used bamboo shafts to build a water-supply system to our camps, sometimes piping water over a distance of five hundred yards. I required all the men to sleep on beds, and severely punished those lazy or hardy enough to doss down on the ground. Apart from the danger of snake and insect bites, lying on the ground also increased the risk of catching even the common cold. Where sheep and goats were kept in camp, they were always housed a good distance away from the men. Indeed, most camps had a designated "health inspector" to watch over all such matters.

Another omnipresent element of forest life was the "scout." Whether men or women, the scouts displayed great courage and loyalty, many times contributing to our victories. They often ran enormous risks, and in some ways their task was more difficult than that of the actual fighters. Their job, basically, was to study the enemy, to learn what they could of Government troop movements, strength and so on. At the same time, they had to know the forest and to be able to contact us swiftly.

A scout had to be something of an actor, able to disguise himself as a peasant and mix freely with local people, arousing no suspicion. Other times he would have to pose as a KAR soldier, a policeman, or a Home Guard. Even more challenging was to pose as a woman—this required a man to be clean-shaven at all times. Self-discipline too, was necessary, for one had always to be on guard, to pay taxes regularly, to avoid alcohol for himself but to use it freely to gain information from another person. Female scouts had the special assignment of fraternizing with the members of the Home Guard; if they discovered important information about troops, armouries, or battle plans they passed it on directly to their company commanders.

Girls found it simpler to disguise themselves, or at least be inconspicuous—nurses or agricultural workers' uniforms were frequently used disguises; a woman could always pretend to be gardening when the enemy arrived. But her real task was to coax information from the enemy, or to lead them into traps where we could ambush them. The parties which our girl scouts arranged for police and Government soldiers often yielded valuable supplies of arms and ammunition. At the same time, girls were forbidden to associate intimately with our own soldiers, especially with rank and file. A woman who became emotionally involved with a forest fighter and then quarrelled with him might neglect her duty, either deliberately or unwittingly. Perhaps in so restricting them we did them an injustice, for the women at all times did a fine job, but we could not afford to take unnecessary risks.

We shared with the scouts some of our most important secrets. They knew, for example, that two feet beneath the cooking place of a deserted camp-site they could find directions to the new camp. Since they often carried messages or letters, scouts were required to destroy them, if necessary by swallowing, should they be caught by the enemy. We shared with the scouts, too, a special code of imitated bird cries which we used to guide them to our camp-sites or warn them of approaching danger.

There was also another special code, which was only used between myself and few trusted colleagues. The code gave the appearance of childish algebra, and was not likely to attract much attention if found by someone unfamiliar with it.

(The basis of the code was the use of numerals to represent consonants, and the separation of these "consonants" from vowels in o the parts of a fraction, that is, numerator and denominator. There were two variations on this system: in the first, the numbers one through thirteen represented the consonants B, C, D, G, H, J, K, M, N, R, T, W, and Y; in the second, the numbers 3, 6, 9, ... 39 represented the same consonants in the same order. Vowels were written in the usual way. Since the Kikuyu alphabet does not include the consonants F, L, P, Q, S, V, X, and Z, they were not included in the code.

As an example of the code's use for writing English, the following example should be adequate. If you wished to write "Kenya our country," it would look like this in code:

Code One— 7 9 13 o u 2 9 11 10 13
            e    a     10 ou    —
Code Two— 21 27 39 ou 6 27 33 30 39
            e    a      30 ou    —

Where two consonants were joined, as in TH, a minus sign was used; thus, TH in the first code was 11-5, and 33-15 in the second code. Although it appears complicated at first, when someone got used to it he could read and write as fluently as with ordinary letters.)

For those of us involved in the struggle for freedom, life in the forests, in the "Reserves" and in the towns took on a quality of excitement and challenge in the days preceding the Emergency and during its early stages. Those of us with experience of military combat had known the thrill of battle, but never the taste of command; in the fight for our own independence, we were thrust into positions which called for new skills and new ideas. Those below us, with no knowledge of modern weapons, tactics, or military organization, faced an even greater test. The opportunities for heroism, ingenuity, loyalty and failure were great, and I was continually surprised and thrilled at the deeds which many of us performed. Chronology here is less important than the substance of what happened, and I would like to relate some of the more memorable events, and to describe the people who made them. For the sake of convenience, these stories fall into three groups: contacts with the enemy, generally in battle or through arrests; the problems of acquiring weapons; and the urban adventures of one of our most renowned heroes, Mr. Paul Mahehu.

# Chapter 12
# The Naivasha Raid

If one were to make a list of the most exciting battles of the Emergency, the attack on Naivasha would rank near the top. Muraya Mbuthia, now an officer alongside me in the National Youth Service, was in command of the Nyandarua Army in 1953, and played a major role in the Naivasha raid. Born in Murang'a in 1931, Mbuthia came from a fairly prosperous family. His father opposed his education, but at fourteen Mbuthia enrolled and received three years' schooling. At the age of nineteen he took the oath and was elected Locational leader of the KAU. In 1952 he joined the revolutionaries, inspired by the anger he felt at the Government take-over of a school in North Kinangop of which he was Chairman. The sight of some 200 children being forced out of school was enough to send Mbuthia into the forefront of the fight for freedom.

His first action was to group thirty fighters around him; he was presented with a pistol by the Kinangop Division elders and ordered to use it against the settlers: "they have ravaged our property, beaten and killed our neighbors, calling them 'Mau Mau.'" Armed with spears and *pangas* [machetes], the men entered the forest. Mbuthia trained his men well in the art of forest-fighting, and in addition linked them up with other groups and obtained additional weapons; within four months, the troop had three .303 rifles, a shotgun, one pistol, and forty-five bullets.

The youngest member of Mbuthia's company was Mungai Thiga, who at one time had predicted that when the forest fighters attacked Nairobi Prison and freed its inmates, the white man's rule would come to an end. For this he had been arrested by the Home Guards, but he managed to escape to the forest, armed with a *panga*. By good fortune he fell in with the "bush" of Mbuthia (at that time, small groups or companies of guerillas were known as "bushes"). At the age of sixteen, he became the seventy-fifth member of the company. Shortly afterwards, Mbuthia handed over supreme command of the group to Mr. Mbaria, who had also escaped from Government authorities, and who was senior to Mbuthia in age; Mbuthia became second-in-command.

Early in March 1953 an attack was planned on the Naivasha Police Station; the date was set for March 22nd. Mbaria, Mbuthia and young

Mungai led the battalion reinforced by thirty men under Mr. Kibira Gatu, a leader from Othaya in Nyeri. After a long and tiring march, in which the dangers of meeting wild animals or enemy troops were very great, the band reached the South/North Kinangop crossroads. Mungai's mystic sense of the future touched him again, and he foretold that a bright star would appear and give them the light and guidance they needed; incredibly, a brilliant star soon appeared. Later, Mungai predicted that no danger would be met on their journey, and when the men reached Karati they rested for the night.

The next day, Mungai, whom all respected for his ability to foretell the future, assured the older men that it was safe to continue. He asked Mbuthia to inform the vanguard soldiers, and advised that anyone who was frightened should remain behind at Karati; anyone who entered the coming battle with fear or apprehension would be killed, he warned.

On the evening of March 26th the group surrounded the compound of the Naivasha Police Station—their courage must have been immense, when you consider that they had only five guns and very little ammunition. With the element of surprise on their side, the men were well-directed by Mbuthia, who knew the layout of the camp perfectly. They cut through the wire fence around the compound and killed a guard with their *pangas*. Firing a few shots into the air they broke into the armoury and Mbuthia began distributing weapons.

There was, in fact, surprisingly little resistance. One policeman, Sgt. [Sergeant] Kiniyia Nene, fired a few shots at them, but harmed none before he was shot himself. The Superintendent of Police escaped by Police aircraft, and some two hundred British troops fled to a nearby swamp. The policemen who had been resting in their houses and tents within the compound shouted out that they were prisoners, not soldiers!

Mbuthia directed the loading of several police vehicles with weapons, and sent them on their way to the forest. Then he released more than two hundred and fifty prisoners and fired three shots into the air, to mark the end of the operation. As the men began to leave, however, one loaded vehicle remained, and Kuria Chege ran back to drive it away. A European officer killed him with a Sten gun. Apart from Maina Thiong'o, who was killed next morning by security forces when he left his hideout, this was the only fatality of the Naivasha raid.

Most of the men made for the Aberdares, travelling as fast as was possible in the darkness. Some could not keep up the pace, and Mbuthia decided to stay behind with them—a decision which, but for his youthful appearance, might have cost him his life. When he dropped back to wait for the stragglers, he went into a village on the route and was arrested immediately by an alert Home Guard. Fortunately at Njabini Police Station, he was not recognized as a forest fighter, although by this time the entire area was being searched for those who had participated in the Naivasha raid. The police decided that his youth warranted repatriation to his home district (he was only twenty-one but looked much younger), but Mbuthia had enough money to bribe one of the police inspectors into taking him as far as Longonot in a police van and issuing him with a schoolboy's pass. With this he was able to reach Nairobi safely, where he met the Central Province party leader, Mr. Gicohi Githua. With a new company of fifty men, Mbuthia returned shortly afterwards to Nyandarua.

The new group was better armed than usual, with seven pistols, a .303 rifle, and a number of *pangas*. Despite the strict controls on personal movement at the time, the unarmed men travelled by bus to Thika, while Mbuthia himself and a few others walked with their weapons to Thika. A day later they entered the forest and joined the companies of Kago and Stanley Mathenge, at a place called Kiama. They went on to Kangema, Location 13 and rejoined Mbaria's original company, by then well-armed with the fruits of the Naivasha victory. It was at this stage that I started working with them.

In April 1953, Stanley Mathenge fulfilled a long-standing promise to take me to Nanyuki, where I was to meet the special committee to the *Kuuga na Gwika* ("say and act") Council. Both of us were armed with pistols, and when we reached Nanyuki we went directly to a KAR camp and were entertained in the sergeants' mess; among the KAR there were many men who were friendly to us and our cause, and others who were actively helping us. After some food and beer, we prepared to go by taxi into town but the driver, Kinyua, warned us that the place was "boiling." In spite of the danger, I insisted that we go on, partly because of a personal desire to see the town, but also because we were anxious to meet with the Council.

The driver took us to the market place. Mathenge got out to buy me a hat, for I always ran the risk of being recognized as a forest fighter by my plaited hair (this was simply a way of keeping the hair and scalp clean in the forest, where lice were abundant). With my head covered, we went into Mr. John's hotel for a rare treat, hot buttered toast and tea. Our pleasure was cut short, however, when a comrade dashed in with a warning— an informer had told the Europeans that I was in the area and white troops were about to surround the market. It seemed incredible that I could have been recognized so quickly, for only a few trusted people knew of my presence, and I was a complete stranger in Nanyuki.

Three elders, John, Muthai and Nduhiu took me to the hotel's newly built dance hall, which the soldiers overlooked in their subsequent search. John was beaten, and the others threatened with torture, but they refused to reveal our whereabouts. After four hours, the troops left, and I came out only to learn of Mathenge's remarkable escape from arrest. He had taken cover in a latrine and was discovered almost at once by an African KAR soldier. He seemed sympathetic, and for a thirty-shilling bribe he agreed to stand guard outside the latrine until the operation was over. The starvation wages paid by the British to their African soldiers were always a factor in our favour; even the most loyal men could rarely resist the chance to earn a few easy shillings, and our men were often able to "escape" from them for as little as five shillings.

When the excitement of the search had died down, we decided that our chances of meeting the Council were better now than before, since it was unlikely the troops would return. What with the distance we had travelled and the risks we had taken, it would have been foolish not to finish the job. The meeting served mainly to introduce me to members of the Nanyuki committee, and to solidify relations between the town and the forest fighters. Afterwards we returned to the KAR camp, delighting in the thought that the same European officers who had searched for us earlier were now relaxing only a few yards away, while we fraternized with their troops. When night came, we collected a large quantity of ammunition from our friends and returned to the forest.

## Omitted section: Chapters 13-14

Itote—now "General China"—continues to discuss the sorts of raids and missions that took place almost every day in the forests. Many of these were carried out with the express purpose of procuring guns or ammunition, often from the homes of European settlers.

## Chapter 15
## Weapons—Home-made

As it became more difficult to acquire weapons accidentally or by theft, we decided to try our hands at making our own guns. Our first experiment, early in 1953, was suggested by General Tanganyika (not yet then a general, however). We succeeded in exploding a .303 bullet by using a nail; the shot went wild, and so did we, as we realized the potential firepower we had. We called in two men, Ngoma and Waiwai, to help us in the construction of the first "home made" guns.

Car type tube rubber, water pipes and rough hewn wood stocks were combined to make a manageable, though not always reliable, rifle. The stock itself was fashioned from the wood of the *Muthiti* or *Thirikwa* tree, which never cracks under any weather conditions. The barrel, generally made from water pipes, was fastened to this, and a smaller pipe or piece of iron, one which would fit smoothly within the barrel, was used as a hammer. The hammer was released by a mechanism built out of a barbed wire spring and a piece of car or bicycle tube. Eventually we progressed from single-shot to "repeating" rifles, using magazines made from the iron of drums, and springs made from the metal bands which sealed boxes shipped overseas. Better triggers were fashioned later as well, using springs from chicken-weighing machines. With all the proper materials, and enough time, there is no telling the limits our imaginations would have reached.

We sent our first two rifles, with pride, to Dedan Kimathi. To our annoyance, he gave the guns names and then sent them into the "Reserves." We were perturbed at this, for if the weapons fell into Government hands they would know immediately of our innovations.

Since General Tanganyika was responsible for sending the guns to Kimathi, we quarrelled with him as well, and as a consequence I opened my own gun factory at our Mount Kenya Headquarters.

Twenty experts began work with me, and each company sent another twenty for training. Ruku, a young man from Murang'a, was in charge of the operation, and no weapon could leave the factory until he signed a release order. His assistants included Mukungi of North Tetu; Kamirig ti from Nanyuki; Kamwana from Mathira; and our original inventors, Waiwai and Ngoma Kagio. As more and more people learnt how to make guns, it was no longer possible to pinpoint any invention or innovation as being the work of one particular person. At the same time, and perhaps more than anything else, the proliferation of this skill and its improvement demonstrated that our men were equal in intelligence to anyone. Had we had the opportunities, many of us would have gone far in such fields as engineering.

Although we were able to manufacture guns in the forest, we never produced our own bullets. We did have techniques, however, for multiplying the use to which those we had could be put. We filed down bullets to fit them to different size weapons, and we frequently opened shotgun shells to remove a bit of the powder, which we replaced with crushed glass: ten shotgun shells could provide enough powder to fill five new shells.

We were always careful to collect empty cartridges, which we either refilled or exchanged for new ones with sympathetic policemen or soldiers. Indeed, one of our main sources of ready-made guns was the KAR. Although the majority had not taken the oath, many of the Wakamba, Luo, Meru and Embu men had done so, and within the military camps they operated their own secret committees, supplying us with arms, ammunition and money. In addition they provided us with KAR uniforms which we used for disguises. Most of these supplies were transferred with the help of women, who would go to the camps on the pretext of visiting boy-friends or husbands; sometimes they dressed as Muslims, draping themselves amply in cloth, under which they could smuggle out guns, bullets and uniforms. Because of the danger of such work, the identity of the women was known only to a few leaders, and they themselves rarely knew their comrades. Over and over again, during the Emergency, I noticed that a woman could keep a secret much better than a man; even under interrogation, relatively fewer women than men would break down and reveal information.

Not all of the KAR helped us, by any means. Some of the tribesmen, notably the Boran, Turkana, Rendille, Nandi and Lumbwa were openly antagonistic, although the latter two groups understood the nature and purpose of our activities. But quite often, where we met a company of soldiers in the absence of white officers, they would fire high and wide, and then exchange their bullets for our empty cartridges, reporting later to their officers that the ammunition had been expended in a severe encounter. Other times they would advise us as to the best course to take to avoid meeting less sympathetic forces. Where whites were present, of course, they were often the only genuine targets!

The Northern Frontier District was another good source of arms. Abdul, a fighter stationed at my Mount Kenya Headquarters, frequently took a group of men with him into the District to collect food and weapons. Bullets could be had for thirty cents each, and pistols, mostly of Italian origin, for two hundred shillings. The success of such expeditions gave me greater ambitions and I decided to send a large group of men directly to Ethiopia to purchase arms. Of the eighty men who set out, fifty turned back before reaching the border. Two of those who pressed on were killed in a battle with border troops, and nothing was heard again of the remaining twenty—whether they were imprisoned by the Ethiopians or decided to settle down there rather than return, which I doubt, is unknown. The fifty-eight who dropped out nevertheless did a handsome business for us before returning. They brought with them twenty-nine guns, six thousand bullets and twenty-one Italian hand grenades. In the District, our Mount Kenya company alone spent Shs. 26,000 for a hundred and thirty-four guns, Shs. 20,400 for 68,000 bullets and Shs. 200 for forty grenades.

Trading in weapons, however, was an extremely dangerous business. Everyone who helped us with so much as a bullet risked his life; to be found in possession of a gun or bullet, or at times even in the company of an illegally armed person, was punishable by death. This provided a vicious temptation to Home Guards who were not above planting a bullet in the pocket of a man whom they wished to see dead; against the denials of the most innocent suspect, the word of the Home Guards was virtually law.

The dangers of carelessness in the handling of weapon transfers caught up with Kefa Wanyonyi of North Nyanza. Kefa was a member of the Mount Kenya Chief Committee and leader of the North Nyanza members who assisted us. Although he was not actually found in possession of bullets, he died as a result of having once possessed them. In November 1953 Kefa sent 1,000 bullets through a messenger, who failed to hand over an accompanying letter. Instead, he abandoned the letter, along with some other documents and books, during a nasty battle at Kianjau, near Kanyota market. The next morning, Government forces found the books and the letter, which named Kefa as one of our suppliers. Eventually he was brought to trial, and the written evidence was bolstered by the testimony of his foreman, a Muganda [Ugandan], who chose to become a State witness. Both Kefa and our courier, Kagume, were clearly damned, and they were hanged; Mwangi, from Murang'a was released for lack of evidence. The foreman was repatriated to Uganda, for had he remained in Kenya our own forces would undoubtedly have revenged themselves for his disloyalty.

Aside from guns, we used and manufactured our own arrows. Kamiruri, who was with the Hika Hika company, was the first person among us to produce arrows; but we didn't find this method of warfare very satisfactory, for arrows required considerable work and were rarely retrievable. At first we poisoned them with certain herbs, such as *Mung'athu*, and later we discovered a virulent poison which, to the best of my knowledge, had no antidote. Even a scratch from an arrow tipped with the poison produced a speedy death. I soon banned the use of this poison entirely, for just as the armies in European wars had banned poison gas and germ warfare, we too knew that this terrible weapon could be turned against us, and against the innocent people of the reserves. As our gun manufacturing flourished, in fact, we ceased entirely to make arrows. The first and last workshop was at Sagana, in a place known as Nguniu.

## Omitted section: Chapters 16-17

Chapters 16 and 17 are about Paul Mahehu, or "Brigadier Nyamanduru" as he was known in the forests. Mahehu carried out a variety of daring forays to steal weapons and bullets—including from the house of the chief native commissioner—and organized the escape of one Mau Mau suspect from the High Court before his trial could take place. Mahehu was finally arrested.

# Chapter 18
# "Should Women and Children be Spared?"

The organization of our troops and military actions on Mount Kenya was handled by a number of different committees, composed of the leaders of the companies which were fighting in the forest. In addition to our own Mount Kenya companies and committees, there was a joint committee of Mount Kenya and Nyandarua, known as Committee No. 4. The scope of this Committee's powers covered all matters connected with the war throughout Kenya; this Committee had the power to authorize war or to end it; it was responsible for enacting all rules and regulations regarding the conduct of war and personnel (see Appendix B, where some of the Committee's regulations are listed). No other committee, in either of the two areas, superseded Committee No. 4, and it had the right to review the decisions of all the other committees. Twelve leaders, six from Mount Kenya and six from Nyandarua (the Aberdare Mountains) sat permanently on Committee No. 4:

- *Mount Kenya:* General China (Chairman); General Tanganyika (Vice-Chairman); and Generals Ndaya, Ruku, Kaleba and Gachuma.
- *Nyandarua:* Field Marshal Dedan Kimathi (Chairman); General Stanley Mathenge (Vice-Chairman); Generals Kago, Ndungu and Kimbo; and another leader, Mungai.

The records of this Committee were always kept in duplicate, with one copy given to the representatives to each theatre of the war.

The meetings of the numerous committees and councils of the Army of Freedom were always lively sessions, both in terms of the amount of business covered and the freedom of expression which was permitted. Debates ranged over such topics as ethics, tactics, promotions, political and economic history, morale, organization, individual rights, supplies, defections and so on. A glance at the agenda for a typical meeting (in this case one which took place between 18th and 22nd October, 1953), reveals the following points for discussion: (a) how to increase recruitment to our forces; (b) how to increase food supplies in particular areas; (c) how to secure the co-operation of non-members; (d) how to convert the police and KAR to our side; (e) how to assist our spies and special police; (f) the conditions for negotiating with the Government on a cease-fire or surrender; (g) the rewards for those who had helped supply weapons; (h) how to aid our men currently held in Government prisons and so on, including questions which might be raised at the conclusion of the scheduled agenda. This meeting, which was held in the Karuthi area of Ruguru Location, was guarded by three hundred and sixty Forest Fighters and attended by such leaders as Field Marshal Dedan Kimathi, Generals Kaleba, Tanganyika, and Ndaya, and Commanders Gachuma, Rui, Rhino Boy (Ruiru), Mohammad Mwai, Githee (Kinyori), Kimbo, Mungai, Kago, Ruku, Kanji, Kaiurgo, Rigatho, Kabiu, Kenneth, Batabatu, Mburukenge and Mathari Ndubu—twenty-one leaders altogether.

One of our most interesting meetings took place on July 8th, 1953, beginning in the evening and continuing through until the afternoon of the next day. Those present, besides myself, were: Dedan Kimathi (Nyandarua), Gitau Matenjagwo (Murang'a), Ndaya (Embu), Makondu (Kamba), Kinyeri (Meru), Ruku (Meru), Kubukubu (Embu), Mburukenge (Dorobo), Kirito ole Kisio (Kenya-Tanganyika boundary), Ng'ethe (Kiambu), Gitundaga (Thomsons Falls), Kahiu Itina (Nyandarua), Gachuma (Mount Kenya) and Njoroge (Kiambu).

After greetings, especially to the Masai delegate, from Dedan Kimathi and myself, I read the proposed agenda. The most important topic was a resolution passed by the Executive Committee No. 4 two months earlier, which read: "that no women or children whatsoever should be killed because such actions limit the future growth of our population."

Kimathi rose to explain the basis for the resolution. Following the Lari massacre, he said, it was evident that both the Movement and the country had suffered a great loss.

"Many children as well as adults were killed, and others were hanged later. I can't see how this had any humanitarian benefits; it could not be compared to the attack on Naivasha Police Station, for example, which was a reasonable operation of the war and one which deserves praise from all those who support our cause. But I would like to ask one of our elders, such as Ng'ethe, to relate the full story of Lari to us, so that we may understand it."

Ng'ethe, who was representing Kiambu, began on a somewhat defensive note.

"I have the feeling," he said, "that leaders of Embu, Meru, Nyeri, Murang'a and Nyandarua have no confidence in Kiambu members. Let me reiterate that Kiambu is the mother wing of the Liberation Movement, and all those who fight for freedom today have been influenced by us. Kiambu gave shelter to those who worked in Nairobi; it provided oath administrators for the city; it is in fact the gateway to Nairobi."

Ng'ethe went on to say that even though the people of Kiambu might form a minority of those in the Liberation Army, they nevertheless had played and continued to play an important role in the struggle for Independence.

"We're not here to discuss the merits of Kiambu or Nyeri or any other place," I interrupted. "We have important problems to deal with, so let's not sing praises but instead let's get on with the business at hand."

Yet I couldn't refrain from adding a few words of my own: "You ought to bear in mind, when you talk of Kiambu, that it was the people of that area who betrayed Mr. Kenyatta, not those of Embu, Murang'a, or Nyeri; nor of the Masai, the Meru or the Wakamba. We must keep things in their proper perspective when we start to praise one District at the expense of others."

Ng'ethe, unperturbed by my strong words—for this was the way we conducted our meetings—turned to the Lari question, as we had asked him to do.

"The root of the trouble at Lari was lack of land, and nothing else. You all know Chief Luka was the only one to go to Mweru—all the rest refused to co-operate with the European Government. He lived alone in the forest, making money from the timber there. Of course, when people saw how he was prospering, some thought they would follow his example and started cutting and selling trees. But when they moved into the forest, Chief Luka labelled them all as 'trespassers,' and 'taxed' them at a rate of a hundred shillings, a fat ram, a debe of honey and a needle from each man. When the Emergency started, thousands of our people who had made their homes in the Rift Valley were 'repatriated' to Kiambu. But when they got there, the Home Guards and Chief Luka did not permit them to live in peace. They accused them of belonging to 'Mau Mau,' without any attempt to find out who had taken the oath and who had not. Many Kiambu people suffered hardships because of this attitude, and their feelings against the Chief grew bitter: they finally decided to destroy him, his family and all the Home Guards. And this was the cause of the so-called Lari massacre."

After Ng'ethe resumed his seat, Njoroge, who was also from Kiambu, rose to express his own opinion.

"I don't intend to praise Ng'ethe's speech," he said, "but I want to add that after Luka was killed, most of the people involved returned quietly to their homes, and a few escaped to join the Forest Fighters. But the Government forces didn't stop to enquire who was guilty or who was innocent when they entered the villages. They killed *anyone* whom they suspected of being a 'Mau Mau' member. Limuru is a land of settlers, as you yourselves well know. The vicious Home Guards of the area hacked and slayed our people, infants as well as grown-ups, indiscriminately. So many people lost their lives through the actions of Government troops that when the Governor visited Limuru he issued a law preventing the authorities from further slaughter. Of course, the authorities gave their usual excuse, claiming that all the deaths were the responsibility of 'Mau Mau.'"

Njoroge added that he had a few more words to say about the costs of such actions.

"I want you to know that some people are now being taken from the villages to the edge of the forest, on the pretext that they will be given land; instead, they are killed, and the blame laid at the feet of 'Mau Mau,' who are supposed to operate at the edge of the forest. Undoubtedly the

British Government believes we are responsible for these atrocities, and as long as they go on believing that they shall never listen to any of our just demands. So let us all be careful, in the future, not to harm women and children, or innocent people, so that our own people will know that such evil deeds are the work of the Government troops."

Gitau Matenjagwo followed Njoroge's moving speech with one of his own.

"Avoid such a massacre again," he asserted, "but as far as I'm concerned, I don't agree with the resolution that women and children should be spared at all times. We all know that some women have served as traitors; since we have no prisons to detain them in, and if they know we shall not kill them, what will deter them from continuing to work against us? But once they are certain that a traitor is always punished by death—whether man or woman—they won't betray us so easily. I'm not saying the Committee's resolution is wrong, but I'm just giving my opinion."

The Masai delegate, Mr. Ole Kisio, then got to his feet, and since it was his first time to speak to a meeting on Mount Kenya he greeted us all, and me in particular as the leader of the Mount Kenya forces. He then pointed out that even when the Masai had fought the Kikuyu in tribal warfare, women and children were captured but not killed.

"I call upon you therefore to catch women spies and traitors, and to take them to the forest and teach them the correct beliefs so that they can work for our cause. Let them carry food and other supplies. And when they realize they have done wrong, and have learnt the correct line of thought, then release them to go home if they wish.

"Women aren't strong," he concluded, "they can be influenced and easily persuaded to see their mistakes."

Kubukubu disagreed strongly.

"I can see no reason why women should be spared. They utter charming words when they meet our soldiers, but they are not sincere. I call upon our people to shoot them dead whenever they cause chaos, for their double-dealing always leads us to battle and sometimes to death. Women like this aren't important to the nation, they are the supporters and servants of the Europeans. Our battle has got to be fought on all fronts, without mercy; let them die as we must die, for this is war. But as for children, I don't think they should be killed."

Some of us were surprised when Kahiu Itina stood up and told us: "I want everybody associated with a traitor to be slain—not only the betrayer himself, but his entire family. Maybe my views are too harsh, but I believe that if you kill only the husband, then the wife will tell his children what happened and in time they will grow up with a wish to avenge their father. I say, if you kill the father, kill also the wife. And if you've killed the parents, the children will be left to suffer, to turn to robbery and other misdeeds in order to keep themselves alive. They will grow up as rebels against society, and recalling the death of their parents will work against our future African Government. So they too must be killed. Show no mercy to a bad family—finish them all, for is this not what the Colonialists themselves do? When they drop a bomb on a village, does it hit only the men? Does it even pick out the 'guilty' from the 'innocent?' Let's not waste time considering the welfare of those who hunt us like dogs, who work against us. Perhaps in future I shall mourn the cost of it all, but for now, let us fight without mercy for the liberation of our nation."

It came as no surprise to me when, after this stirring call, Mburukenge of Dorobo rose to support Kahiu Itina.

"I want to say briefly, for we've got many other important things to discuss, that women spies and traitors should *not* be spared, and those who advocate this are wrong. Such women should be brought before village committees for judgment, and if found guilty should die. But if they are found innocent, they must be released, for otherwise we may kill many women who are unpopular for personal and not political reasons."

Dedan Kimathi, our Chairman, suggested that we vote on the matter, but Gitundaga wanted a chance to speak, and also called on me to say a word before the voting. Kimathi agreed to this, and Gitundaga picked up the argument in a new direction.

"Think back to the days when famine swept our land and men died like flies; when people lived on banana stems and bitter vegetables and roots. Women were left without husbands, and to escape the famine they fled to the forests and lived there in groups, without men. When a man appeared, however, they caught him and detained him by force, if necessary, until they were all heavy with children. Then they freed him. Thus did the Kikuyu tribe rebuild itself and increase its numbers. We must recall such incidents, for when our women die it pleases the Europeans greatly, for it saps our strength and will one day reduce our population so much that we will not be able to demand our Independence and our land. Is it not the aim of the slaughters which the Government carries out and then blames upon us?"

Gitundaga went on with this interesting speech, bringing in a few statistics.

"Is it not the truth that if a thousand men and only ten women survive a disaster, it will take them centuries to build up their tribe? But if a thousand women and even five men are left alive, it will not take long to fill the land once more. Forget what the British did centuries ago when they liberated themselves from the slavery of the Romans; let us instead do what we have proved right, without imitating other nations."

At this stage, my secretary, Wamaitha, a girl from Meru, asked for permission to speak. I opposed this and said that her work was to record our discussions, not to join in them; she was not a leader and since not every view had been put forward, she had to remain silent. A majority of those present disagreed with me, however, and so she was allowed to speak.

"It is an honour to have this permission," she said, "and I hope General China understands that we no longer live in the days when a woman could not eat meat before men. Although I'm not a leader, I am responsible for writing down your speeches and your secrets, and I have never revealed anything. If General China didn't trust me, I could not even be in your presence, let alone speaking to you. Besides, this is a war of men and women; since I'm the only woman here I must represent them. I've been to many meetings and have never before asked to speak; but when you are discussing women, you've got to listen to their representative; even fighters such as yourselves can make mistakes about the war."

This was all something rather unusual for our meetings, but we were very much caught up with her words.

"You all know that when the world was made, Eve was created from Adam's rib. Yet it was she and not Adam who was tempted by the serpent and then in turn tempted her husband to eat from the Divine Tree. You can see how delicate is the heart of a woman, even though she can work and think like a man. It is her nature to be easily seduced, and this must be kept in mind when discussing women.

"Now, women in the 'Reserves' are treated as badly as men, and sometimes even more harshly, for the men can escape to the forests. Some are restricted and imprisoned. But even if we have taken the oath, we can't look on another woman's child and let it die of hunger when our own children are eating—in this we are not at all like men. Even white women help African children if they find them sick or hungry, while the white men find this strange and kick our children as they pass through the 'Reserves.' Men mistreat women by raping them and by other bitter actions. Instead, it is up to you to teach women to be faithful and loyal to our cause. I say you should concentrate on killing our enemies, the white settlers, and leave our women alone. The European is like a teacher, while women are like students; if you wipe out the class today he forms another one tomorrow, but if you kill the teacher, the pupils cannot suffer evil from him, and you can replace him with a teacher who does good."

Wamaitha made a final plea: "Forget about killing women; wipe out your enemy and the foreigners and so liberate our country. Then all our sorrows shall disappear. And as for women traitors, when you catch one take her to the forest to work for our Movement, but do not allow her to know any of our secrets lest she be captured before she is loyal to us."

After Wamaitha's speech, I had the privilege of being the last to address the gathering.

"I can only say that I have completely and absolutely rejected the idea of killing women. Instead, I agree with Wamaitha that whenever a woman traitor or informer is discovered, she should be taken to the forest by our fighters and held prisoner. In the meantime, our village leaders can report to the authorities that a certain woman has gone into the forest and been killed by the 'Mau Mau.' Then, when she returns unhurt after two weeks, the authorities will arrest her, suspecting that she has joined the Movement. In that way, she will be punished for her wrong deeds and we shall not be guilty of harming her. She will have been cooked in her own oil."

The Committee then voted on the resolution, which was supported, ten to five. From that time on, we avoided the killing of women and children. The meeting continued with discussions dealing with enemies in the reserves, tactical co-operation in the event of attack, and the use of such animals as monkeys as warning devices.

# Chapter 19
# "The Komerera"

One of the continuing problems of our forest army was to maintain its integrity against those who wished to use it to further criminal purposes, or for other reasons unconnected with the liberation struggle. Such people were called "*Komerera,*" and a major discussion of how to deal with them took place at a meeting on 20th November, 1953. Those in attendance, including myself, were: General Ndaya, General Tanganyika, Major Ruku, Captain Kanji, General Kaleba, Major Rigathi, Major Mapiganyama, Adj. Achieng (Mundia), General Rui, Brig. [Brigadier] Batabatu and Major Kubukubu.

In the course of the discussion, we found that men in the forests could be divided into three groups as far as their loyalty to our Movement was concerned. First there were those of us who had taken the Oath of Action and were organized into companies and who operated according to the rulings of the committees of officers and leaders. Then there were those captured by force to fight with us, people who feared to return to the "Reserves" after being with us because of possible reprisals. And finally there were the so-called *Komerera*, those who ran away from their homes for fear of being killed or detained, no matter what the reason. Some hid in the gardens during the day and returned home at night; often, if they were killed by "security" forces, they were identified as members of "Mau Mau," when in fact many of them were not connected with the Movement at all.

The *Komerera* had expected the Emergency to end quickly, and planned to return from hiding as soon as it was over; they also expected the quick release of Kenyatta. But when they saw that things were getting worse, some of them thought it better to throw in their lot with us, hoping at least to get food and protection. But those who succeeded in this were also the first to reveal our secrets if and when they were captured. Although some of them had taken the oath, they were not really committed to our cause and so they fell easy prey to the offers and persuasions of the Government side. Of course, those whom we had forced to fight with us were even more eager to expose our secrets if they fell into enemy hands. We decided that our best defence against such traitorous actions was to prevent the *Komerera* and forced fighters from knowing any details of our activities, and to change our pattern of behaviour and camp immediately [when] such people were captured.

One of the sources of these so-called "forced fighters" was another *Komerera* group, who pretended to be "Mau Mau" fighters and who went round the "Reserves" beating people and taking their money. Many times these people were in the pay of the Home Guards; but regardless of their inspiration, they gave the true Forest Fighters a bad name with the people. We had decided to instruct our village committees to arrest or detain such people, and we would then bring them, under guard, to the forest, where they were often punished. After two weeks, they were given permission to leave, but many of them refused to go home because they feared both the ordinary people and the policemen and Home Guards.

It was unfortunate that we, whom the Government and spokesmen called "thugs" and "ordinary criminals," sometimes found our activities hampered by just such groups of people who wished to take advantage of the tensions which existed in the reserves and in Nairobi. Whereas such elements, as well as the ordinary *Komerera*, were simply operating on a day to day basis, we were planning night and day to bring the war to a successful conclusion. We knew what our aims were, and for us it was better to be dead than to be slaves in our own country. Our aim was the return of our land and the achievement of freedom from foreign rule. And our chief motto was the famous Kikuyu proverb, *Gutiri wa Ithegi utuire*, "None of our ancestors is alive." By this slogan, we meant that we must all one day die, and therefore we would fight until strength failed us, until our death, or until we were victorious.

As for *Komerera*, we decided we would have to wage war against them just as much as against our other enemies, for they threatened not only our Movement but the safety and well-being of innocent people in the "Reserves."

# Chapter 20
# "Loyalists" v. "Mau Mau"

In January 1954, there was a large meeting of "loyalists" of the Kikuyu, Embu and Meru tribes. Chiefs, local government heads, church leaders and Members of Parliament attended in an effort to find ways to stop the "Mau Mau" war and to demolish "Mau Mau" activities. Among the speakers were some who preached that "Mau Mau is the biggest enemy of Kenya," and that they had witnessed how "Mau Mau" slaughtered the people, drank their blood and ate their meat. They accused "Mau Mau" of burning houses and crops and schools, of blocking the country's political and economic progress, of taking money from people for their own use. The "loyalists" called on the people to fight against "Mau Mau" and to help the Government.

Others at the meeting claimed that "Mau Mau" caused the leaders of the country to be disobeyed; that it took young men into the forests where they lived like animals but were told they were fighting for Independence; that there could be no Independence in Kenya unless Africans, Europeans, Indians and Arabs united together to demand it; that if one tribe claimed Independence alone it could not succeed and thus "Mau Mau" would lead to nothing. Those who fought against "Mau Mau," the people at the meeting were told, would be remembered for generations for their peaceful and gentle actions, while "Mau Mau" leaders would forever be cursed by forthcoming generations for their evil activities, and they would never be allowed to return to normal society. The meeting went on for twenty-four hours and passed resolutions to be sent to the Chief Native Commissioner of Kenya, demanding stern steps against "Mau Mau" leaders and their followers.

Not long after this meeting was held, when its resolutions had become known to the public, Field Marshal Dedan Kimathi addressed his own meeting of officers and men in Nyandarua. As an example of the educational use to which some meetings were put, I shall quote some excerpts from Kimathi's address. At all such meetings, extensive minutes and notes were made, which now makes it possible for me to set down publicly, and accurately, what we said more than ten years ago.

"A short time ago," Kimathi began, "a meeting was held in Nairobi of

Chiefs, leaders of churches, MPs [Members of Parliament] and so on, with the aim of weakening our Movement. Let me tell you what they said, so you may see how falsely they challenged us. First, they said 'Mau Mau' is the enemy of the people and that it murders them and drinks their blood. Now, we all know that these people want to please the Government; some of them even betray us, for they have taken the oath. Not even a child can agree to drink human blood or eat human meat; you know that the blood used in our ceremonies comes from animals. We have our order that bloodstained clothes cannot be worn; if we cannot even dare to wear clothes touched by blood, how can human blood be swallowed? To fight these lies, it is up to us to make the truth known.

"They have said we burn houses and crops. But where we only burn the property of our enemies, the chiefs and Government agents burn the property of all, including peasants; they confiscate the property of those whom they dislike and then falsely prove them guilty of some crime. We can never do such things.

"They say we refuse to let children go to schools and that we burn schools. Yet the Colonialist Government itself burnt more than three hundred KISA [Kikuyu Independent Schools Association] schools, depriving sixty-five thousand children of their schooling. Where do these pupils now learn? And where is the equipment which was removed from those schools? There could be no more open robbery than this. We don't hinder children from going to school, but the children of parents who are connected with 'Mau Mau' are expelled from schools. Didn't some of our Members of Parliament agree with the resolution to deny our children education?

"The elders said that 'Mau Mau' blocked the wealth and trade of the country. But which 'Mau Mau' member issues business licenses? Which African distributes jobs or profits? Jobs and business are in the hands of whites and Asians, and the black man is given no chance. Those elders know very well that the European Government has blocked the way of the African, but because they are heavily loaded with fear and their bellies have grown fat, they want to collect their wages and escape detention. They are worth nothing to the country.

"They say that 'Mau Mau' deprives people of their pastures. But think, which African, whether 'Mau Mau' or not, has taken away a piece of land which people now lack? Wasn't it the white settlers who took away our land in the first place? Isn't that the very reason we are fighting today? We can see how foolish these elders are. The settlers who grabbed our land and who said, 'step into the *shamba* [farm] and you will go to prison for trespass' are the very same people who put forward this meeting, at which the 'loyalists' pledge themselves to fight against 'Mau Mau!'

"The leaders accuse us of collecting money from women, which they have saved through selling grain. Now, the Government has refused to allow Africans to plant maize in the Kikuyu 'Reserves,' and this is causing our people to starve. Where then do the women grow this maize which they are supposed to sell? The Government's aim is to force the Kikuyu to starve, but those 'trusted' leaders do not seem to be aware of this.

"The elders assured their meeting that there would be no African Independence alone, that all races had to fight together for it. But then, may I ask, why didn't India accept an 'Indian-British' Independent Government? Or, when Britain herself was under Roman rule, why didn't they agree to a 'coalition' government, instead of their complete independence? Our country does not belong to fools, and chiefs. Church ministers and Members of Parliament of 1954 should bear in mind that they are selling our country and nation. But I, Kimathi Waciuri, urge you to fight to the last person—and the last should take cover until he regains his strength, for we shall never stop the war until our Independence is assured.

"Finally," Kimathi said, "those leaders at the meeting said that people fighting against our Movement would be remembered forever. But I say that our Movement, known as 'Mau Mau,' will be remembered and respected forever when we gain our liberty, and generations will celebrate the heroic deaths of those who gave up their lives for the nation. In the big cities of our country will stand the portraits and statues of our heroes, and those of the Colonialists which stand there now will be pulled down. Those given medals for their good work in beating 'Mau Mau' will throw them away when we are free, and those pretending to be good now will hang themselves after Independence. Their children will be ashamed, while the children of 'Mau Mau' will walk strongly.

"'Mau Mau' leaders who are living at that time will bear proudly their medals and honours, respected for the excellent work they did in liberating their people from the hands of the Colonialists. Do not think," Kimathi concluded prophetically, "that we shall all die and that none will remain to reveal our activities to the people at a time when they shall be free to applaud them."

## Omitted section: Chapter 21

This chapter describes China's trial at the hands of Executive Committee No. 4. He was accused of stating that the British would ultimately defeat Mau Mau but was found innocent of these charges by Dedan Kimathi.

## Chapter 22
## "Peace Demands"

Apart from confirming a number of rules governing conduct in the Forest Forces, the meeting on January 4th, 1954, had the most important purpose of discussing the report of our Peace Committee, of which I was Chairman. For some time, we had been considering the question of negotiating with the Government about the conditions for ending the war, and a committee had been appointed to draw up a list of demands and a timetable for initiating peace talks. Kimathi called upon me, after the session began, to present the committee's report.

After greetings, I told the members of the Executive Committee that a thorough investigation had shown that a continuation of the war would not be wise unless we revealed our aims both to the other tribes in Kenya not connected with it, and to people throughout the world.

"Unless people understand what we are fighting for," I said, "they will find it harder and harder to support us. Right now we have no political organization in Kenya to speak for us, and none of our own leaders dares approach a civil servant to put our case—this would be the same as asking for imprisonment or death. With all our political leaders in prison or detention camps, however, it is up to us to begin some kind of discussions with the Government. Even if this doesn't stop the war, at least it will show the people in Kenya and throughout the world that our battle is not aimless, and that we are not the cause of the troubles in our land. We think it wise to try and find a way to fight the Government with reason as well as with weapons."

I then went on to list the eight principles which my committee thought should be discussed in any talks with the Government. These were, briefly:

1. According to speeches and leaflets issued by the Governor of Kenya and by General Erskine, in which people were asked to surrender, we would demand that the Government show its sincerity by removing its forces from the "Reserves," whereupon we would end the war and seek an agreement for the future.
2. All arrested leaders were to be released to participate in peace talks.
3. African Independence must be complete, and not under British rule.
4. Land must be given to those who have none.
5. Racialism in all forms must be abolished in Kenya.
6. Business and trade must be open to Africans.
7. District Education Boards must be dissolved and an intensive development of African education begun.
8. All Kikuyu schools must be allowed to re-open.

"There are many points on this list," I said after reading them, "and none of them will be easy to settle. Our committee, however, after considering which person should represent our forces in any talks with the Government, has chosen me, depending upon both the approval of the Kenya Army of Freedom Executive Committee, and any amendments or additions which may be made to the eight principles. The committee has decided to go on investigating the possibility of peace talks and has decided that June 1954 would be the proper time to hold such talks for by then we shall have prepared ourselves completely. Now that everything has been explained, it is up to the Executive Committee to accept or refuse our suggestions."

The discussion which followed was terse and to the point. Mungai thought that the proposed date was good, but emphasized that all adequate preparations and precautions should be made. General Ndaya agreed with him, and pointed out that since we were only at the report stage, there might be other demands to be added. Ruku, of Meru, wished to amend the list by adding a ninth point: that Africans should be a majority in the Legislative Council and that Members of Parliament should be elected by the people they represented; Kago seconded his points. Gachuma raised a tenth demand, that the building of villages should end, as it was almost like imprisoning people.[5] Stanley Mathenge agreed with Gachuma, and added an eleventh demand: the special tax must be cancelled.[6] Ndaya called for an end to the forced employment of women in aimless and difficult work. General Tanganyika requested a thirteenth point, that the destruction and clearing of crops such as maize and bananas must be halted.

Then Kago took the floor, asking for a fourteenth demand.

"Warn the Government to stop shooting people who surrender with their hands raised above their heads. Many people are forced to hide themselves these days for no reason, except that they fear to be seized, arrested or killed by the Home Guards and Police; when innocent people approach these forces with their hands raised they are often shot dead.'

"I support Kago's point fully," General Kaleba said, "and indeed I agree with the current fourteen points in our list. But I think there may be others, and I would suggest that China should go round the 'Reserves,' talking to our village leaders and compiling all the grievances of our people so that they may be placed before the Government. I fully support China as our representative, but I think it must be absolutely certain that when he goes to talk with the Government in June he will not be arrested.'"

The conference chairman, Kimathi, took the floor.

"Our committee has twelve members, and we have raised 14 points. I think each of us has made at least one point or supported one particular demand. This in itself shows that you are pleased by the idea of pursuing the peace talks further. But before voting on the Peace Committee's report, I would like General China to comment on the six points which have been added just now."

I said that I welcomed not only the new ideas, but also the suggestion that I visit the "Reserves" to talk with local leaders about their opinions not only on our fourteen points but on any others which they might wish to add. I told the conference that I had already spoken to local leaders and that they were all pleased with our plans.

Kimathi then summarized the discussion. "We decided to form a committee to deal with the question of achieving peace and of formulating our demands; that committee has now given its report and we have agreed with its suggestions and have added some points to it. No war is fought without discussions and explanations of the cause of the war, and we must do as other nations do in time of war—fight and discuss. Although we are not voting on the resolutions of the Peace Committee until May 1954, I would like you to decide at this meeting whether General China shall serve as our representative to the Government. Personally, I don't like the idea, for if the Government refuses to let him return, or if he is hurt or imprisoned, it will be a great loss to us. But if the committee decides to send him, I will naturally support its decision. If the committee does choose him, then he is like a lamb of sacrifice, and he will have to swear to obey. Is there any discussion on this before we vote?"

There was not much to say, and Kago seemed to speak for most when he said, "We cannot send anyone else, for the Peace Committee has chosen General China. Whether he will be killed, I don't know… but then, none of us can lock our lives in a box. Why don't we get on with the voting?"

Nine favoured my going, three opposed it.

"I have offered myself for this job," I said, "and have authorized General Tanganyika to take over command of the Mount Kenya Battalion, should anything happen to me. In such an event, General Kaleba will replace General Tanganyika as commander of the Kabaru Headquarters."

The meeting was closed by Kimathi, who said, "This committee of twelve agrees that General China should seek means to consult with the Government in June 1954. This committee sends General China to tour the 'Reserves' gathering public opinion, guarded by a force of at least 100 men. General Tanganyika has no authority to take any action in General China's place until we hear that something has happened to General China. We shall now ask General China to swear an oath before this committee."

I was then given the following oath by Field Marshal Dedan Kimathi: "I swear that I will not object to anything passed by this committee. I swear that I will never fear to speak of African difficulties, on the day I am dying and even in hell shall I fight for our cause. I swear that I will not reveal to the Government any of this Council's secrets or any of the secrets of our Movement. I swear that I will give my life rather than betray Africans."

# Chapter 23
# Wounded and Captured

The day of my capture began as many before it—in an operation to obtain weapons. The previous night, January 14th, 1954 I had taken sixty men to Mathira Division to collect arms and ammunition from a secret store in a deserted house. I left my men posted about a mile away and continued on, accompanied by General Tanganyika and two other men. We spent the entire night ascertaining the condition and type of weapons which had been stored there, and dividing them for distribution to different groups. As we were taking tea just after dawn, one of my scouts came in to warn us that the police were approaching.

I went out to warn a company of forty soldiers to prepare for a fight. They had arrived from Embu a few hours before and had taken up positions on the northern side of the house. As we waited together in an ambush, another scout arrived with the revealing information that the police had not raided the house where we had spent the night, but had simply passed by. I ordered the Embu men to stay at the ready, and returned to the house with General Tanganyika. My cup of tea was still warm, but before I could finish it I heard gunshots and the sound of a bugle. It turned out to be a brief engagement between General Kaleba and the police, who had been driven back. Nevertheless, our position now seemed rather serious: we were only a mile from Kiawarigi where a 7th [battalion of the] KAR camp was located; it was a mile to Kiamachimbi, two miles to Tumutumu and four miles to Karatina. In each place KAR soldiers, police, Home Guards and tribal police were based. If the Government forces co-ordinated their attack at all, we would be surrounded completely.

Our only chance of escape was to fight our way out of the circle.

"Get ready with your poor weapons," I shouted, "the battle must continue!"

A strong contingent of police attacked us, but we sustained their fire rather well. About 9 o'clock, after an hour's fighting, I was shot through the chin and neck. At first it did not seem to affect me, and I went on fighting for a while, encouraging the men to get on with the battle and not worry about me. It may have been an hour later, probably less, that I began to feel weak and faint; the wound bled continuously, and I was in some pain, but the worst problem was difficulty in breathing—my windpipe must have been injured, for fluid seemed to be entering it.

It suddenly seemed like the end of the game for me. I handed over my rifle and ammunition to other men, as well as the books in which we had noted the allocation of arms the previous night. I removed my battle uniform and remained in short pants and a shirt. Four men cut a piece of *Mutundu* tree and used it to support my weight while they carried me by the shoulders and feet about half a mile from where I was wounded. We came face to face with a group of KAR soldiers, and one of my men was shot as we all ran for cover. It seemed pointless for them to risk their lives to save a man who was nearly dead, and I told them so. It was better for them to rejoin the others or they might all be killed.

So I was left alone in the bush, and began to crawl along until I reached a path leading to a house. I saw an old woman by the door and got up to walk towards her. She must have watched me sink down unconscious from loss of blood, and then come out and poured water over me. When I regained my senses she went with me to collect the body of the dead "stretcher-bearer" and we dragged it into the bush and tried to cover it. I went off a bit further to hide in the hut of Migwi, but someone must have been on my trail because within a moment of lying down the house was sprayed with bullets. Out in the open again I confronted two KAR men among the banana trees. I followed their command to raise my hands. One of the men recognized me immediately: we had served together in Burma.

"Since you've fallen into our hands," he told me, "we'll take you out of this dangerous area, across the Kiamachimbi-Karatina road."

I was warned that if we met any Government forces along the way, I was to say I had surrendered.

We headed for Kiawarigi KAR camp, but even before we reached it, at the home of ex-Chief Muhindi, I collapsed. White fluid poured from my throat, mixed with blood. Yet I did not lose consciousness, and I shall never forget the kindness of those two soldiers who ran for water to wash the wound; after risking so much, they carried me nearer the camp and advised me to try to reach the gate on my own, and to tell the soldiers there that I was surrendering. It was wiser at this time to surrender rather than be captured, for at least I would have a chance to speak before being shot.

Crawling on a bit further alone, I lay for a moment in the grass, recalling a prophecy made in July 1953: I would be wounded and arrested, but not killed. This prophecy had been made during a ceremony in which I was anointed with oil and a flag bearing our freedom colours was hoisted. Although there was little reason for optimism, the recollection of that day, at that moment, gave me a shred of hope. I raised myself from the ground with a certain confidence that I was not going to my death, and staggered on a few yards, until some Kamba soldiers ran towards me and brought me into the camp, to Mr. Young, their officer. He was, in fact, the man who had shot me.

It must have been after 11 o'clock by now. The officer in charge of the camp knew me from the days when I had worked as a fireman with the Railways, and so there was no question as to my identity—or my value to the Government! He gave orders that I should not be harmed in any way. I was thoroughly searched, and to my dismay a small notebook was found in my pocket, one in which I had made notes during visits to the "Reserve"; this was a regrettable oversight on my part. Later, as well, another notebook was brought in by the local headman; it must have been dropped during the fight, but it contained nothing of any importance except the names of my companies and their commanders.

In spite of my wound, or perhaps because of it, I was suffering from a terrible thirst. I offered twenty shillings to someone to buy me a bottle of soda, but I was unable to swallow it and again lost consciousness. I woke up again in Karatina Army Camp Hospital, where I was fortunate to have a good doctor to treat my wound. I say "good" because many Europeans and Africans at the camp hospital tried to persuade him to let me die, but he silenced them all by saying, "I'm not a doctor who ends lives but one who saves them."

Not even my intense pain prevented me from feeling a wave of gratitude for his mercy.

Lieut. [Lieutenant] Walker, RAMC [Royal Army Medical Corps], Karatina, closed the tent flaps and started to work on me. I was fully conscious as he cleansed and stitched my chin and throat, while medical orderlies held my arms and legs. It was a brutal way to have to operate, but I preferred it to death. Afterwards I was helped out of the tent, where I found a crowd of people waiting to see me; some seemed furious to see me alive, and a few shouted aloud, "Let him die!" I was driven by car to Nyeri Provincial Hospital, where another search of my person was carried out. This time my money was removed: Shs. 160 from one pocket, Shs. 20 from the other. When the Tribal Policeman who fished out the Shs. 20 went to hand it over to a CID [Criminal Investigation Department] officer, he was told to keep it.

At Nyeri Hospital I received an injection and fell off to sleep. At 10 o'clock that night I awoke in King George VI Hospital in Nairobi, with my hands and legs chained to the bed. My guards said I had been brought by aeroplane, but of the journey I have no memory whatsoever. On the morning of the 16th, [Assistant] Supt. [Superintendent] Ian Henderson, whom we had nicknamed Kinyanjui, came to my room with a secretary and the two notebooks found with me in Karatina. I did not deny that they were mine, but since they covered the period 1952/53 I was not concerned; there was nothing really secret in them. Notes such as "Embu-Meru," made during a visit to the "Reserve," were meaningless to anyone but me. In neither book were any civilian names listed, so there was no chance of implicating any of our friends through this oversight.

After four days in hospital, during which time I gradually recovered some strength, I was transferred to Nairobi Prison. I suppose it was an "honour" to find that all my escorts and sentries were European. Every two hours, the one inside my cell exchanged places with the one outside. Such security-consciousness for a sick man was inexplicable—I could hardly swallow, let alone attempt to escape. They must have realized this, for they placed a bell in my cell so that I could summon attention should I take a turn for the worse. Eventually I could get down soft, mushy foods such as rice mixed with milk, or mashed vegetables. Although the wound itself healed slowly, the teeth in my lower jaw were loose and they ached constantly.

With a measure of health came also a need to locate myself to calcu-late my strengths and weaknesses vis-a-vis my captors. I discovered that my cell was just by the kitchen, and after some thought I hit upon a way of telling people where I was being held prisoner. I began to sing rather loudly, so that the men in the kitchen could hear me.

"Surely we are in trouble and discomfort," I sang in Kikuyu, "but let us not worry. Give a cough, you in the kitchen, to show me that you lis-ten. Then I'll tell you a word or two."

The reply came back, and I continued: "You may know, I have fallen into strict hands. It is up to you to let other people know I am here. And when you want to tell me something, just sing it out and know that I am listening."

This system was frequently used by prisoners on their way to court, and it helped me a great deal. I was able to exchange news and keep in touch with the outside world, and also to inform my wife and my com-rades of my condition.

Once captured, I knew in the back of my mind that I would probably be hanged as the leader of the Mount Kenya forces. For a while, howev-er, I was kept alive by God's mercy and the desire of the Government to learn what they could from me.

"Why did you surrender?" I was asked over and over again, and "Why did you become a leader in this war?" The authorities also wanted to know why the people refused to surrender, as the Governor and the Commander-in-Chief had asked them to do in August, 1953. All they had to do was hold up green branches as a sign of peace.

My basic reply to these questions went like this: "I had come out," I said, "to hold discussions with the Government and to determine whether their surrender offer also meant a willingness to comply with the demands of the people and the fighters. Our first demand was the release of Kenyatta and other imprisoned leaders, so that they could substitute peaceful means for violence in the fight for freedom. Next, the Government had to remove the prohibitions on the growing of maize, and to cease the wholesale and indiscriminate destruction of Kikuyu proper-ty and homesteads. People in the "Reserves" were starving, homeless and liable to illness and disease because of the Government's so-called secu-rity measures. These were the issues I wished to discuss with the Government," I said.

The interrogators remained sceptical of my intention to surrender at the time I was wounded; this point was to figure prominently in my subsequent trial. Why hadn't I informed them in advance about my surrender? They asked. And why did I not carry a green branch as a signal at the time of my arrest? I told them I hadn't been connected with the battle which took place that morning, but had been shot as I came out to surrender. It was true, of course, that I had only accidently "surrendered" on the 15th January; nevertheless, I had made arrangements prior to that date actually to come out of the forest and negotiate with Government.

I persisted in this description of the events of the 15th, but the authorities found it unacceptable, particularly as regards the claim that I was shot while on my way to surrender.

"If you think that I'm lying," I said, "then who arrested me? I came to the camp alone, if you remember."

Their reaction to this indicated that they knew nothing of the two soldiers who had helped me to a point near the camp. At least one point was fairly clear in my favour.

We wanted our Independence, and the return of our lands which had been taken by white settlers—these were the basic reasons for my taking part in the fight, and for the fight itself. With Independence, I said, the colour-bar would end in all respects; we would not permit racial discrimination of any kind in a free Kenya. Every channel would be open to everyone who belonged to the country, without regard for his colour. With our land, I went on, we would have the means to life; in those days, for us, wealth simply meant having the means and ability to grow enough food for one's family. But neither Independence nor land would be enough, I reminded them, unless Kenyatta and our other leaders were released.

The argument went on for some time. The Chief Native Commissioner, of course, disagreed strongly. There could be no connection between the aims and activities of "Mau Mau" and the winning of Independence. "Mau Mau," he said, had in fact brought disaster to Kenya by such actions as maiming and slaughtering cattle, and by burning schools. He cited the Timau cattle slaughtering of 1952 and the razing of huts in Aguthi Location on Christmas in the same year as just a few examples.

These discussions generally ended with the realization that each side claimed it was fighting for what was right, while the other side was in the wrong. The point of these otherwise useless exercises in debate was that the Government wished to sound me out as to the feelings of other revolutionary leaders. If they could hold a reasonable discussion with me, they could hope to do the same with a group of our leaders. I was asked whether I thought I could persuade others to meet with Government Officials. There would be little difficulty in arranging such a meeting, I said, if the Government guaranteed the safe conduct of our leaders and if the Forest Fighters were allowed to choose their own representatives.

The Government agreed to these terms, and I said I would undertake to arrange peace talks—I still had to await my trial, however, before any action could be initiated. I was not as optimistic at heart as in my words about the possibility of arranging for the Forest Fighters to leave their sanctuary for a meeting with their enemy. Nevertheless I felt I had a chance. In any case I felt satisfied in the knowledge that I had said nothing to betray our members or any of our secrets. In addition, my authority over many of our leaders, my familiarity with them and with our activities and organization, would be in my favour. Personally, though, I was sure my own fate led to the gallows and therefore, in whatever conversations I had with Government representatives, I tried to put forward our aims and purposes. If I could do anything to convince the Government that it was incorrect to call members of the "Mau Mau" Movement "criminal gangs" or "terrorists" who fought for the love of it, without motivation or logic, it would help our cause and those who had to go on fighting for it.

# Chapter 24
# Brought on Trial

Before my trial, my meetings and discussions with Government Officials were kept highly secret, for the white settlers would have been enraged had they known what was going on—they were indeed already clamouring for my death. They did not have to nourish their hopes for long, for on February 1st, 1954 my trial opened in the Nyeri Assize Court under Justice JL MacDuff. I was brought to the court in a jeep, handcuffed to an

African constable and constantly guarded by a European police officer. To an outsider, the authorities must have seemed much more nervous than the accused: six armed *askaris* [soldiers] were placed round the dock, all communicating doors into the courtroom were locked, and a squadron of armed troops took up positions outside the court building itself. I was encouraged, however, by the friendly faces of African *askaris* peering through every window, and from the calm confidence of my lawyer, Saeed Cockar, a young Indian recently admitted to the bar. On the other side were Mr. AJ Somerhough, Kenya's Deputy Public Prosecutor (who had played a similar role in Mr. Kenyatta's case in 1952), and the full force of a State determined to get a conviction. The press, of course, was well represented, and photographs of me in the white hospital shirt and shorts, my hair still plaited in the forest fashion, my leg bandaged and my throat wound half-healed, were flashed to all parts of the world.

I pleaded "not guilty" to the two charges—(a) consorting with persons carrying firearms, and (b) being in possession of two rounds of ammunition. Two other charges against me had been dropped by the prosecution. The first was that I had taken part in the attack on Chehe Timber Mill, an Italian operated mill—this charge failed because I could not be identified in the police "line-up" of suspects. The second charge, that of killing a policeman on the day of my arrest, was withdrawn because of evidence which showed I had been wounded early in the battle, before the death of the policeman. Lieut. Young, hidden behind a tree, had fired at me as I rose from cover to collect a gun dropped nearby; I saw him clearly as he ran off afterwards, and even fired a number of shots at him. This evidence contradicted a claim by a 7th KAR officer that he had shot me later in the fight between the police and General Kaleba at Gaturiri village (*"kwa Mbari ya Kiritu"*).

Mr. Somerhough opened the Crown case by describing the events of January 15th at Kiawarigi. A headman in charge of a Home Guard post had heard shooting, and Lieut. Young accompanied by several *askaris*, had come to take charge of the counter-operation. Somerhough said that a number of Africans, some armed, were seen leaving a nearby banana plantation. When the security forces opened fire, the gang scattered in all directions. The headman then inspected the spot where the gang had broken up and found a blood trail leading to a hut. A notebook and other objects were found in the hut, but nothing else, and the *askaris* returned to the camp.

Somerhough then reached the time of my own arrest, when I was challenged as I approached the camp.

"He was carrying his shirt and wearing a blood-stained vest; a scarf round his neck was soaked with blood," he told the court.

When my identity was established, I was taken to Karatina headquarters and then to Nyeri Hospital, where two rounds of ammunition were found on me. This sounded rather convincing, and even more so when the prosecutor defensively added that "It was impossible for any evilly-disposed or unscrupulous person to have planted the ammunition" on me. He was simply anticipating our claim that the ammunition had been put in my pocket after I reached camp—this was a common practice, and I was certain I had been a victim of it.

The first prosecution witness was Murakaru Gichera, the headman. Under cross-examination he agreed that the blood trail which led him to the camp was not necessarily mine; that is, others besides myself could have been wounded during the fight, especially when Lieut. Young came into action with his Bren gun. Pte. [Private] Kioki of the 7th KAR then gave some significant evidence. He was the first to challenge me when I approached the camp, and he verified that I had been searched at that time by Lieut. Young. Nothing could have been planted on me at that time, for I would have protested; yet it was strange that the bullets I allegedly possessed were not discovered then, for I was wearing only a pair of thin shorts and a vest.

Lieut. Young then took the stand, and described fairly accurately what had happened on the 15th.

"I directed my Bren gun towards the banana plantation," he said, "and fired two bursts at five men dressed in black coats and khaki trousers. One man seemed to stumble. Five minutes later I saw what I thought was a man at the edge of the plantation. I fired two more bursts and then decided to sweep the area."

Later, he said, he saw me walking towards him, badly wounded. At first he doubted my identity, but then came to believe it.

"He asked me when we would end this war of ours," Lieut. Young continued under questioning, "and I replied that it was entirely up to them.

He did not say where he had come from but stated he had been wounded in the valley."

He added that there had been no opportunity for anyone to slip anything into my pockets before I was handed over to the police at Karatina.

Taking up in a skillful cross-examination, my lawyer revealed the hypocrisy of the Governor's so-called surrender offer. This had been announced in a widely circulated pamphlet which read something like this: "Come in and surrender yourself. If you do, you will not be liable for prosecution for carrying arms and ammunition. Save your life now. This especially applies to those who have not committed murder. Run away from Mau Mau. Surrender as quickly as possible. Bring your arms with you. To gang leaders: you can come in safely to surrender your men and arms. Come in daylight to any police or military post carrying a green branch. Your men will be fed and treated justly."

This offer had been taken up by many of the Forest Fighters, but I was having my first practical exposure to its meaning. Both charges against me, "consorting with armed persons" and "carrying ammunition," were not grounds for prosecution according to the Governor, guided by the Commander-in-Chief, General Erskine. It was true, of course, and I admit it, that I had committed other acts which were regarded as criminal and had I been charged with them I could not have complained of injustice. The State, however, was unable to charge me with anything but these two offences and in spite of the "surrender" offer they wanted a death sentence.

Lieut. Young admitted that carrying a green branch was not a compulsory condition of surrender. Anyone could surrender to the security forces—provided he was not wounded! This was something which had not been mentioned in the pamphlets, and my lawyer then attempted to hand over a copy of the pamphlet to Lieut. Young. Mr. Somerhough objected on the grounds of "irrelevancy," but the judge, who was in my opinion an impartial and fair man, commented that if I had denied being with the "terrorists" and arrived at the camp of my own volition, then surely it *was* relevant. My defence was that I had surrendered in light of the offer, and Mr. Cockar told the court I would explain my actions more fully when I came to testify.

Next, the relevant witnesses described my treatment at Karatina by Lieut. Walker and the search through my clothes at Nyeri Hospital. The tribal policeman who allegedly found the ammunition admitted that, "Waruhi was not shown the bullets but I think he had seen them." This was the same policeman who had been told to keep the Shs. 20 note found in my pocket...

It was getting late in the afternoon, but before the court adjourned my lawyer hinted that he might be calling on General Erskine to give evidence regarding the surrender pamphlet. The possibility of calling the Commander-in-Chief as a defence witness in the biggest "Mau Mau" trial to date obviously did not appeal to the prosecution, and they agreed to accept a copy of the surrender pamphlet. Following on the adjournment, I was returned to Nyeri prison under heavy guard. Although the case against me did not seem very strong, it could have only one conclusion. Still, I slept peacefully that night.

Coming back into court the next morning was like returning to a long familiar room. The previous day's experience had etched itself in my mind, and the faces of the *askaris* were those of old acquaintances, the chairs and benches of the courtroom were the furnishings of a house I knew well. I was in a strange state of mind about the outcome of the trial—although no one wants to die, I did not really fear death. Yet an instinct of self-preservation, whatever it was that had kept up my strength in all the dangerous situations which preceded my arrest, led me to want to try my utmost to evade the death sentence. Whether or not *my* case was hopeless, I could still speak freely, within limits, to put *our* case firmly and clearly before the world. I knew that what I said in court would be read by thousands of people, and it was ironically an opportunity I would never have had before my arrest, to tell the world why we were fighting and what our objectives were. Still, I knew I must be careful, for one thoughtless word could hang me. In short, it was a question of speaking the truth, if not the whole truth.

I elected to give my hour-long statement on oath, in spite of my mental reservations. Stepping into the witness box I experienced a touch of "stage fright." I was used to audiences of comrades, of friends speaking together in a spirit of mutual trust round some warming campfire. Now I was in a bright, open courtroom, surrounded by the grinning faces of Europeans and weighted down by the remorseless atmosphere of legal proceedings in which my life was at stake.

# Chapter 25
# The Death Sentence

I began with my early history, and said I had gone to Karatina in 1952 to find that my wife had been arrested for taking an oath. I went into hiding in the forest because I was told I too was in danger of arrest. This was true so far as it went. I described my election to the position of "general," which had followed from my leadership in collecting funds to aid the people. I told the court that my men and I remained in the forest because we feared beatings, imprisonment and being killed—not because we wanted to fight. This too was true, for the Kikuyu were fighting only because our backs were to the wall, as a famous British soldier had once put it. The British had taken our land, our rights and our freedom; then when they locked up our political leaders we had a choice of complete suppression or resistance; our militancy was literally forced upon us.

I went on to tell the court that on December 28th, 1953 I had summoned our leaders to a meeting and told them it was time for me to surrender. I had thought that since no group had ever met the Government, I would attempt to do so. Before such action, however, I planned to go round the forests and then the reserves to learn the feelings of the people and the grievances which had to be rectified. After familiarizing myself with the overall conditions, I had thought I would surrender under the Government's offer. Two weeks after the meeting of 28th December during my period of investigating the reserves, I had been involved accidentally in a skirmish and had been wounded as I went in to give myself up.

Whether anyone tells the whole truth in a court which is trying him for his life is doubtful; at least, I doubt it. I do know that most of what I said was true—in the forest we had several times discussed the questions of meeting Government Officials to present our demands formally and to talk peace. We knew we were not politicians; but with our political leaders locked up, we also knew that we had some responsibility for more than fighting. Peaceful discussions, we realized, might both end the fighting and bring about the release of the very men who could speak for us. Obviously, though, I had not intended to surrender myself on the day it happened—but the court was there to judge my actions, not my intentions.

Mr. Somerhough's cross-examination was thorough and probing. First he wanted to know where I got the name "General China." I explained that in the forest many men preferred to use pseudonyms rather than reveal their real names. "China" was the one I thought up for myself, but the "general" was a title bestowed upon me by the committee. I agreed that I had taken an oath and that I had led the Mount Kenya group.

Somerhough then wanted to know what I meant when I said I had gone to the forest after "our leaders" were arrested; which leaders did I have in mind? This was a question I certainly could not answer, and I claimed to be unable to recall all their names—but even as I spoke I recalled that stirring meeting with Kenyatta, and his words continued to comfort me during the cross-examination. The judge intervened to ask whether I could recall *any* of the names of the leaders; I had to admit sadly that I could not! Strangely enough, the colonial mentality was such that an answer of this kind was probably believed—after all, Africans were traditionally stupid, lazy and so on. My dissembling behaviour certainly must have convinced Fred Majdalany; in his book, *State of Emergency*, I am described as "a puzzled youthful delinquent" with the mental age of an eleven-year-old. Although some of the answers I gave the prosecution that day would justify Majdalany's observation, the motivation behind them obviously would not. In the context, he might have done better not to have taken me at face value.

Speaking at all was for me still painful, as well as tiring. We went on through seemingly hundreds of questions, covering my knowledge of the surrender pamphlet, my role in the supplying of arms and ammunition and so on. A diary in my own handwriting was produced and the entry, "10 *askaris* killed; some guards and whites 6," was read to the court.

"Did you think the surrender terms applied to you?" Somerhough demanded.

"Yes," I said. "Nobody was killed on my order."

I maintained that my trial was unfair in that odd bits of evidence which did not relate to the charges were being brought in throughout, prejudicing the assessors (three Africans—there was no trial by jury for Africans in Kenya then).[7] Somerhough, for example, produced a notebook showing amounts of ammunition received in December and a note in my writing that "nine women should be finished because they are enemies of the public."

"I thought you told us one of the reasons you accepted this leadership was because there were to be no more attacks on women," the prosecutor said. An explanation of such notes was difficult in a reasonable context, and I could only curse to myself the traitors who had passed on such evidence. "Yes," I replied, that was true, and the note had been written only to show to the committee. I could not put to him a larger question in my own mind: "what about the thousands of innocent women, children and old people who have suffered or lost their lives at the hands of the 'Security' Forces and white settlers? This is a war and we did our best to ensure that only genuine traitors were killed, unlike you, who killed first and thought afterwards."

We then went on to the circumstances of my surrender. I was asked why I had not sent a note in advance to the Government announcing my intention. This seemed a foolish question, for had this been known by the public in advance I probably would not have lived to surrender when I came out, so great was the animosity towards me in some sections. But I replied that the pamphlet said nothing about sending notes, and I had not carried a green branch because as a military man I knew that by raising my hands the soldiers would understand my intentions. I denied leading a gang on the 15th January, and maintained I was about three hundred yards away from the "terrorists" when I was shot. I also had a chance to condemn one of the more infamous practices of the Home Guards; I had not surrendered to them, I said, because they often killed a man after catching him; therefore, I had gone directly to the military camp.

After nearly three hours of cross-examination, I returned exhausted to the dock to listen to Mr. Cockar's summation. Both offences with which I was charged, he submitted, were excused if a "Mau Mau" fighter surrendered.

"I admit this surrender does not excuse murders," he added, "but if the Crown is in a position to prove this man committed murder or directed murder then it is at liberty to proceed on that count."

But the charges against me were both unfair, for on the one hand the Government offered conditions to people in the forest and on the other hand, when they accepted them and surrendered they were brought to court. The prosecution had failed to prove its case by any reasonable standards of criminal justice. Mr. Cockar also cited letters produced during the cross-examination in which I had urged that my seat on the committee be given to someone else; this he pointed out, was a clear indication of an intention to surrender. In addition, I had requested the permission of the committee to take a brief rest. All these things pointed to a prior intention to surrender which, for various and relatively obvious reasons, I could not reveal in advance to my men. I began to feel a certain optimism as Mr. Cockar finished his speech—the prosecution case suddenly seemed rather weak.

These feelings were deflated soon after Somerhough began to address the court. There was no point of law in this case, he argued, simply one of fact; the surrender pamphlet was irrelevant for it was not part of the law of the country. The evidence showed that I was found in my own operational area, during a battle; my tracks were among those of the scattering fighters and it was only because of my severe wound that I had to surrender. He used my own words against me by pointing out that I was frightened of falling into the hands of the Home Guard and so sought safety at the military camp.

My hopes were further destroyed when the judge addressed the assessors. He reiterated that the surrender leaflets had no basis in law. So far as the court was concerned they did not excuse any person for a crime committed. This was tantamount to a verdict of "guilty," for the assessors were already prejudiced against me as they were against the "Mau Mau" Movement in principle. It was not surprising when all three found me guilty of consorting with persons carrying firearms—"he did bad by bringing war with him," said one—and two found me guilty of possessing ammunition.

While judges sometimes disagreed with a "not guilty" verdict of assessors, it never worked the other way round. What followed the next morning at the sentencing was therefore not unexpected. The judge noted that I had admitted to being General China and a member of the "Mau Mau." When I was found guilty on both charges I was asked if I had anything to say or why sentence in accordance with the law should not be passed against me. I neither desired to show any emotion nor did I have much left in me after two days in the dock; I simply leaned forward and replied that, if convicted, I would like to appeal.

Ritually the judge placed a black cap on his head and pronounced the death sentence; I was deeply moved, despite my earlier resignation to it.

The judge's words to me were morbidly humorous: "I do not propose to address any homily to you," he said, "because so far as this court is concerned it will have little effect on your future. The sentence in respect of this court leaves very little chance of reformation." With about three weeks' time in which to "reform" myself, I had to agree with him. Mr. Cockar requested the granting of a certificate of appeal; the circumstances of the trial were very peculiar, he argued, and pointed out that the Court of Appeal had, as yet, given no ruling on the surrender leaflets. The judge refused the request, but Mr. Cockar assured me he would appeal on a point of law.

With the sentence uttered, I felt relaxed, I chatted and joked with the constables guarding the dock. Outside the courtroom I passed by crowds of people hoping for a chance to see me. Under a heavy guard of well-armed Europeans I was taken back to Nairobi Prison on the same day, February 3rd; the authorities still feared an attempt to rescue me.

## Omitted section: Chapters 26-27

In these chapters, China recounts how after his arrest he tried to procure the overall surrender of Mau Mau by writing letters to—and meeting with—forest fighters. He then describes how he was transferred to Lokitaung Prison in northern Kenya, where he was detained with the "Kapenguria Six."

## Chapter 28
## "Hero of the African Nation of Kenya"

During my first year at Lokitaung, in September, I was allowed to receive a letter concerning a meeting held the previous April by "Mau Mau" leaders on Mount Kenya. This was of great interest to me, first because it gave me some idea of how things were going in my absence, and second because my behaviour in the peacetalk procedure was discussed at the meeting. The gathering had taken place on April 20th, just ten days after the second scheduled conference between our leaders and Government. It was held at Gen. [General] Tanganyika's headquarters, just above Kabaru, and was attended by more than eight hundred people from Nyandarua, Meru, Embu and Nanyuki.

General Kaleba was Chairman of the meeting, and opened it with an explanation that "many things have been passed without the presence of our soldiers," and that it was time to review what had happened in a general meeting.

"You all know General China was arrested and then found a way for our leaders to meet the Government. After his hard struggle with the Government, we held a meeting at the PCs [Provincial Commissioner's] Office, Nyeri, on March 30th, and announced another one for April 10th. This second meeting never took place, for we had arranged to meet on April 7th to prepare for the talks and on that day our armies were savagely attacked by Government forces at Kagua-Mutu, just at the foot of Itiati Hill. During the incident we lost twenty men, and seven were captured, including Brig. Gatamuki. Because of that action," General Kaleba concluded, ' many people were angry with China, Tanganyika and with me as well. Now General Tanganyika is here and will explain what led up to the meetings with the Government; after that, as Chairman of the committee to arrange the meetings, I shall explain to you what our policy was, and what resulted from our first meeting on March 30th."

General Tanganyika then rose to begin an extensive review of events from the time of my arrest. After thanking the group for permitting him to speak he began with a warning: "I'm sorry to hear the rumours that Gen. China and I negotiated to end the lives of our soldiers. Such words show that you don't trust us—but whether or not that is the case, it is better to speak the truth even at the risk of breaking a friendship. So what I tell you now will be spoken frankly."

Tanganyika described the events of the 14th and 15th January; how we had worked together distributing arms, medicine and some ninety pounds of gunpowder to various company commanders, before the police arrived in the morning.

"We hid in thorny bush at the back of the house, waiting for the police to search the place. We were with Commander Kourugo's company. But the police passed by to another area, where Gen. Kaleba attacked the police and we went to help them when we heard a trumpet call. By the time we arrived the police had fled, and when we pursued them we were met by KAR, home guards and tribal police. In this battle, China was shot in the jaw and neck, but went on fighting bravely. When his strength failed him, he handed over his Sten gun, clothes and books to Mr. Ngomore."

My progress through the bush and the assistance I received from the friendly KAR soldiers were described, as was my arrival and interrogation at the KAR camp. "The Government told China that 'Mau Mau' never sent any demands to them, and they said that when some Forest Fighters are captured they claim they were forced to enter the fight against their will. So the Government took 'Mau Mau' to be simply a gang of thieves, with no demands or objectives. They asked China whether he could ask other 'Mau Mau' leaders to meet with the Government authorities and present their demands; this might help them to appreciate what the Africans were fighting for. China assured them that Africans wanted Independence, land and a chance to progress; these things alone were what made us carry on the war."

The safety of all leaders at any meetings was assured, Gen. Tanganyika went on, and he told the meeting that this agreement was signed by the Governor, by General Sir George Erskine, and by myself.

"On February 14th," Tanganyika said, "China was brought secretly to Nyeri and sent us letters explaining the proposed meetings. He asked Mr. Muriithi Mathai to meet him, and then sent him to us. When Muriithi came to us, he said China had changed his outlook and was now serving the Government. I could not believe this, for China had knowledge of all our stores, our members, the location of our headquarters and so on, and I knew that none of this had been revealed. A committee was selected to discuss China's motives, and afterwards China sent Miss Njoki Mari to us with assurances that it was right to hold the meeting. We sent a letter to China agreeing to meet, and on March 6th, China and a European policeman, nicknamed Kinyanjui, met with our fighters under the leadership of Wamai Waithu. They talked for an hour-and-a-half and then brought us a full report. Our delegates had shaken hands with China and Kinyanjui and were impressed by what China had accomplished. This encouraged me to go ahead with the meetings, even if it meant risking my life, for I had to answer our leader's call and to show him respect."

Tanganyika went on then with his own story.

"I left my hiding place on March 7th and on my way to see China I was caught by Home Guards. I was taken to China, and met him and the European, Kinyanjui, who is a clever man. China explained to me that if we refused to meet the Government officials they could go on saying that we didn't have any aims to fight for, and this would lead foreign nations to blame us instead of encourage us. This made sense to me, and I agreed to co-operate with China and Kinyanjui. On March 28th, General Kaleba left the forest and a KAR vehicle picked him up at Gatung'ang'a and brought him to Nyeri, where the three of us met Kinyanjui. At this conference we learnt the Government wanted all 'Mau Mau' to surrender and withdraw from the war. We took their proposal to study until the meeting on March 30th, which General Kaleba will talk about in a little while."

At this point, before he sat down, Gen. Tanganyika spoke a few words on my behalf.

"When we were with China," he said, "he told us how to keep his books and clothes. I can assure you that China has revealed nothing to the Government and has not changed his mind about this fight. When he was answering accusations during his trial, he challenged the Government's policy of burning houses and destroying the crops of both the guilty and the innocent. He did not hesitate to plead 'guilty' to being a 'Mau Mau' leader, and this showed he really loves his people and is not selfish. When he called on us to meet the Government leaders he was not hoping to save his life but wanted to try to save the lives of our people and to let us live peacefully. In my opinion, General China was not wrong at all in what he did, and he must be thanked for his devotion to the people and remembered by forthcoming generations. If you believe that Gen. China and I caused the death of our twenty beloved soldiers and the capture of seven others, I won't deny it—but the committee and other representatives will judge the truth."

Commander Kourugo asked to say a few words as one of those who had accepted the peace-talk offer and had helped to choose representatives.

"If men are required to meet again," he told the meeting, "I will be the one to lead, for fear puts you into a hole. I disagree with those who blame

China or any other committee member for the death of our soldiers. No village member has been arrested because of reports by China, no secret books have been discovered—how can we blame him for being captured?"

He then called on Gen. Kaleba to present the findings of the "Board of Inquiry into the Meetings Between Our Leaders and the Kenya Government." Kaleba asked Kahiu Itina to read the report, which went as follows:

1. "The Board selected to investigate the meetings proposed by General China agreed to the conference whatever happened;
2. D. Kimathi as well as the Kenya Army of Freedom Executive confirmed the meeting;
3. Our Board directed that eight representatives should be sent to the meeting, to show that we feared nothing;
4. The Board agreed not to reveal its objectives until it had seen what the Government wanted, therefore we planned simple demands to draw out the Government; the demands were:
   a) Government forces to be removed from the 'Reserves';
   b) building of villages to be stopped;
   c) special tax to be abolished;[8] and
   d) all arrested and imprisoned people to be released;
5. These demands were sent to us by our superiors, and if the Government accepts them we would halt the war and fight with words only; we decided to omit two additional and most important claims at the first meeting:
   a) our national Independence, and
   b) landless people to be provided with land.

We also agreed to let General China speak for us at the meeting."

Kahiu then went on to the details of the March 30th meeting, as contained in the Board's report.

"On the night of March 29th, the representatives went to a certain *Mukurue* tree, near General China's home, where we had promised to wait for the white men who were with China. Just after the dawn they arrived, unarmed; Mr. Henderson seemed to have no fear, although 'Mau

Mau' was his greatest enemy."

Kahiu told how they travelled together to Nyeri and found me and General Tanganyika still in our rooms.

"When these leaders saw us they were very happy, and after greeting us, General China said, 'I know now that even if I die I cannot be sorry, for there are real men behind me.' Mwangi Kamitha produced ten shillings and sent for handkerchiefs, which we gave to Gen. China as a present. Mr. Mutebu also handed Gen. China ten shillings which he accepted reluctantly. In the meantime, [Assistant] Supt. Henderson ordered tea and bread, which we received with gratitude."

At this point we had sat down for our private talks, and Kahiu told the meeting about the discussions: "We representatives showed our demands to Gen. China, who accepted them. He said that we must be careful and in this first meeting we should just see whether the Government would accept or refuse our demands; then we would have to have a second meeting to make definite decisions. General China then told us the proposals which he wished to make to the Government. China said that the first request would be for the release of our leaders now in detention or prison, and for the convening of a meeting between political leaders and the Government. Two representatives to this meeting would come from each of the following areas: Kiambu, Murang'a, Nyeri, Embu, Meru, Nyanza and Rift Valley. This would be a meeting for the discussion of politics. Besides this meeting, we would also demand the following from the Government before we would end the war: (a) the removal of soldiers from the 'Reserves'; (b) the right of Africans to vote for their own representatives in the Legislative Council and an increase in their number; (c) the abolition of the special tax; (d) the release of all 'Mau Mau' prisoners; and (e) the ending of the curfew."

Kahiu told the meeting that we had left out certain major questions at this first meeting, mainly African Independence, the land question, education, and freedom of trade and business. We omitted these points because we wanted to wait until our political leaders were released to deal with them correctly. "We had no right," Kahiu said, "to deal with such matters while our elders suffered in prison. General China and General Tanganyika had agreed to this plan," Kahiu informed the meeting, "and we agreed to it. It was clear that his only aim was to save the lives of our people, and he cared very little for his own life.

"We then went to the PC's Office and [Assistant] Supt. Henderson, and found the Government Officials friendly and respectful. The Government agreed to consider our proposals, but said they could not withdraw security forces from the 'Reserves' until people had ended the war. We did not sign anything with the Government, but told them we would return to our leaders and then come to another meeting, which was fixed for April 10th. The meeting agreed to a cease-fire: the Government would stop bombing attacks on Mount Kenya and Nyandarua and also in Nyeri, and no Government troops would enter the forest to hunt for us. On the other side, the Government said that if any man put his finger into the 'Reserves' it would be cut off, but no fighter would be guilty for being in the forest. The Government also released Generals Tanganyika and Kiihuri to return with us, and we were pleased by their sincerity. We had a feast after the meeting, and were given cigarettes."

Kahiu's report was extensive, and he continued with a description of the return of the representatives to their assembly point.

"On the way back to China's house, General Kaleba remembered one point which had been overlooked in our demands, about the expulsion of all Europeans from Kenya. He wanted to know why this had been left out, and returned with Henderson to see China. China laughed when he heard this question, and gave the example of India which was independent in spite of the presence of Europeans. 'After our Independence,' China told him, 'Europeans will remain under our flag because we shall need them to train our people for high positions and to invest in industries in our country. We can't discuss such matters now, for the kind of Independence we want is not like that. In fact, we shall be dependent on the British for some time, until we have gained the strength to run our own Government.' General Kaleba agreed to this point, after a long discussion, and the next day, March 31st, he was returned to his home by Henderson.

"General Kaleba went to see Kimathi and other officials of the Kenya Army of Freedom Executive, and they were pleased by China's negotiations. On April 7th we called a meeting at Ngiaba just near Itiati to select members to attend the April 10th meeting, but at that time we were heavily attacked and some of our soldiers killed. The wrath that filled our hearts then caused us to ignore the proposed April 10th meeting, but we sent a letter saying we might meet at another time. General China replied that he was to be removed from Nyeri but whenever he called us again we should be ready to come. Since then we have not heard from him but are waiting to learn where he has been taken."

Kahiu concluded his report with the decisions made by the Board of Inquiry: "(a) The day China calls, we shall definitely go; (b) If the Government calls a meeting without China and we consider its aims honest, we shall go; (c) General China did not act incorrectly and to respect him, we shall stand silent for a minute at each of our meetings; (d) General Tanganyika did not make a mistake in acting as he did and he should continue his leadership; (e) General Kaleba and General Tanganyika deserve promotions for their leadership and for the risks they have taken; (f) Some copies of our books should be kept where Gen. China can recover them so that in future he can show Africans the activities of the Forest Fighters. These are the resolutions of the Board," Kahiu said, "and it is up to you to approve or reject them."

The Chairman of the meeting, General Kaleba, then asked all those who agreed with the resolutions to raise their hands; there was unanimous acceptance. The meeting broke up on a humorous note when an old man, Twananu from Meru, proposed that [Assistant] Supt. Henderson Kinyanjui be captured and searched, and then released unharmed, with the warning that it was only his courage which saved him. Everyone broke into laughter at this, and what was, for me, a very important meeting came to an end.

I did not learn all these details about the meeting until I was released from detention, when I had access to the records. The letter from Dedan Kimathi and the Kenya Army of Freedom Council, which I received from a Turkana policeman on September 24th, 1954, and which was dated July 8th, contained only a brief message. This in itself was a reassurance that my colleagues continued to support me, even in prison:

"Dear General China," (Kimathi wrote), "I am thankful to God for this chance to let you know how we are since you left us. When you sent a letter home we learnt where you were and Mr. Mohammed Mwai found a Turkana soldier who promised to deliver this letter; that was good luck, and I hope you will reply with the same man when he returns to Nyeri

"The KAF [Kenya Army of Freedom] Executive Committee met on July 8th; the twelve elders of the Council were Dedan Kimathi, Mathenge, Kaleba, Ndaya, Tanganyika, Gicane, Wamutundu and Ruku, joined by the new members Mohammed Mwai (replacing Gen. Gachuma who was killed), Githee (replacing Gen. China), Kimemia (replacing Kago, who was killed) and Nyoro (substituting for Mungai who was absent). These elders send you this letter:

"'We are thankful to you keeping your promise at our meeting with Government on March 30th that even if you fell into hell you would not desert our cause. Now that good luck has brought you together with Mr. Kenyatta you can speak freely with him and ask for his advice. Without word from you we shall not change the demands which we made in March. We have agreed to attend further meetings, if they are called, but if the Government asks only for people to surrender and does nothing for us, we cannot do so unless our detained leaders give us good reason for it. We trust you, for you are with our leaders and can decide the way to be followed.'

"On September 23rd, 1956, we shall have completed four years in the forest and at that time we shall put forward a new protest, for now the first one has fallen through. Until then we shall not raise any attack, but only harbour ourselves and allow people to be calm, until we regain power again. The leaders who are alive on the proposed date will organize the new protest.

"This committee has confidence in you and gives you the honoured title of 'Hero of the African Nation of Kenya.' Greet Mr. Jomo Kenyatta, F. Kubai, B.M. Kaggia, P.J. Ngei and K. Karumba and tell them we are all right (signed) The K.A.F. Executive Committee, by Chairman Dedan Kimathi."

# Chapter 29
## English Lessons from Mzee

The time passed, the year passed and we entered 1955. I no longer bothered to keep track of the days. But at a point sometime near the first year's anniversary of my arrival at Lokitaung, a new District Officer was

appointed and life cha       the better. Colonel Robeck had
come from the Sudar          fore, and we had served in
Burma together. One          release me from solitary
confinement and allov

"Why should he b                              He assured the
warders I was not a "bad" man. I had                him, he
said, and "you cannot fear someone who fights for m        't
want to see him kept alone again."

It was an entirely new reunion we held on the day I was first permitted
to cross the yard to the others. Talk became a sustenance, and we had
much to say to each other. They had access to newspapers but no first
hand news of the forest; my year away from the fighting seemed to van-
ish, and I spent hours answering questions and trying to satisfy their
curiosity. I recounted our battles and tragedies, our victories and defeats,
and described how much support we had got from the people of Kenya.

To sit among friends again, after so many months, was wonderful. To
watch them laugh and joke, to join them in debates, to ask and answer
questions, was like rediscovering life. Above all it meant that I could talk
with Mr. Kenyatta—this was the greatest source of happiness. Now that I
was treated as a human being, prison no longer seemed intolerable and
my spirits revived; I might be sentenced officially to life imprisonment,
but in my heart I was sure that victory would soon be ours, and we would
be free men again.

One evening in my cell, to which I was still returned alone at night,
another stroke of luck came my way. I managed to smuggle into my room
a piece of newspaper which I had found in the yard. Earlier I had found a
pencil stub on my way to work. Using my mug of water, I rubbed the
newsprint with a dampened finger, gently and patiently removing the ink
and turning the paper into a soft pulp. I was going to dry it and then write
a letter! Without warning the key turned in the lock of my cell and Col.
[Colonel] Robeck came in; there was nothing for me to do but sit there
with the paraphernalia on the floor beside me. I knew Robeck was a fair
man, but he might not be able to overlook this; for a moment I saw myself
in solitary confinement again. I looked into his frowning face and
explained that, although I had had only a limited education, I was anxious
to teach myself. I was practising my writing, I said.

I don't know whether he believed me, but in any case he showed me nothing but kindness. He asked me to follow him into the yard, and to get into his car which was parked nearby. When one of the warders rushed over to get in beside me, Col. Robeck waved him away, saying there was no need. "China doesn't have to be guarded when I'm around." We drove to his own home, along a bumpy track. He took me into the cool and spacious lounge and went over to the bookcase, where he took out seven paperback books and gave them to me.

"Just because you're going to be in prison for a long time doesn't mean the time must be wasted. If you study now, you'll be able to find a good job when you're released. I think you should have a chance to use this time for study," he said, "because I think you are a brave man. As a fighting man and a soldier myself I think I understand you."

These were unexpected and moving words, and I tried to thank him. Then I suggested an idea which had just come to me—perhaps Mr. Kenyatta would agree to teach me English! Col. Robeck thought this an excellent idea, and he found an exercise book and a pencil for me before we drove back to the prison.

The next day, when I saw Kenyatta, I told him what had happened with the DO [District Officer] and what I had suggested. Although I did not think he would refuse, I was nevertheless delighted when he agreed.

"You've done much for our country," he told me. "If I gave you money in return, no matter how much it was, one day it would be gone. But if I give you education, it will serve you for the rest of your life."

"An illiterate man," he went on, "is almost like a blind man, missing so much that is of value, and nearly helpless to improve either himself or his community."

Then I had my first lesson in English.

Each day, when I returned from my work, we sat down together— sometimes for twenty minutes or so, sometimes for as much as an hour. Time was really no object to us, and I was taught slowly but thoroughly. Mzee would select two words a day and explain them to me exhaustively, their spelling, pronunciation, meaning, application and use. The rate may seem slow, but it added sixty words a month, seven hundred and twenty words a year to my basic vocabulary, and of course once I had got some grasp of the "basic" it went much quicker. Soon I was able to turn to the paperback books which the DO had given me, detective stories and light romances, and I found I could understand whole sentences. Mzee was a wonderful teacher, and were it not for those early lessons I doubt this book would ever have been written, for I knew only a few words of English at that time and no grammar at all.

Nothing was more serious to us, though, than a period when Kenyatta fell ill. We were all deeply worried when he developed a painful eczema on his legs and arms, and his legs swelled up alarmingly. We learnt later that it was due to acute vitamin deficiencies, brought on by the prison food in general and also by Kenyatta's own dislike of *ugali* [maize meal], which he found extremely difficult to eat. Perhaps because of his long years in Britain he was no longer in the habit of eating it—at any rate, try as he would, he could not manage more than a mouthful or two at any meal. Consequently he suffered more than the rest of us from malnutrition, and this helped to bring on his illness. When his eldest daughter, Margaret, heard this, she managed to send some more nourishing food, which later helped him a lot.

A European doctor was called in to treat him but Kenyatta, naturally distrustful of his enemies, refused to take the medicine prescribed; he accepted it, but would later ask one of us to discard it in the latrine, or throw it out of a window. Thus his recovery was slow until a trustworthy Asian doctor, Dr. Bakshi, was called in; then things improved. But what really seemed to start him on the road to recovery was a small tin of black soil which Margaret sent him. I had no idea where it came from, and since I was not very superstitious I had little faith in its healing powers; Kenyatta was even less superstitious than I. Nevertheless he smeared it on his legs and soon the painful rash began to heal. It may have been that medicinal herbs were mixed into the soil; whatever it was, to our great joy and relief we saw him recovering, and after about six weeks he was nearly as fit as before.

Yet he still could not be persuaded to eat *ugali*. He used to save his portion and then persuade the Turkana warders to give it to the small children who sometimes stood outside the barbed wire compound, staring at us and sucking their thumbs, not daring to approach the fence too closely. Some of them were thin from malnutrition, with swollen bellies and pathetic matchstick arms and legs. I doubt that Kenyatta would have eaten his *ugali* even if he had enjoyed it, in the presence of those hungry children. Yet we pressed him to take care, for we knew that Kenya without Kenyatta would be a hollow victory, and we grew worried when his strength and health were endangered.

Throughout the pain and fever, and even when he was confined to his bed, Kenyatta refused to halt my English lessons. He insisted on giving me "homework," and each day I went to him while he corrected it and set me more work. I protested against this, for I felt he should devote all his energy to recovering his health, but he was adamant. I was encouraged to work doubly hard—with such a teacher I had to be a model pupil! At the same time I was proud and happy to experience his concern for me.

Margaret's affection for her father was also something to witness, and we were all impressed with her steadfast concern for his well-being. She was working at the time, and I am sure that every penny she earned was spent on him. Each day the local and overseas papers arrived by air— Kenyatta had now been given special permission to receive them—and this alone must have cost her a small fortune. No one who has not lived within a prison can imagine the profound pleasure which reading a newspaper from the "outside world" can bring. Besides this source of "health," Margaret supplemented her father's diet with food parcels whenever she was able. None of us will ever forget her love and thoughtfulness.

## Omitted section: Chapters 30-34

In these chapters, China details the poor conditions of confinement that he and the others endured at Lokitaung. He then describes his detention in several other camps, before he was finally released on June 14, 1962. Once free, China was sent to Israel for military training, which caused some controversy in the midst of independence negotiations between the Kenya African National Union—Kenyatta's political party—and the British.

# Chapter 35
# I Return to Kenya and Talk with the Forest Fighters

At last, on November 16th, I received a message from Mzee advising me to return ten days later. I left Israel under strict security precautions on November 26th, and flew via Athens, where I spent the night. I arrived in Nairobi on November 27th, and went directly to the Prime Minister's Office. Mzee Kenyatta was anxious to have the full story of the rumours, and I was equally anxious to explain them. It did not take long for us to straighten out matters, and it seemed more than ever that some people had been eager to destroy my future as well as my friendly relations with Mzee.

A few days after I arrived in Nairobi, I was interviewed by the Press I expressed my pleasure at the changes which had taken place in Kenya while I had been away, and added: "Nobody should think of the whites as being enemies of Africans. The war we fought is now over and we have much to learn from them for the future of our children."

I told them I was distressed by the large scale of unemployment among youth, and that Kenya had much to learn from Israel in this sphere. Of course, I clarified once again the unfounded allegations about my future status in Kenya's Army.

People at my home in Nyeri were anxious to see me, for some worry had been caused by the delay in my return. I decided to spend some quiet days there before our Independence Day on December 12th—but those days were to lead to one of my most important and exciting tasks in the service of the country. On the 10th, I received word from Mzee asking me to go to Meru, to meet the veteran Forest Fighter, Field Marshal Baimungi, who refused to come out of the forest despite our political achievements. I had already had some contact with the question of the treatment to be accorded to former Forest Fighters. This had occurred the previous August, when I learnt that people still in the forest had requested permission to form their own battalion in the new Kenya Army, and wanted their own tents, uniforms and mess hall. I wrote to the Prime Minister at that time, to the effect that, although I favoured the fighters, it would be wiser for them to postpone their claims until Kenya was fully independent. Charges of "Mau Mauism" could have been made, had these people been absorbed wholesale into the army, and to set them up outside the regular military establishment would have been useless as well as dangerous.

Thus, when I was called upon in December to meet the Forest Fighters, I felt as though I had a great responsibility both to them and to our new Government. My disappointment at having to miss the celebrations in Nairobi was more than offset by the importance of the task I was to undertake. I asked Mr. Ngatia Mugo, of Nyeri, to accompany me, since he knew many of the current Forest Fighters' camps. Ngatia had gone into the forest after my arrest and had been an oath administrator and scout. We left Nanyuki on December 11th, in a police vehicle; at a pre-arranged spot near Meru, we were met by a group of fighters. Ngatia went with them to obtain permission for me to meet Baimungi, and this was granted for the following day—the long-awaited day of our Independence!

It was a rainy morning when we entered the Mount Kenya forest—on foot, since no vehicle could negotiate the slippery paths. Being enclosed again by the dense and awesome trees, feeling the weight and wetness of my boots and clothes brought me quickly back to those heroic days on the other side of the mountain, when we had fought for our freedom. Now the forests were no longer the only refuge, for on that day the whole of the land became ours. We tramped along little-used paths, meeting no one, until after two hours or so, we had covered about seven miles, and were at Baimungi's Headquarters.

The camp was guarded on all sides by Freedom Fighters, just as we had guarded our camps in the earliest days of the Emergency. Some of the men were anxious to know why I was there; I am sure several must have thought I wanted to discuss "surrender," as I had before my capture and imprisonment in 1954. Most of them had reservations about approaching me, and their true feelings stayed hidden behind fierce glances. I was searched for arms, and then led into the camp. Round a large campfire were both men and women soldiers, armed with guns or knives. It looked as though the same tight organization and discipline prevailed, and in addition the camp was "modernized," with army tents and some temporary houses. I was struck by the cleanliness and order of the base, and by the apparent good humour and health of the soldiers.

To my great and pleasant surprise, I found my old colleague, General

Chui, in the camp. He had been based in a cave near Meru when I was in the forest, and then had joined up with Mwariama, and eventually with Baimungi. We exchanged brief but exciting reminiscences, and then he asked me to wait a moment while he completed a job which had just been assigned to him. This gave me a chance to look more closely at the camp and at the soldiers. There was a joyous mood running through the place, with the knowledge that the *Uhuru* [independence] for which many of them had fought and suffered over a long period was at last achieved. The old miseries, grievances, pains and despair were forgotten and replaced by a new sense of hope, a feeling that at least they would no longer suffer for having a black skin, that the world was now open to them.

Yet the problem for many of the men was that the only world they knew was their tiny camp in the forest. And this was what I had come to discuss with Baimungi. Finally, a soldier directed me to his office, and we shook hands like old comrades. Actually, I had not known Baimungi before; he had worked as a DO's driver while I was in the forest. A guard was instructed to bring food for us—*ng'araga ndihoyogwo uhoro*, you do not question a hungry man—and we sat down to a meal of *njahi* (black grams), gruel, meat and Kikuyu liquor. We chatted about the current situation, and about the camp organization until we had finished, and then got down to more serious matters.

I explained that our Prime Minister wanted all those Freedom Fighters still in the forest to return to normal life by the 16th December—within four days of Independence.

"And what is the Government going to give us as a reward for our devotion to Kenya's freedom?" Baimungi was a man who lived his rank and status; he expected to be head of one army or another, and his expectations were great and demanding. But at this point it was still difficult to make a big splash about "Mau Mau," either in the form of rewards or special decorations. In Israel the people who had fought for freedom were not rewarded immediately, and any special attention to "Mau Mau" fighters at that time would have doubled the difficulties of returning to a normal situation in Kenya.

I tried to clarify these points for Baimungi. It was unwise for Forest Fighters to expect money, although arrangements would be made to provide them with land. After all, I said, the reward of *Uhuru* should be enough for the present—we had all fought for Kenya's freedom, not just for the freedom and advancement of ourselves or the Kikuyu people. It may have been unfortunate, but nevertheless any special rewards for the Kikuyu would have looked like favouritism at that particular time. Baimungi's eyes wandered away from me—he had been counting on much more than this.

"If our new African Government will not permit Freedom Fighters to join the Kenya Army as leaders," he said, "and if it doesn't give land to those who fought and suffered during the struggle, we shall all be very dissatisfied. When we come out, we want to hold on to our arms and our domestic animals, and to establish ourselves in our own camp where we can live like normal soldiers."

Baimungi added that he could not imagine anyone but himself as Chief of Staff of the Kenya Army. General Chui, who had joined us after the meal asked whether it was true that I had been sent to Israel for training to become Kenya's Chief of Staff.

"I went to Israel for agricultural training," I told them. "I'm too old to go to war again."

"But aren't you a general?" Baimungi asked.

"I was a general when I had men to command, but I have no army now," I said.

Baimungi had his army, he was a Field Marshal, and he could go and talk with the Prime Minister himself, if he wished, I told them. "But whether you are a Field Marshal or a General, you've got to follow the instructions of the leader of the Government, for it is the Government which appoints officers. If you don't agree with the Prime Minister, it is evident that you weren't appointed by him."

I could not speak for the Prime Minister as to whether or not the fighters would be rewarded—I was sent only to put the Government's point of view on the return of fighters to normal life, and to hear the demands of Baimungi and others. No one faced any punishment, I assured them, and indeed their weapons would be placed in museums for future generations to see. Under our own African Government there was no need for private armies.

It was important that the leaders and their men should come out of the forest, if only to facilitate negotiations between them and the

Government. Outside, they could explain their problems, and organize themselves in a group to present their demands to the Government. Inside the forest, they could only appear as dissidents and indeed as a potential threat to the peace and security which had been our objective from the earliest days of the struggle.

"If you refuse to come out, I told them, "the African Government might easily think that your aim was not to fight for our freedom, but for something else. It is up to our Government to decide how you will be treated, but you can do a lot to help your cause by coming out and dealing openly with our political leaders."

Neither Baimungi nor Chui was totally convinced of the Government's desire to help them return to normal life, but finally Baimungi accepted the government's request, although he asked for more time to contact his men and organize their departure from the forest. He then launched into a bitter attack on Field Marshal Mwariama, claiming that he himself was the only Field Marshal in Kenya. Baimungi demanded to meet the Prime Minister and Mwariama "to discuss who is the head of all the Freedom Fighters in Kenya."

Such personal quarrels were to hamper not only relations between the fighters and the Government, but the advancement of the fighters themselves. I told Baimungi that, if the men came out of the forest, the Government would give them two offices in which to organize themselves and sort out their problems. We left the discussion more or less at that point, and I returned to Nairobi to report to Mzee Kenyatta. At my request, he extended by two weeks the deadline for leaving the forest.


## Omitted section: Chapters 36-37

In Chapters 36 and 37, China exhibits his frustration with some forest fighters who refused to ally themselves with Kenyatta's government at the time of independence. He is similarly frustrated, however, that Kenya's new government was doing little to support those who had fought for freedom. China then describes the military evaluation he underwent in Kenya for a possible position in the new nation's army (which never materialized).

# Chapter 38
# The National Youth Service

Finally, on our passing out day, I was informed that in spite of my great success during training and in the exercises, I had lost two points due to my age and lack of educational background; thus I became Number Three cadet, instead of Number One. In the official Gazette, I had been accorded the rank of 2nd Lieutenant in the Kenya Army Reserve. On being presented with my certificate, I learnt that I would rank as a Captain in the Kenya National Youth Service [NYS]. Eleven of the thirty-one who had been in Israel, including myself were seconded to the Youth Service; three remained in the Army and five went to the Air Force; the others are no longer in military or Government posts, and some are unemployed.

Those of us who went to the National Youth Service were surprised to find that our military ranks were ignored. I, as a Captain, and the others as Lieutenants, became "Section Commanders"; some of the NYS authorities claimed that we had failed our army training and had been dismissed. It was again a matter of remaining patient in the face of certain lingering hostilities. Yet there were memorable and pleasant events. The day we reported to the NYS Headquarters in Nairobi we were met by the Assistant Secretary to the Ministry of Labour and Social Services, Mr. S.A. Tongoi (now Deputy Director of the Service), who handed up Public Service Commission forms to complete.

"May I know who 'General China' is?" he asked after a moment.

When I moved forward he shook my hand and offered to complete the forms for me, and added that he was pleased to meet me because of my prominent role in the history of Kenya's struggle for Independence.

A few days later, towards the middle of August, I called on the leader of the National Youth Service, the Hon. Josiah Mwangi Kariuki. I was anxious to learn just what my rank would be in the Service. I had gone from Captain to Section Commander, according to some of the European officers in the NYS. These men were simply trying to annoy me to the point where I would resign, so they would not be forced to serve with me. Mr. Kariuki assured me that no matter what the difficulties, a solution would be found whereby I would receive the correct status.

At this time I also met the Permanent Secretary to the Ministry of Labour and Social Services, Mr. M. Ndisi. He told me he was aware that many Europeans in the NYS were suspicious, if not hostile, towards me, but advised me to ignore this by working hard. The role which I had played in Kenya's struggle would be taken into account in determining both my rank and remuneration in the Service. He added that with my wide experience, I was in an excellent position to assist the youth of Kenya, and that his Ministry would rely very much upon me for the success of the Service. Although at first only Mr. Ndisi and Mr. Tongoi seemed pleased to have me in the Service, my relations with the European officers soon changed for the better and life became much more normal.

Working in the National Youth Service is a job I have come to love very much. The idea itself was an excellent national undertaking, in which youths from all parts of the nation help themselves and others towards a better life. Young people from different tribes learn to live and work together, they learn the customs of their fellow citizens, they develop a loyalty and devotion to their Government and Nation. Basically, the NYS helps the young unemployed, or those who have not passed the Kenya Preliminary Examination. They receive school lessons and also learn such occupations as driving, mechanics, building and farming. Some learn to wear shoes for the first time; others put on trousers as a new experience; at evening campfires they sing, debate and develop a new appreciation of their own culture.

Perhaps the most important thing which the young people receive is a sense of discipline. When they finish their training they are better young men, who display a distinct personality and a good character. If we had the means, I would not hesitate to recommend to the Government that all school leavers should be required to serve in the NYS before looking for employment. This would help to develop the self-discipline which is so necessary at our present stage of national development. I have observed with dismay how many young men who leave school to go straight to work soon find their lives in a turmoil. Exposure to the discipline and demands of life in the NYS would help many of these young people to take better care of their lives and their future.

Indeed, the young men and women who go through our programme have a good chance in the future. We try to find jobs for those who successfully complete the training, although this is not always possible. Nevertheless, it is right that we should consider idle youth as a waste of a great national asset. We should do everything possible to give our young people the skills and the confidence to strengthen the nation which they will one day lead.

## A NOTE ON THE TREATMENT
## OF FORMER FOREST FIGHTERS

For certain historical reasons and circumstances, the Kikuyu, Embu, and Meru tribes were the spearhead of the militant wing of Kenya's nationalist movement. For understandable reasons, members of other tribes may be envious of this position, although praise for those who fought has often known no tribal boundaries. Even within these three tribes, some of those who served on the side of the Colonial Government as "Loyalists" are, not surprisingly, apprehensive about the attitudes of their former opponents, and some may even fear revenge should former Freedom Fighters acquire power. Thus, in many high places, there appears to be a basic apathy towards the plight of those who fought and sacrificed. Some of those who now enjoy the fruits of Independence, who sit in places made available to them partly through the blood and sweat of those who fought, look down upon the fighters as fools. They prefer to give them no opportunity at all to come up, to regain what they sacrificed.

There are many children alive today whose fathers died during the Emergency; their mothers may still be living as well. Very little has been done to help them. Yet many politicians claim in public that "we all 'fought' for *Uhuru* and no credit should go to any one tribe or individual." But there are different degrees of fighting.

In many countries of the world, those who served in the armed forces are recognized in a number of ways. The families of those killed are looked after by the government; those who return alive but injured receive pensions or special loans to establish themselves; others have special opportunities to attend schools, and are given medals and honours. Kenya itself has known the settlement of British soldiers under special schemes after both World Wars.

While the former Freedom Fighters do not seek big jobs for which they may not be qualified, they at least deserve free land on which to maintain themselves—this is what they fought for. Their widows should be aided, and their children given free education. Many of those who were detained lost their land rights in the "Reserves," either through the land consolidation programme or through outright confiscation—they should be compensated for this. Those who lost their property, their shops, their cattle and sheep and goats should also come under a plan for compensation. Similarly, those who were disabled should be housed by the Government, and provided with whatever employment they can manage in the face of their particular handicaps. The graves of those who gave their lives for *Uhuru* are scattered throughout the country, particularly in the Kikuyu "Reserves" and in the Mount Kenya and Aberdare forests. As a gesture of appreciation, and where it is possible, these graves should be located and clearly marked, with memorials to those who lie there. The Government might also establish some form of award for those who distinguish themselves in the service of the country—past, present, or future.

These remarks should not be misconstrued as a sign of dissatisfaction with our African Government; on the contrary, I am indeed most satisfied with it. Rather, they should be seen as a reminder to the Government that it has not recognized the Freedom Fighters in the same spirit with which the struggle for freedom was prosecuted. Those who sacrificed everything cannot be expected to receive nothing in return, or to be made the laughing stock of other, more successful men.

Many former Freedom Fighters remain disappointed by the efforts of the Government to help them, and others deplore the attempts to make everyone's contribution to Independence appear of equal weight and importance. While I do not foresee any undue threat to security arising from the dissatisfaction felt by some former fighters, it would probably not be wise to assume that they will tolerate their present position indefinitely.

# Appendix A
# The Meaning and Use of Oaths

The word "oath" in connection with the "Mau Mau" Movement has somehow been associated in the minds of many people with "savagery," "atavism," and the most imaginative stories about human beings gone "mad." Yet the same people will have only the most solemn thoughts when they hear the word "oath" in connection with legal testimony, where it stands for "honesty," or in connection with allegiance to a country, where it stands for "devotion" or "commitment." For those of us in the Movement, oaths had the same solemn and peculiar "binding" quality as they have had for other groups and organizations throughout history. We used them for many purposes, and we had many different oaths for these purposes.

Rather than try to figure out why so many western writers have been able to see nothing but blood, sex and bestiality in our rituals, I would prefer to describe some of our oaths, how they were administered and what purposes they served. I shall leave it to others to deal in the same way with the western writers and their products. Here, of course, I can speak only of what I myself did or observed being done, both before and during the Emergency, in the several hundred ceremonies at which I was present.

From the point of view of our fighting forces, the most important oath was the Action Oath, which was given before a man joined our army. Those who had taken the oath were identified by means of an armband of animal skin. Ordinary members, that is, non-Forest Fighters, often feared the Action Oath (*muma wa ngero*) because they knew so little about it. Wild rumours often circulated about this oath, stimulating enemy propaganda. With the need to record the history of our struggle so that our children may understand how we achieved freedom, I can now describe the Action Oath in its entirety.

While the potential Forest Fighters waited nearby, but out of sight, a he-goat all of one colour was slaughtered. Kikuyu custom was followed, and the goat was strangled quickly by pressure on its windpipe. As soon as the animal was dead, it was stabbed in the breast next to the heart, and the blood which ran out was allowed nearly to fill a gourd. Typical

Kikuyu foods, such as milk and millet, were then mixed in with the blood, and bile added to give a bitter taste. The goat's carcass was dismembered and place[d] on a flaming fire but the head was put to one side and the fluid from its eyes added to the gourd. Special slaughter knives (*rau*) were used throughout this procedure. Finally, the goat's skin was cut into small pieces (*ngwaro*) to be made into armbands for the new recruits. One long strip of hide was cut to tie around the stone of sacrifice.

With these presentations completed, a place was cleared for the ceremony itself. Any place would do and it was always well-decorated with banana plants, sugar-cane stems and other plants, placed in a wide circle around the stone. On the stone itself were placed the *mugere* stick and seven black plants, within which rested a bunch of bananas, the full gourd and the meat of the goat. The men about to take the oath were brought naked into the circle of sacrifice in such numbers as the oath administrator decreed; the latter wore ceremonial dress but no shoes.

When the men entered the circle, they first walked round it seven times and then stood still, while the administrator took the gourd and the goat's meat and passed them round each man—again seven times. The men were then given a small ball of soil or clay, which they had to hold in their hands. The jaw of the goat, which had been placed in the gourd, was removed by a piece of string tied round it. Each man in turn took the jaw bone, tied it round his neck with the string, and held a *mugere* stick in his hand as he repeated the oath:

> If I reveal our secrets, let this oath turn against me;
> If I spy falsely, let this oath turn against me;
> If my father, my mother or my child betray the nation and I refuse to kill him or her, let this oath turn against me;
> If I leave any comrade in danger, let this oath turn against me;
> If I kill a leader to gain promotion or a higher post, let this oath turn against me;
> If I surrender before we have gained our Independence, let this oath turn against me;
> If I see a weapon of the enemy and fear to take it, let this oath turn against me;

If I hand over my gun or our books to the enemy, let this oath turn
against me;

If I kill a fellow soldier out of enmity, let this oath turn against me;

If I betray our country or our nationalists, let this oath turn against
me.

While repeating these words, the man would strike the jawbone with
the stick, and when he had finished he would pass them to the next man
in line. When they had finished, the administrator took the meat and went
to the first man, who was told to repeat the following words:

I swear in truth before God and this Council that I will obey
the laws of the Council and will be a steadfast soldier who will
obey the Council's and the commander's orders. If I disobey
or fail to fulfill any commission, let this meat turn against me
and let my legs be fractured;

I swear that if I become a commander I will judge all cases
fairly, without fear or favour to any person, whether friend or
relative. (Again, he bit and swallowed the meat);

I swear that I will never forget our people, our women and
children, or those killed in the forest or in Government camps.
If ever I refuse to help them when I am able to do so, or if I
forget them, let this meat turn against me;

I swear to give my life as a sacrifice for the nation in the
fight for Independence, without demanding any reward except
our freedom. If I speak falsely, let this oath kill me;

I swear that if I am sent to cut off the head of a European or
any of our enemies and I return without doing it, due to fear or
cowardice, let this oath turn against me;

I swear that if we attack any place and capture money or any
other article and I hide it for my own use, let this oath put an
end to me;

I swear that if I form my own private committee without the
knowledge of this Council or my commanders, and commit
such offence willingly, let this oath put an end to me.

At the end of each statement, the man would bite a small piece of the goat's meat and swallow it whole. The other men in turn would each swear the seven oaths. Then the next part of the ceremony began, as the troop commander held the point of a sharpened *panga* against the back of the first man. The administrator held the gourd to the initiate's lips, dipped a knife into it and drew a cross on the man's forehead, saying: "I mark you with the mark of Gikuyu and Mumbi,[9] who were granted this country by God for themselves and their generations. Be brave and firm, knowing that if you die in the fight to liberate your land, God will preserve you in heaven. If you die like a coward, you will be punished by God." While these words were being spoken, the *panga* rested on the man's neck and at the conclusion of the speech he sipped the blood from the gourd. (This part of the ritual may indeed have led to the common misunderstanding of the whole ceremony—that it was performed with human blood. Since those taking the oath had not been present at the slaughtering of the goat they had no idea what kind of blood was in the gourd).

The administrator continued: "This is blood, and whether it be of man or beast, make it a cup of love and drink you all from it. Drink knowing that this cup is for trouble and restraint, sorrow and tears. But we who drink from it are united together and hope for that joyous day which, when it comes, will always be remembered. This is your remembrance, whether you are in difficulties or in pleasure.

Each man then sipped from the gourd, and was given an armband of skin (*mi rerema*), and a *mwembaiguru* round his hand. He then took a hammer and a goat's leg and said: "If I fail to fulfill my oath let me be smashed like this leg," and he hit the leg with the hammer. When all of the men had completed this, they put on their clothes and turned to face Mount Kenya, saying: "God bless this sacrifice." The men were then registered as soldiers in our official books, and the Action Oath was over.

A similar but slightly modified oath was taken by women scouts who worked with and for us. They, however, did not remove their clothes during the oath, and if at any time they were ordered to do so, those involved were committing a grave offence. They were required to wear only woven clothes, and could not be adorned with such things as jewellery, rings, bracelets or wristwatches. Finally, women swore fewer point commit-

,elves to the punishment of the oath generally for the following

1. acting as a spy;
2. refusing to come when called at night;
3. failing to take advantage of an opportunity, or failing to report it to our men;
4. neglecting a wounded soldier;
5. reporting a soldier to the enemy;
6. neglecting to report secrets of the enemy which she had learnt;
7. betraying the nation, or resting before Kenya was Independent.

While the oath was being administered to women they were not allowed to stand up, but sat upon a small pot placed in a traditional basket. At the conclusion of the ceremony, they did not receive goatskin armbands, as did the men, for they were reserved for fighters only.

Oaths also played an important role in the promotion of soldiers to leadership ranks. Up to a certain point, company commanders controlled promotions, but above RSM [Regimental Sergeant Major] rank it was awarded only by Headquarters. Anyone promoted to the rank of major had to take the leaders' oath, for he would be attending highly secret meetings. But even before taking this oath, a potential leader had to undergo a rather difficult and tricky test. A number of soldiers from another company would be dressed in police uniforms from our own stores. The man tipped for promotion would be taken to a house or meeting spot, where an unexpected and unavoidable "arrest" would take place. He was told by our policemen that he faced immediate death unless he revealed everything he knew about the Forest Fighters, their hiding places, camps and so on.

At first sight, this may look like an unfair trick to play on an innocent man; yet this was exactly the position in which a leader might and very likely would find himself sometime during his career. We had to be absolutely certain of the courage and integrity of any man entrusted with our secrets. If we failed to assess his character correctly, or even gave him the benefit of the doubt, all our lives, as well as the success of our Movement as a whole, might one day be endangered. It was better to show from the outset a man's strengths and weaknesses.

If a man passed this test, he was then given the Oath of Leadership, a highly secret ritual known only to the commanders. In addition to swearing the oath, the officer was also taught a number of basic principles of leadership. The oath was not always taken by high ranking officers, however, especially in cases where a junior officer stepped into the place of a more senior man who may have been arrested or killed. In the administration of the Leaders' Oath, the candidate did not remove his clothes, and only the head officers were present. Only after the oath was completed was the promotion announced to the rank and file, who were summoned and introduced to their new officer.

Among the basic provisions of the Leadership Oath were the following:

1. I swear that I will not reveal any secret of the committee to the public or to any non-member, or before the committee allows it to be known;
2. I swear that I will not judge unjustly any soldier of lower rank;
3. I swear that I will not challenge the word of my commander in front of junior officers, nor will I accuse him publicly before other commanders;
4. I swear that I will not reveal any secrets to the Europeans or sell any information for money;
5. I swear that I will fight to my last breath and until we get our Independence, and will never cease to challenge the whites who robbed us of our land.

At the conclusion of the ceremony, the new officer was instructed in some basic rules of conduct. The four most common rules dealt with discipline, women, communication of plans, and morale. On matters of discipline, where soldiers were found to be unruly or disobedient, the officer was told to take them to the reserves and through the help of the local leader, find a suitable house in which to administer the oath. The officer would then tell this man, "I know why we have no co-operation or peace in our company—we have forgotten our oaths and must take them once again." The obedient members of the company would then lay down their arms and be taken to a separate room, and an oath administered; when the same procedure was repeated with the disobedient men, their arms would be given to the recently oathed obedient group. Those who were guilty of misconduct would then have two days in which to correct their behaviour and then had to come individually to the officer to obtain their weapons. Those who refused to meet their officer would either be taken to head-quarters or posted to another company, unless their behaviour warranted a judicial inquiry.

As regards women, officers were instructed to avoid relationships with a woman who had any connection with an ordinary soldier, and to pre-vent their affairs from becoming public. New leaders were told that if they wanted to meet a girl, they should contact the chief woman scout of the village, who would at least ensure that the girl was safe from a secu-rity point of view and assist the officer in meeting girls. We also urged officers to exercise great caution in dealing with attractive but unknown women, who might easily be enemy scouts. Indeed, we advised our offi-cers to restrict their relationships to women leaders only, although this was not always possible.

Communication of battle plans to soldiers was to be reserved until the last possible moment. Junior officers could be informed of the route to be followed and bivouac points, but soldiers should be given no details at all, since they might reveal this information, even unintentionally, in the "Reserves." Once a march was begun, soldiers could be told their desti-nation so that they could regroup in case of attack. But once the destina-tion was revealed, no one could speak to any civilian, not even his wife or mother.

Finally, as regards morale, officers were asked not to reveal to their men the total number of deaths and casualties in any battle. They should train their men to bury their dead discreetly, so that supporters would not be discouraged when there were heavy losses. Optimism was a keynote of leadership, even if it meant playing down defeats and setbacks. While liquor of any kind was forbidden both to leaders and to rank and file in the forest, the use of opium, *bhang* (Indian hemp [cannabis]) and similar drugs was not prohibited where men were already accustomed to it. The majority of leaders in the forest, including myself, disapproved of such drugs, but we found that some men gave a much more reliable performance if they were not denied it prior to battle. There was never any question either of encouraging its use or of relying upon it as a stimulant to battle—we usually had more than enough cause for that.

I have not touched on oaths administered in the "Reserves" to non-Forest Fighters; although they were similar, they were generally briefer and less complicated. My colleague, Josiah Mwangi Kariuki has already written of them in his own autobiography, *"Mau Mau" Detainee*. The main point is that we looked upon all oaths as a natural expression of people who already felt a common bond of anger and hope in their lives. For most people, taking an oath was the final, not the first, expression of their devotion to our cause. Participating in the ritual ceremony gave people a chance to attach their feelings and devotion to a sacred part of their own society; they did not have to take an oath to know that they were suffering and that they wanted to do something to help themselves, but rather many people took the oath just to show how *deeply* they felt these things. To me, there is nothing strange about people who already feel strongly about their freedom wanting to sanctify those feelings openly by taking part in a sacred oath.

Apart from the solemnity which it gave to a man's devotion, taking an oath also helped our organization and morale. Those who refused to participate obviously had loyalties elsewhere, and we knew just how far we could trust them. Oath-giving ceremonies were, however, more than ritual initiations. We also used them for the opportunity they gave to educate new recruits about the history of their country, about our objectives, about military tactics and so on. As an important experience in their lives, the oathing ceremony was an excellent time to impress upon our young men the reasons for our struggle.

Claims that oaths were used for other purposes, such as satisfying the "perversions" of certain individuals, or "debasing" the men who fought in the forest, have never been substantiated in fact, and there is no reason to think they are true. To say, for example, as some people would have done, that we used human blood in our ceremonies makes no sense. We Kikuyu have a horror of human blood which has its origins in some of our most sacred tribal traditions. One of our forest laws, in fact, laid down that if a soldier attacked an enemy with a *panga* and blood touched his clothes, he must wash them before mixing with his comrades. This rule was so carefully observed that a man would have to wear wet clothes, which he had just washed, if he had no change of clothing. Cleansing rituals after a killing were also observed. A man would cut Kikuyu grass and place it on the spot where the death had occurred, and then walk across it; if it were near a village, an elder was called to pour a little milk on the grass and then onto the soldier.

# Appendix B
# Rules of Conduct in the Forest

With so many men in the forests of Mount Kenya and Nyandarua, and with military type organization of ranks, companies and so on, we were naturally faced with such problems as discipline, settling disputes over property or personal rights, keeping records, setting up standards of good conduct and establishing some basic rules of behavior which could be understood and followed by soldiers of all ranks. Although these regulations were added to and changed, over the time we were in the forest, many of the most important ones were codified in the meeting held January 4th, 1954 by Committee No. 4, the joint Executive of Mount Kenya and Nyandarua. The meeting was under the chairmanship of Dedan Kimathi, and took place at Thigingi, near Nyandarua. The following rules of conduct were approved at this meeting and thereby became laws, enforceable by commanders and by our own judicial system:

1. Any soldier or leader who disobeys the order of a more important person, will be prosecuted.
2. No soldier may object to any order given by his superior.
3. Soldiers or leaders should not object to orders given by our "Special Police" when, for example, they are refused permission to travel a certain path, or to spend the night in a certain village; our "Special Police" are the eyes of our soldiers when they are in the villages.
4. If a soldier or guard falls asleep while on duty, he will be prosecuted.
5. A spy who reports false information will be prosecuted.

6. No one may fire bullets when there is no battle, even if he is alone in the bush and does not know the whereabouts of the others.

7. No one may shoot any wild animal except when soldiers urgently need food or unless the animal attacks our people.

8. No one may speak during a night march, and rifles must always be kept at the ready, not hanging from the shoulders.

9. No one may enter any house without a thorough search for the enemy, no matter whose house it is.

10. No soldier has the authority to go to his home without a permit from his commander; even then, he must be accompanied by other soldiers.

11. Without permission, no soldier may sleep in any house.

12. A soldier may not abuse his comrades or commander.

13. A soldier must always assist any of our men or women scouts and respect them, especially women scouts.

14. If a soldier meets a policeman, KAR soldier, Home Guard, or tribal policeman and the enemy turns his gun butt towards him, the soldier must spare him for this is a sign that he belongs to us.

15. If a soldier meets any enemy troops or policemen who stand still and then leave their weapons, he should not attack them nor should he take their arms.

16. If girls or older women are heard preparing a feast for enemy forces, no soldier should show himself or approach nearby, for that is a snare planned by our women to obtain weapons.

17. No soldier may leave his company to join another without permission of his commander, except where his company is defeated and he is unable to find his comrades; in such a case, he must report to another commander and rejoin his own company if it reassembles.

18. It is not permitted to allow people into the forest without the approval of the village leaders. This will avoid infiltration by enemy CID agents.

19. If a soldier recovers a gun he may not retain it for his own, nor may a soldier have two rifles, a pistol and a rifle, or two pistols to himself, except in Nairobi where fighters may have two pistols.

20. There is no authority to kill any person under eighteen years, for this would show us to be unwise.

21. No one may be killed without the approval of village leaders, for they are responsible for reporting traitors.
22. No one is authorized to write a letter to a person demanding his head, for that will only make him watchful.
23. No soldier will receive any reward for capturing weapons, as was the case initially, only village leaders and members will continue to receive rewards.
24. There is no permission to beat civilians for that will turn them against us.
25. Soldiers have no authority to collect any tax without the permission of their commander.
26. Attacks on any prison are not permitted unless the prisoners and prison soldiers are firmly united behind the action; such actions otherwise are dangerous, for the Government will take stern measures against the villagers and relatives of the prisoners.
27. No hospital should be attacked, but wounded people in hospital may be recovered and returned to the forest; nurses should not be harmed for they are friendly to all; any soldier found molesting a nurse will be punished severely.
28. Villages under construction should not be burned, for people will turn against us.
29. There is no authority to burn any school, even though ours were burnt by the Europeans and their agents.
30. No child should be hindered from going to school.
31. There is no authority for any soldier to rape a girl or woman.
32. No soldier has the right to fall in love with his comrade's girl-friend; a soldier who falls in love and keeps it a secret is liable to prosecution.
33. No one is permitted to bring a woman into the forest unless she has been kidnapped for traitorous activities, in which case permission must be obtained from the Executive Committee or from company commanders, and there must be a good reason why such people should be kept in the forest.
34. No one may smoke in the forest except when resting; smoking is permitted in villages only within houses; at night, cigarettes must be covered or smoked within a house.

35. No one may drink beer without permission of his company commander.
36. No one may leave his excreta uncovered, for the waste may help the enemy to know where people are, or the time they were present in a certain place.
37. No one may refuse to undergo a medical examination; anyone found suffering from venereal disease will not be permitted to leave the forest until allowed to do so by the doctor.

The following regulations were especially applicable to leaders and officers:

1. A leader has no right to abuse a soldier.
2. Whipping of soldiers as a punishment is not permitted.
3. No officer may judge any soldier unfairly; such an offence is liable to prosecution.
4. Leaders may not choose the best food for themselves; food will be the same for officers and soldiers, and will be distributed to both by the Food Commissioner; however, if an officer goes to a village and a special meal is cooked for him, he is free to eat it.
5. An officer is not permitted to play about with girls in front of his soldiers, and should not fall in love with a girl-friend of any soldier; an officer may not hunt for a girl but must meet her through our women commanders.
6. Every company commander must have his own judicial council to deal with minor cases.
7. A commander who meets with a lost soldier must help him locate his own company.
8. No leader may prevent his home area from giving support to another leader.
9. Officers must always be ready to assist women scouts in case of difficulty.
10. If a soldier reports difficulties to his commander he must be helped; if there is no money available, the commander must give him a letter authorizing him to receive money from his home leaders or from Headquarters.

11. A commander is not authorized to accept any soldier from another company without a certificate from the other commander.
12. If a commander wishes to increase the number of his soldiers, he must first report to Headquarters of Mount Kenya or Nyandarua; but if he is given some additional soldiers by village leaders, he must report their names immediately to one of two H/Qs.
13. Every commander must send a monthly report to H/Q on his activities, the state of his supplies and the number of his own and enemy forces wounded, killed or captured in action.
14. Every commander must obtain a certificate from H/Q to obtain supplies from village leaders; but every commander must try to be as self-sufficient as possible concerning food, clothes and ammunition.
15. A commander may not receive supplies from village leaders without signing their receipt book.

## Omitted section: Appendix C

This appendix explains how the Mount Kenya fighting forces were organized.

# The Interrogation of
# Waruhiu Itote (General China)

*General China was captured on January 15, 1954. His interrogation began on January 26 and was conducted by Assistant Superintendent of Police Ian Henderson.*

Secret.

Office: The Special Branch, Kenya Police
Time: 68 hours.
Language of Interrogation: Kikuyu
Nairobi: 26th January 1954

## China's Biography

Waruhiu son of Itote was born in 1922 in Kaheti, Muhito location, South Nyeri. During his childhood his father changed residence and came to live near Ichuga, Konyu location. He is a member of the Mabati circumcision group and was circumcised on the 5th July 1939.[1] His clan is Muchakamoyo.

Schooling: First went to the CMS at Mihuti.[2] From 1936 to 1937 he studied at the CSM [Church of Scotland Mission school] Ichuga. Later studied at the old CMS School close to the Native Civil Hospital in Nyeri, which he left in 1938. He then came to Nairobi and worked as a vegetable seller. Speaks a little English.

Last occupation: Fireman in the EAR and H [East African Railways and Harbours]

Training:    a) Civil: Qualified tailor. Drives motor vehicles.
             b) Military: Intelligence. General small arms training and
                fieldcraft.

Brief details of military service: Enlisted in the army in 1942 at Langata from where he was posted to the EAMLS[3] at Nanyuki. Then joined the 36 (TT) KAR [36th battalion of the King's African Rifles, based in "Tanganyika Territory"] at Yatta. Trained at Moshi and in 1943 he proceeded to Ceylon [modern-day Sri Lanka] as part of the 26 Brigade, 11 East African Division. Visited Calcutta [Kolkata today] and then went into action against the Japanese in the campaign down the Kabaw valley [in Burma]. During this time he was employed as a corporal in the Intelligence Section of HQ [Headquarters] Coy [Company], 36 KAR. He returned to Kenya in 1944 with a leave draft. On completion of his leave he proceeded with the Unit to Jinja [a town in Uganda on the shore of Lake Victoria], employed as a General Duty corporal in the HQ Company. Then took his discharge at Gilgil, passing out with an "exemplary" ticket.

Countries visited: Tanganyika, Uganda, Ceylon, India, Manipur, Burma.

Criminal history (stated):  a) Civil convictions: Nil.
                            b) Army: 7 days CB [confined to barracks]
                               at Nanyuki for being late back to camp.

Land: Contends he owns no land whatsoever in the reserve.[4]

Religion: Church of Scotland

Ever a "squatter"?[5] No.

Mau Mau: Has taken all grades of the Mau Mau oath. First initiated in 1951 at Kabete, under compulsion. "At that time I did not know that it was a good thing," he says.

Ever cleansed?[6] No.

Membership of political associations: Was an *askari* [soldier] for KAU [Kenya African Union – see Introduction] and attended many of Jomo Kenyatta's mammoth KAU meetings in the Central Province in pre-Emergency days. Was a paying member of the Transport and Allied Workers' Union.

## China's Characteristics

China is a complete fanatic. He has no fear of execution, is completely self-exposing and cannot be convinced that Mau Mau is doomed, however long the battle may last. He is an arrogant and ill-tempered Kikuyu, possessed of a good brain and remarkable memory. He regards himself as a "martyr to the cause" and, whilst concealing nothing against himself, is anxious not to supply information of a nature likely to lead to the destruction of Mau Mau. Fortunately, being a fanatic, he is easily excited, particularly when drawn into discussion concerning Kikuyu national aspirations, and when in this state he inadvertently reveals what he would normally conceal. Once he starts talking, it is difficult to stop him. At the time of his interrogation, his sole wish was to expound his political testament before Legislative Council[7] and then walk to the gallows without trial.

Reliability: Much of the information contained in this paper is undoubtedly true. Part is supported by documentary evidence by way of papers and books found on China and in the area where he was engaged. Other matters he mentions are already known, having been the subject of reports by independent agents prior to his capture. I would add that, throughout the lengthy interrogation of the subject, he at no time indicated that he was attempting to paint either a brighter picture of his command than was the case, or that he was intentionally misleading his questioner.

Definitions: The militant wing is that part of Mau Mau which commits acts of violence. The Passive Wing is that part of Mau Mau which, while supporting the movement fully, including the policy of violence, does not itself engage in violence.

# Compartment A—The Militant Wing

China as a leader: China was popular with the militant and passive Mau Mau in his region, primarily because he did not remain in hiding in the forests. His courage and ability to argue convincingly, at least in the eyes of the Kikuyu, placed him higher than his associates in violence. It is no over-statement to class China as one of the most cunning, vicious, determined, and powerful terrorist leaders in the country.

China's sphere of influence: China was regarded as the supreme head of Mau Mau in the following general zone:
   a) The whole of the Mount Kenya forest region.
   b) The Embu reserve.
   c) The Meru reserve.
   d) The South Nyeri reserve in so far as the following are concerned:
      i) Mathira Division, ii) Gikondi, Muhito, and eastern Othaya locations, iii) Aguthi.
   e) The Nyeri Settled Area (which includes Nanyuki) east of a general line drawn from Nyeri Township to the Lol Daiga hills.
   f) All areas east of the main Nairobi-Nyeri road down to, and including, Nairobi City.

The boundary between Dedan Kimathi and China, in respect of the South Nyeri reserve, was formerly the Sagana river. On the 11th September, 1953, "Generals" Rui and Gachuma broke away from Dedan Kimathi's command on account of Kimathi's refusal to allow the former sufficient physical latitude in the area immediately west of the Sagana river. The two "generals," with their troops, then registered under China, bringing the general area of Gikondi, Muhito and Aguthi locations into the Mount Kenya sphere.

Such is China's sphere of influence. In reality, however, Nairobi and the area to its north as far as Sagana had drifted from China's control although, in theory, it still belonged to him. To some extent the same applies to Othaya location.

## MILITANT HQ—MOUNT KENYA

China's static HQ was at Barafu 25, high on the bamboo of Mount Kenya.[8] Barafu 25 camp was discovered abandoned by security forces some weeks ago. China contends that he had forewarning of the military patrol, and had moved his HQ some four miles further north, again calling it Barafu 25. The distance of the new site from Hombe is 18 miles by foot.

Static HQ staff: Only five terrorists remained at Barafu 25 when China was absent, and this was for most of the time. These were under one Major Nyaga (real name Thuita of Konyu). China's records accompanied him wherever he went. Barafu 25 is thus evidently of little interest, being unlikely to contain more than five terrorists and, possibly, a small number of food-carriers.

Former static HQ: Prior to March, 1953, China had his static HQ with the Hika Hika (described below), the HQ of which was situated in the Chieni forest. This was abandoned on the score that homemade firearms were then put to the test of manufacture high on the mountain and he wanted his static HQ close to the "factory." China's HQ proper, however, moved with him wherever he went.

China's personal staff: China's HQ (roving) staff consisted of:
   a) Captain Faranja (real name Kahiu s/o [son of] ? from south of Tumutumu. Faranja accompanied China for many months as his personal secretary. He was with China on the day of his capture.
   b) Lieut. [Lieutenant] Mahua (real name Maina s/o Karoki, an ex-squatter from Ngunio) who was normally China's orderly.
   c) 20 men acting as a bodyguard, made available by the nearest terrorist unit to his position.

It was not uncommon for China to move about with Faranja and Mahua alone.

Personal arms: China always carried a Lanchester [submachine gun] with three magazines of 9mm, one of the weapons stolen from Naivasha Police Station.[9] On the day before his capture he had given the weapon to one Sgt. [Sergeant] Rongu who had gone to Aguthi to deliver a message, and taken over a .303 rifle from another terrorist. Capt. [Captain] Faranja similarly carried a Lanchester while Lieut. Mahua carried a BSA [Birmingham Small Arms] Sporting .303 rifle and one 36 fragmentation grenade.

When China entered what he considered to be a "risky" area, he insisted on having the bodyguard of 20, all of whom had to be armed with weapons proper.

In the fortnight preceding the date of his capture (15th January 1954) China had been continuously in Mathira Division save for a brief visit to Ndia in Embu district. Since July, 1953, he had spent longer in Mathira than in any other area.

## CHINA'S COMMAND:
## THE MOUNT KENYA COMMITTEE

The supreme body governing both militant and passive wings in the Mount Kenya sphere is the "Mount Kenya Committee" which consists of 20 leading militant personalities drawn up on the following basis:

| | |
|---|---|
| Nyeri District | 6 |
| Embu District | 6 |
| Meru District | 6 |
| Chairman | 1 |
| Secretary | 1 |
| | 20 |

Representatives of the Mount Kenya Committee:

| | |
|---|---|
| Nyeri District | General Tanganyika |
| | General Mapiganyama |
| | General Gachuma |
| | General Kaleba |

|                | General Rui |
|                | Brigadier Kinyori |
| Embu District  | General Ndaya |
|                | General Kassam |
|                | Brigadier Kubukubu |
| Meru District  | Brigadier Ruku |
|                | Brigadier Mtu Anampio |

Note: The vacant "seats," three in the Embu and four in the Meru groups respectively, have *never* been filled as the two areas do not possess the required number of high-ranking and sufficiently trusted leaders of a calibre acceptable to the Mount Kenya Committee as a whole.

| Chairman  | General China (until captured) |
| Secretary | Captain Faranja |

The Mount Kenya Committee is primarily a policy formulating body and is regarded as the "War Cabinet." It does not deal with detail. Its business usually consists of, for example, matters such as: recruitment, overall prosecution of the "war," etc.[10]

This Committee has met on a number of occasions, the last two of which were the 26th November, 1953, and 28th December, 1953, at Barafu 25 and near the Karinga river in Location 7, Embu, respectively. In the case of the former, the venue was changed from Gachuero, where it was to have taken place on the 27th November 1953, to Barafu 25 on the 26th on account of security forces having found a summons on a courier. (This is correct.)

The Committee also acts as the "Supreme Court for Mount Kenya" and can deal with offenders, but cases are few as only high-ranking terrorists are "tried" on this level.

If half of the recognised representatives of the Mount Kenya Committee attend a meeting, the Committee is regarded as properly constituted and can proceed with its business. For obvious reasons, most meetings are attended by six to eight members only.

Decisions of the Mount Kenya Committee are executed by the attending members who, being commanders of various militant units, put the decisions into practise on their return to their respective commands, wherever they may be. In the case of absentees, the decisions are conveyed to them by couriers.

The Mount Kenya Committee will select a successor to General China. It is likely to be one or other of the following:

a) General Tanganyika
b) General Mapiganyama
c) General Kaleba

It is very obvious that on major issues, such as a decision to move large forces from the forest to the reserve, China is bound by the Committee. Nevertheless, disagreement is most unusual.

The chairman, formerly China, is responsible for calling meetings, the method of summoning members being left to trusted couriers. Any member, however, having some major item for discussion, is entitled to call a meeting.

General discussion is the main theme of Mount Kenya Committee meetings, views being exchanged on tactics, members voicing their difficulties and generally pooling information concerning successes and reverses. All details are recorded by Capt. Faranja.

As will be seen in the ensuing sections of this paper, members of the Mount Kenya Committee are the hierarchy of militant Mau Mau in the Mount Kenya sphere, thus the governing power of the Committee over the militant wing requires no further explanation. The Committee, however, also controls the passive wing of Mau Mau in the reserves. Such control is achieved by *influence* and although the passive wing is not represented at meetings, orders given by militant leaders to individuals of the passive wing are quickly obeyed as they are regarded as emanating from a "committee of generals" with whom nobody would venture to disagree.

# CHINA'S COMMAND:
# THE EXECUTIVE COMMITTEE

From representatives of the Mount Kenya Committee an Executive Committee is elected. The Executive Committee meets as and when it considers it necessary to do so and deals with the prosecution of the "war," within the general policy of the Mount Kenya Committee, but in far greater detail. It has authority to switch troops about, to direct supplies and to concern itself far more closely with terrorist activities as a whole.

Members of the Executive Committee: The Executive Committee consists of the following eight leaders, all of whom are already members of the Mount Kenya Committee:

    (1) General China as chairman (captured)
    (2) General Tanganyika
    (3) General Ndaya
    (4) General Kassam
    (5) General Gachuma
    (6) General Rui
    (7) General Mapiganyama
    (8) Brigadier Ruku
      · with Capt. Faranja as clerk.

The Executive Committee does not appear to meet more often than the Mount Kenya Committee, and, like the latter, its business can be transacted with only 50% of its members present.

The difficulties in arranging a meeting are considerable and while it is intended that the Executive Committee should meet fortnightly, the fact that it cannot do so has caused its members, and Mau Mau militant commanders as a whole, to enjoy far greater latitude in their respective commands, Executive Committee rulings arriving both irregularly and infrequently. This committee seems to have become, therefore, more or less a "sounding box" for the Mount Kenya Committee, reviewing in greater detail what the latter has already reviewed.

All Executive Committee meetings take place in forest areas for some reason it being considered unlucky to meet in the reserves.

# THE MILITANT STRUCTURE

China's militant wing is composed of nine independent units:

    (1) The Hika Hika battalion

    (2) The 195 Tanganyika battalion

    (3) The Ruheni battalion

    (4) The Kaleba battalion

    (5) The Embu battalion, Ndaya

    (6) The Embu battalion, Kassam

    (7) The Ruku battalion, Meru

    (8) The Engineers

    (9) The Hika Hika 210 battalion, Nairobi

Each of these battalions is dealt with separately, commencing with the Hika Hika battalion.

### The Hika Hika Battalion

This battalion is commanded by General Mapiganyama (real name Gaitho s/o Mathenge, a Kikuyu from Chief Eliud's location, Iriaini) and has, as its assigned area, the region from "Eliud's location at Karatina, to Chehe and to the border of Ndia," thus the eastern sector of Mathira Division. It has, as will be seen, some companies outside this region.

It was originally called the "Hika Hika No. 1," but when its ranks increased, it was raised to "battalion" status.

Battalion HQ: The HQ of the Hika Hika battalion is in the Muthea forest area, above Chehe, some 8 miles into the forest of Mount Kenya from the Chehe sawmills. The HQ is above-ground, consisting of a number of "hides," and is manned by:

    (1) Captain Achieng (real name Mundia s/o ? of Kiangai, Embu, but formerly of Iriaini, Mathira) who is the HQ clerk.

    (2) Col. [Colonel] Kubai (real name Kinaro s/o ? of Ruguru). This man may have been killed recently by mortars.

    (3) Lieut. Mwitira (real name Muthee s/o Migwi, of Mugoiri, Fort Hall).

(4) Sgt. Major Konyeki (real name Kiriru s/o Kabii of Kahiga, Magutu).

(5) Cpl. [Corporal] Kahoki (real name Munandi s/o Kagui, of Chief Eliud's area, near Chehe).

General Mapiganyama spends about one day a week in this HQ, travelling around his companies, mostly in Mathira, in the balance of the time.

2 i/c [second-in-command] Hika Hika battalion is Colonel Ngomari[11] (pronounced like "Montgomery"). The battalion is divided up into the following six companies:

*The Rumuri Company (formerly known as No. 1 Hika Hika Coy)*

|  |  |
|---|---|
| Commander: | Brigadier Kafiu |
| Staff: | (1) Col. Gakuru |
|  | (2) Major Gathechani (real name Kagume s/o Mare of Ichuga, Konyu, brother of deposed headman Mengo). |
|  | (3) Staff Sgt. Baranja, clerk (not to be confused with Capt. Faranja). |
|  | (4) Major Kagume. |
|  | (5) Capt. Kenya. |
|  | (6) Sgt. Major Githerangi |
|  | (7) Sgt. Major Wangamsemi |
|  | (8) Sgt. Kaka |
|  | (9) Cpl. Mechiria |

Assigned area: Particularly the area between Giagatika and the railway line at Kianguruwe. Generally, Iriaini and Konyu locations of Mathira Division.

Strength: Personnel: approximately 450.

Arms: 3 automatic rifles, 84 firearms proper, assorted. 160 "home made" weapons.

*The 77 LMT Company*

Commander: Brigadier Kinyori (real name Kinyori s/o Muhindo, of Magutu location), alias Githee

Assigned area: Roving commission, now mostly assisting Brigadier Ruku in the forests above Meru.

Strength: Personnel: approximately 700.

Arms: 1 Sten [submachine gun], 12 shotguns, 14 .303 rifles, 8 pistols, about 60 "home made" weapons.

The above company was formed on the 12th April, 1953.

*No. 3 Hika Hika Company*

Commander:  Brigadier Batabatu
2 i/c:          Brigadier Kanji (real name Gachemi s/o ? of Kariko, Magutu, near Giakaibii).
Staff:          (1) Lieut. Uganda (real name Kahuria s/o Kainira of Kabiru-ini, Chief Muhindi).
                (2) Lieut. Kanyoni Kanja (real name Mwangi s/o Kuhuria, clerk, of Magutu, Chief Ndoria).
                (3) Sgt. Major Njogu Kabau

Assigned area: Ngaini, Ihwagi, Karura, Karuthi and generally, Kirimu-kuyu location of Mathira Division.

Strength: Personnel: approximately 550.

Arms: Batabatu has not sent in a return. Believed to be 21 firearms proper, ? number of "home made."

Note: Brigadier Batabatu with a proportion of this company went to Nanyuki on 13th January, 1954 to fetch arms and ammunition (not known from who)

No. 3 Hika Hika company is responsible, *inter alia* [amongst other things], for sending armed parties to all other companies within the battalion for the purpose of collecting reports for General Mapiganyama.

*No. 4 Hika Hika Company*

Commander:  Brigadier Kenes (pronounced "Kennis") (real name unknown but man of Mukore, Konyu)
2 i/c:  Brigadier Waituku.
Staff:  (1) Major Kiihuri (real name ? of Mutathi-ini, Kirimukuyu location).
   (2) Lieut. Hiti Mguu Tatu (real name Mwangi s/o Gatheru, of Gakunyi, Chief Muhindi).

Assigned area: Ranges between Konyu location, Mathira, and Ndia Division, Embu. Now split between Aguthi location and Kariko in Mathira Division.
Strength: Personnel: 420.
Arms: 2 automatic rifles, 3 grenades, 24 rifles/shotguns proper, 80 "home made" weapons
Note 1: Brigadier Masongaleri was OC [officer-in-charge] No. 4 Hika Hika Company but was killed recently.
Note 2: Major Kiihuri is at present leading a gang operating in the area between Giagatika and Tumutumu.

*The B.1 Company*

Commander:  Major Rhino Boy
Staff:  (1) Captain Kuriandamu
   (2) Lieut. Marindono.
   (3) Lieut. Sebeni (real name Muriuki s/o ? of Magutu location)

Assigned area: The border country between Mathira Division and Embu Reserve, penetrating to Location 3, Embu.
Strength: Personnel: 400.
Arms: 2 automatic rifles but these are reported "out of order," 31 firearms proper (assorted), 65 "home made" as at 15 Dec. 1953.
Note: The B.1 Company is an off-shoot of No. 3 Hika Hika Company which still seems to exercise some control over its movements (?)

*The 375 IW Sarema Company*

Commander: Colonel Njune (real name unknown but a man of Aguthi location living near the home of ex-Senior Chief Wambugu Muthangania).

Assigned area: None in particular, but now split between the Nanyuki forest area and the low country north of the Lol Daiga hills.

Strength: Personnel: approximately 600.

Arms: Reported to be better armed than any other company but he has not received the figures.

The 375 IW Sarema is a "suicide company," wearing very little in the way of clothes. When given a target it attacks regardless of loss of life. It is the only militant unit in the Mount Kenya sphere which is permitted to a) smoke *bhang* [cannabis], b) pocket all the money it is able to obtain.

The above six Hika Hika Companies are again divided into sections:

## THE RUMURI COMPANY, SECTIONS

    (1) The Rumuri Section under Brigadier Kafiu himself. Part is in the Kiawarigi area of Mathira, part in the Rititi area of Kirimukuyu.

    (2) The Kuhanga Section under Major Kiihuri part of which is in the Giagatika-Tumutumu area, and part in the Mutathi-ini area of Mathira.

    (3) The Kuhanga No. 2 Section under RSM [Regimental Sergeant Major] Junio (real name Nderitu s/o Kaibii of Gakandu-ini, near Tumutumu) which is in the Kamindo area, Ngaini.

    (4) The Ruguthi Section under Lieut. Ruguthi, which is split between Magutu location and the Thage-ini area of Aguthi location.

    (5) The Faga Faga Section under Sgt. Major Faga Faga. This is "wandering." Was last in the Kagumo School area of Aguthi where it was engaged by security forces.

    (6) The Ya Major Ruku Section under Major Ruku. The majority of these were with China at Kiawarigi at the time of his capture. This section often operates in the Gatiko area of Kirimukuyu.

This section was responsible for the recent "feeler" attack on Gaikuyu Police Station.

The strength of each section in the Rumuri Company is approximately 60, but some have more. The sections are again sub-divided into *"batuni"* ("platoon," but smaller):

*Batuni*:

(1) Rumuri Section has three *batunis*. One is under Corporal Juni (real name Gachahi s/o Gacheru, of Karindundu, Chief Muhind).

(2) Kuhanga Section has two *batunis*. The following are the more prominent members of these:
i) Rank ? Kinyua (real name Muriuki s/o Kabingu)
ii) Rank ? Mwene Tiri (real name Murage s/o Ngure)
iii) Rank ? Butea (real name Maina s/o Kibanja)
iv) Rank ? Matiki (real name Gakuu s/o Mukunji)
v) Rank ? Januari (real name Mwangi s/o Maimba)
vi) Rank? Wagikungu (real name Wanjohi s/o Njaramba)
vii) Rank ? Bako Manari (real name Mwangi s/o Ngatia)
viii) Rank ? Kochi (real name Maina s/o Karume)

(3) Ruguthi Section has three *batunis*, one under Lieut. Rugutlhi, another under Sgt. Koti and a third under Cpl. Mwas.

(4) Kuhanga No. 2 Section has two *batunis*. The following are the most prominent members of these:
i) Rank ? Imajinthi (real name Nderitu s/o Kihuha)
ii) Rank ? Maka (real name Magima s/o Kaguiri)
iii) Rank ? Magani (real name Mwarari s/o Gatheru)
iv) Rank ? June (real name Huria s/o Ngari)
v) RSM Junio himself

(5) Faga Faga Section has two *batunis*, one under Sgt. Major Faga Faga.

(6) Ya Major Ruku Section has three *batuni*, one under Major Ruku. (This Ruku must not be confused with Brig. [Brigadier] Ruku of Ruku Battalion, Meru).

## THE 77 LMT COMPANY, SECTIONS

This company has five sections, sub-divided into 10 *batunis*, all going under the name "77 LMT." The names of section and *batuni* leaders have not been reported, save for one section leader—Major Four Four, a Meru.

## THE NO. 3 HIKA HIKA COMPANY, SECTIONS

This is divided into five sections:

(1) Kanji Section under Col. Kanji—strength approx. 100.
(2) Ruguni Section under Lieut. Ruguni—strength approx. 80.
(3) Kamumbu Section under Sgt. Major Kamumbu—strength approx. 40. Kamumbu is a man of Hiriga, Ruguru location.
(4) Wajuda Section under Lieut. Wajuda—strength approx. 290.
(5) Githuika Section under Sgt. Githuika (real name Ngingu s/o Wainaina of Karii, Chief Josiah's area, Kiambu). Strength: approx. 40.

The above five sections are again split up into *batunis*. Details unknown. The Kamumbu section is now with Brigadier Batabatu in the Nanyuki area collecting arms and ammunition.

The remaining Sections are in Mathira Division and the forest area above Mathira.

The Wajuda Section is responsible for the transport of foodstuffs to all companies operating *in forest* within strength of this section. Three *batuni* leaders under the Wajuda Section are:

i) Sgt. Major Kananda
ii) Sgt. Kiuno
iii) Cpl. Mucheji
iv) Cpl. Baringi (named after HE!)[12]

Cpl. Maniuru Kwigaya, a Kikuyu of Gatongo in Iriaini, is clerk to Col. Kanji of Kanji Section.

## THE NO. 4 HIKA HIKA COMPANY, SECTIONS

This company is divided into two sections, which are again sub-divided into an unknown number of *batunis*.

   a)  The Waituku Section, under Brigadier Waituku, a native of Gathu-ini, Mathira, with approximately 220 men.
   b)  A second section which was being formed at the time of China's capture. No further details known.

Part of the Waituku Section was in the vicinity of Kariko, Mathira Division. Part is in the area between Gatundu and Ndia, Embu.

## THE B.1 COMPANY, SECTIONS

Until 15th December, 1953, this company was in Nanyuki District. Since its transfer to the Embu-Mathira border country, some re-organisation has taken place. China received a letter on 11th Jan., 1954, from Major Rhino Boy, the commander of the company, to the effect that he would send in the names of his section leaders by 12th Feb., 1954, but would first like to see Brigadier Kenes of No. 3 Hika Hika Company and General Mapiganyama, commander of the Hika Hika battalion. No further details are, therefore, available.

## THE 375 IW SAREMA COMPANY, SECTIONS

This Company has six sections, each 100 strong. These are not sub-divided into *batunis*. The sections operate as "gangs" of 100 and are referred to periodically in letters as *mururumo*, meaning "thunder." They are the pick of China's command and are well equipped. China has intended promoting the Sarema commander, Colonel Njune, for many weeks but has not been able to get him over from the Lol Daiga hills area.

The 375 IW Sarema Company has been inactive for eight months. China refuses to be tricked into giving any reason for this inactivity and has not explained the future intentions of this "group." It would appear that they are lying low and widely scattered in bush and forest country. Apart from China's disclosures, their existence is established documentarily.

China says the 375 IW Sarema Company is the only one under his command which is permitted to purchase *bhang* and use any funds it collects. Some of its arms are likely to have been obtained from frontier tribesmen (this is partially supported by a document relating to a meeting that took place near Ngare Ndare in September, 1953). Most of the rank and file of the Sarema are dangerous criminals who have, so it seems, been evading the police for many years.

This concludes material on the Hika Hika battalion.

### The 195 Tanganyika Battalion

This battalion is commanded by General Tanganyika (real name Muriuki s/o Kamotho, of Kahiga, Magutu location, Mathira Division) and has, as its assigned area, the region generally "from Kiamariga to Kanyota market, thence to Kabaru near the 'Island Farms' in the forests of Mount Kenya."

The leaders of this battalion were, up to May, 1953, under the command of the Hika Hika battalion, but during that month General Tanganyika was promoted, and he set up the present unit.

An Italian speaking Kikuyu, known as Sgt. Sitasu, is General Tanganyika's personal secretary.

The *static* HQ of the 195 TN BAT [Tanganyika Battalion] is in the Kabaru forest area, given as four hours walking time (night) up the Mount Kenya forest slopes from the old Kabaru Saw Mills, taking a direct bearing on the peak. This static HQ is manned by:

(1) Major Kibisui
(2) Capt. Karuigi (real name Kariuki s/o Ngare of Magutu location)
(3) Some rank and file

General Tanganyika is not always at his Kabaru HQ. He travels a great deal visiting his units, but is usually in Mathira Division somewhere.

The 195 Tanganyika Battalion is divided up into the following three companies:

## The 195 Company

Commander: General Tanganyika himself
Usual operational area: Magutu location
Strength:     Personnel: 365 on 18th November, 1953
              Arms: 1 Lanchester, 18 miscellaneous firearms proper, prob-
              ably 60 "home made" rifles (General Tanganyika carries a
              Lanchester)

## The Kibarabara Company

Commander: Brigadier Wahura. Was formerly Brig. Njege Kibarabara of
Kiamariga, Chief Muhindi, now believed dead.
Usual operational area: Roaming, but often in the Itiati hill area of
Mathira Division.
Strength:     Personnel: 180
              Arms: 11 miscellaneous firearms proper, probably 50 "home
              made" rifles

## The Kabaka[13] Company

Commander: Major Kabaka (real name Miano s/o Wambugu of Kiamar-
iga, Chief Muhindi)
Usual operational area: The Royal Lodge—Kanyota—Hombe areas.
Strength:     Personnel: 160
              Arms: About 6 shotguns, 2 .303 rifles, probably 50 "home
              made"

The above three 195 Tanganyika Companies are again sub-divided into
the following sections:

## THE 195 COMPANY, SECTIONS
This company has five sections, each approximately 70 strong.
    a)   The Abdulla Section under Lieut. Abdulla (real name Matu s/o ?
        of Gitunduti, Magutu). This section has left Magutu temporarily
        and is somehow deployed in the adjoining forest.

b) The Udongo Section (no details known).

c) The Chui Section under Lieut. Chui, a native of Mihuti. This section is, for the main part, in Magutu location. 30 men of this section were with China at Kiawarigi when he was captured.

d) The Wimbi Section under "Doctor" Wimbi (real name Kinyua Kabi of Kiamariga, Magutu. This section left on 6th Jan., 1954 for the Thomsons Falls area to "recce" [do reconnaissance in] that district.

e) The Githukia Section under Sgt. Githukia, which has been sent to the Kiambu District on a special mission involving the transport of ammunition (no further details).

## THE KIBARABARA COMPANY, SECTIONS

This Company has two sections, each some 90 strong.

a) The Haraka Section, under Sgt. Haraka, a man of Kariko, Magutu location. Now in the one mile strip[14] near Kanyota village or at Njathe-ini.

b) The Nyakundi Section (leader unknown to China) now temporarily in the Ndia-Gichugu area of Embu, or in the forests above that area.

## THE KABAKA COMPANY, SECTIONS

This Company has no sections. Its 160 men are divided into five *batuni*, each about 30 strong. Save for one *batuni*, the Giteru, under Sgt. Major Giteru, a Kikuyu from Fort Fall, China knows no further details. All *batunis* of the Kabaka Company are in the Kabaru forest area. Some of the rank and file of the Kabaka are in contact with "friends" in the vicinity of the Police Training School at Nyeri station from where it is hoped to steal some ammunition.

Like Sections of other Companies, all sections under the 195 Tanganyika Battalion are broken down into *batunis* for action or for security.

The following are other prominent personalities in the 195 Tanganyika battalion who China intended promoting to captain when the next meeting with General Tanganyika took place:

(1) Sgt. Major Konyanga

(2) Sgt. Major Mungania

(3) Sgt. Major Bahati
(4) Sgt. Gatheka
(5) Sgt. Inyasio

## The Ruheni Battalion

This battalion is commanded by General Gachuma (real name Mutahi /o Gichuki, evicted "squatter" from the Rift Valley Province).

The battalion was formerly under Dedan Kimathi in the Aberdares but broke away from Dedan Kimathi's forces on the 11th September, 1953, on account of a controversy between the two leaders as to what action was necessary in the area west of the Sagana river. At that time General Gachuma was operating on the eastern flank of the Aberdare sphere. General Gachuma then registered his forces under China and is now commander of the area which one might call the wedge between Kimathi and China. This includes the general area made up by:

   a)  Gikondi, Muhito and eastern Othaya.
   b)  The Nyeri settled area, including Naromoru and Nanuki.

Before the Ruheni Battalion merged with China's forces, it was known as the "Liberation Army" and captured terrorists may still refer to it by this name.

General Gachuma has no static HQ. He travels widely within his sphere, but not very much in Nanyuki. Like other members of the militant hierarchy, he is in the habit of making an appearance in Mathira Division.

Brigadier Simba (alias Makarange) shot in the Nanyuki area some months ago, originally belonged to General Gachuma's command. Likewise, General Kamwamba (alias Nyinge Gakiye) who was killed in August, 1953, whilst touring Mathira Division.

The Ruheni Battalion is divided into the following four companies:

### B.4 Company

Commander: Brigadier Mohammed Mwai, a detribalised Kikuyu who was born in Mathira Division and brought up in the Nanyuki native locations.

HQ: Somewhere in the general area of Mawingo. Moves the HQ every week.

Assigned area: The whole Nanyuki area from the Burguret river round to the Meru reserve border, including the settled area on the left of this curve and the forest areas of Mount Kenya on its right.

Strength:    Personnel: 600

Arms: 1 Bren [a light machine gun often fired from a tripod], 3 Stens, 12 rifles/shotguns proper, 15 revolvers proper, probably 70 "home made" weapons.

*B.22 Company*

Commander: Brigadier Ligatho (real name Kiama s/o ? of Iruri, near Kanyota, Mathira Division).

Present area: In the forests of Mount Kenya above Githagui.

Strength:    Personnel: 180 approx.

Arms: 1 Sten. No details of other arms. Very few "home made" weapons.

*The Ruheni Company*

No details are known of this company save that it is operating directly under General Gachuma's orders in the general area of Gikondi, Othaya, eastern Thegenge, and Aguthi west. It is probably under Colonel Joel Stephen Mwithiga.

*Jimmie Company*

Commander: Colonel Jimmie, who came over from the Aberdares eight months ago.

Clerk: Capt. Kimunya, enlisted 3rd Dec. 1953.

HQ: Somewhere in the forest above Naromoru. Changes frequently. Usually only about three miles into forest from the SA [settled area]/ forest boundary.

Strength:    Personnel: 130

Arms: 21 rifles/shotguns, 60 "home made" rifles

On 28th December, 1953, the Ruheni Company sent 60 additional men to swell the ranks of Jimmie Company, bringing the total to somewhere in the region of 200. Groups of Jimmie Company are spread widely over the settled area. The majority, however, remain in the forest.

The breakdown of the Ruheni Battalion below company level is obscure. There is, and has been since September, 1953, a tendency for General Gachuma to operate with greater freedom than any other leader under China. China has great faith in Gachuma and does not interfere with Ruheni affairs.

## The Kaleba Battalion

This battalion is a splinter of the Ruheni, having been part of the "Liberation Army" of the Aberdares. In its Aberdare days it was commanded by General Kaleba, from whom it derives its name. General Kaleba has now removed himself from an active capacity and was, until China's capture, his touring "advisor." Kaleba still retains the rank and is usually in Mathira Division.

The Kaleba Battalion registered under China on the 11th September, 1953.

The commander of the Kaleba battalion is General Rui who operates almost exclusively in Aguthi location which is his battalion's assigned area. When Security Force pressure increases, Rui takes his men into the Kabaru forest area "for leave."

HQ: General Rui has his HQ in native houses in the Sagana valley, transferring it about frequently on account of Security Force action.

The Kaleba Battalion, which is some 300 strong, is divided into the following three Companies:

*The Roriondo Company*

Commander: Brigadier Roriondo.
Area: Anywhere in Aguthi.
Strength:     Personnel: 100 approx.
              Arms: 16 rifles/shotguns proper, 43 "home made" firearms.

*The Kaleba No. 1 Company*

Commander: General Rui himself.
Area: Anywhere in Aguthi.
Strength:     Personnel: 100 approx.
              Arms: 1 Sten (broken), 19 rifles/shotguns, 55 "home made"
              rifles.

*The Kaleba No. 2 Company*

Commander: Brigadier Kaurugo.
Area: Anywhere in Aguthi.
Strength:     Personnel: 100 approx.
              Arms: 8 rifles/shotguns, 50 "home made" weapons.

According to China, it is unusual for the above three companies to sub-divide. They usually operate as "gangs" of 100.

In recent weeks the Kaleba Battalion has suffered many reverses and has lost quite a number of its arms. The day before China's capture he wrote to General Rui and advised him to move out of Aguthi until more ammunition became available. He does not know whether Rui will evac-uate as suggested. (This was the message conveyed by Sgt. Rongu who took China's Lanchester.)

### The Embu Battalion, Ndaya

This battalion is commanded by General Ndaya, a native of Ndia whose reserve name is believed to be Wanjagi s/o Ndegwa.

This battalion is assigned the whole of western Embu district, includ-ing the forests of Mount Kenya above this sector. West of Gichugu in Location 6 Embu comes under Ndaya. Ndaya's southern flank extends to the Yattas and Ithanga hills.

General Ndaya's static HQ is given as "Kianjahi," on the hill, some 12 miles from Gichugu into the Mount Kenya forests. Ndaya shares this stat-ic HQ with General Kassam, who has his own command and area.

The battalion is divided into six companies which are again sub-divid-

ed into an unknown number of sections and *batunis*. China is rather ignorant of the breakdown of this command, even to the extent of its principal leaders. He knows only a little concerning three of the companies.

Documents suggest that some re-organisation is going on in Ndaya's
command.

### The B.4 Yatta Company

This is generally commanded by General Ndaya himself. It is now
believed to be in the Kiamwongo hills area.

### The Kubukubu Company

Commanded by Brigadier Kubukubu (real name Njeru s/o ? a native of
Inoi location). The company is scattered over the reserve and forest in a
very wide area.

### J Company

Commanded by Brigadier Kiai Jimi, a native of Ndia who was arrested
some time ago but escaped.

Corporal Gakeno is General Ndaya's chief assistant. His rank seems
rather unusual, under the circumstances.

Strength: China is ignorant of the strength of arms and personnel in
Embu Battalion Ndaya but insists that the battalion is over 1,000 strong,
of which number at least 30% have firearms of some description, the
majority "home made." He states that approximately 15% of Ndaya's
forces are Kamba.

On the 13th December, 1953, China went to Embu to obtain details of
this command, but before he could meet Ndaya his advance guard was
intercepted by a large force and he decided to return to Mathira. On the
28th December, 1953, Ndaya sent China a message from "Kianjahi" to
the effect that he could not attend the Mount Kenya Committee meeting
due to "too many other affairs." In all probability, China is partially ignorant of Embu affairs.

## The Embu Battalion, Kassam

This is commanded by General Kassam. Its sphere of control is from Gichugu in Location 6, Embu, to the Meru border i.e. in a general sense, the *eastern* half of Embu district.

Kassam shares the same HQ with Ndaya [see above].

China is emphatic that General Kassam's strength is well over 800, but, like the case of Ndaya's command, he is very ignorant on detail. There is little doubt that China, due to spending the greater part of his time in Mathira Division, is far more closely versed with enemy forces close to his stamping ground, his knowledge of a unit decreasing proportionately with its distance from Mathira.

General Kassam himself carries a Sten. The strength of arms in his command is well below the same in any other battalion. They consist chiefly of "home made" weapons. China will not be tempted into giving an opinion of the number.

Note: General Communist, mention of whom was made some months ago and who, since that time, seemed to have disappeared altogether, is reported to have enlisted in Kassam's command as an ordinary soldier, having been deposed by the Mount Kenya Committee for "causing too many of his men to be killed." Kassam replaced Communist.

China does not consider that the Mau Mau militant wing in Embu District is weaker than in Nyeri district. There is, however, an acute shortage of ammunition in Embu, so acute in fact that China considers it is inadequate for defensive purposes far less offensive, and because of this he has advised both Kassam and Ndaya to bide their time in hiding in the Mount Kenya forest. China also considers that military forces in Embu reserved areas are very "hot" and "all over the place."

## The Ruku Battalion, Meru

This battalion, which is 600 strong, is commanded by Brigadier Ruku, a Meru, who has his HQ at Kisironi (?) some four miles into the forest from the reserve boundary. (He [China] does not know which point of the reserve).

2 i/c to Brigadier Ruku is Major Mtu Anampio, also a Meru.

The majority of Brigadier Ruku's troops took to the forests in mid-August, 1953, and are still in the process of allocation and distribution. He has received no reports from Ruku of the "order of battle" or of promotions. Of the 600 terrorists involved, China has received the names of 320, these being brought by Ruku himself to Barafu 25 for the Mount Kenya Committee meeting held on 26th November, 1953. He has not seen Brigadier Ruku since. China wrote to Ruku on 8th December, 1953 asking for details of the battalion's organisation. (This is confirmed.) Most of the troops are Meru.

Ruku's battalion is very short of arms, the number of which does not exceed 20 (proper). At the time of China's capture, he was about to send an additional 20 firearms to Ruku from the Rumuri Company which is particularly well off in terms of firepower.

Brigadier Ruku's forces are now supplemented by the 77 LMT Company under Brigadier Kinyori.

The principal task of Mau Mau forces in Meru district is, at the moment and according to China, organising food supplies and generally cultivating Mau Mau in the reserved areas.

## The Engineers Group

This unit, which sometimes goes by the name "Mechanic," is commanded by Brigadier Gatamuki (a native of Gitunduti in Magutu location). It operates as a compact unit in the vicinity of Barafu 25, China's static HQ.

The unit is divided into two sections:

a) RSM Jimi's Section (not to be confused with Jimmie Company) which consists of 20 men.

b) Lieut. Sikungu Satamuki's Section (alias Wagikungu, of Magutu) also consisting of 20 men.

The two Engineers sections are entitled to go wherever they please, charged with the task of obtaining arms, ammunition, and material for the manufacture of "home made" weapons. This unit is responsible for feeding all other units in the Mount Kenya sphere with supplies of arms and ammunition. Its role, does not of course, relieve other field units of their responsibilities towards the aim of obtaining adequate supplies of such items. Weapons, etc. obtained by independent units in battle, or through other sources of their own, are not brought to the Engineers for distribution. The finder is the keeper although a report on the finding must be sent to Brigadier Gatamuki who in turn keeps China posted.

The Engineers group has its own "factory," again situated near Barafu 25, where weapons are manufactured and repairs undertaken. This work is carried out by the following "experts," assisted by a team of 20 labourers:

(1)   Chief Mechanic Kamwana, a native of Gitunduti, near Kariko

(2)   Mechanic Ruku, a native of Fort Hall

(3)   Mechanic Mbirikimu, ex-Nanyuki squatter

(4)   Mechanic Mundo Mugo, of Gitunduti

(5)   Mechanic Hiro Hito,[15] of Kariko

(6)   Capt. Mechanic Ngoma Kagio, reserve name Buri s/o Kamau of Kiamariga

(7)   RSM Mechanic Hiti

(8)   RSM Mechanic Mahiothi

(9)   Sgt. Mechanic Muigwithawa

(10)  Sgt. Mechanic Oluosh (real name Kamau s/o Kibira of Mbogo-ini, Kibugu)

(11)  Cpl. Mechanic Gatomeki

(12)  Cpl. Mechanic Kenda

(13)  Cpl. Mechanic Ukesh (real name Kinyari s/o Kamuiga, of Kanyota)

(14)  Cpl. Mechanic Mugumo (real name Magima s/o Kaguiri, of Magutu)

Batches of men from different parts of the reserves are brought to the Engineers' "factory" for instruction. When they are proficient in the manufacture of weapons, they are reabsorbed into the passive wing where they set themselves up as "one man factories." Somewhere in the region of 400 have received instruction in this way since May, 1953.

Considerable quantities of equipment are obtained by the two Engineers sections under Brigadier Gatamuki and on the latter's instructions, those supplies are buried in various parts of the forest until required. Such places of deposit are known only to a select few in the Engineers. (China professes to know nothing about them.) Those supplies consist chiefly of materials for the production of "home made" weapons which are turned out, by the Engineers' "factory" alone, at the rate of 42 per week, bolts taking 15 minutes to make.

Attempts by the Engineers to manufacture grenades did not prove successful. On the first occasion the article exploded during manufacture, killing a Cpl. Mechanic Gatakaya. On the second occasion the article was completed and then thrown into a ready-made hole for experiment. It did not explode. One of the labourers went to pick it up and it killed him instantly. Nevertheless, the project has not been abandoned. The Engineers are also responsible for the making of stamps such as those which appeared from time to time on China's documents.

Brigadier Gatamuki is at present in the Aberdares, where he arrived on 10th January, 1954. He went there with a party to collect a number of firearms which Dedan Kimathi had agreed to release for use on Mount Kenya.

An interesting feature about Brigadier Gatamuki's set up is that, "by order No. 24 of 1953" signed by four members of the Executive Committee, nobody but Brigadier Gatamuki, his two section commanders, and two selected men of each section, should know the sources of supplies, the routes they normally take to bring the supplies to the forest, and the whereabouts of the hidden materials.

Brigadier Gatamuki's two sections carry weapons proper and not only consist of hand-picked troops but consist also of terrorists who know the Mount Kenya forest region like the backs of their hands.

### The Hika Hika 210 Battalion, Nairobi[16]

In June, 1953, a selected team of "hard-core" terrorists under Brigadier Nyamanduru (real name [Paul] Mahehu s/o ?, whose home is near Tumutumu) was sent from Mathira Division to Nairobi to stimulate terrorist activities in the city and obtain materials badly needed by "fighting men" in the forests. Three months later, in September, 1953, Nyamanduru wrote to China and told him that he had raised a force of 900 which he had called the Hika Hika 210, and that he would, from then on, regularly dispatch, parties of recruits for service in the Mount Kenya sector. Although there has been no correspondence since between China and

Nyamanduru, China is certain that the 210 still exists in some form or other.

It seems highly probable that Nyamanduru and his group has merged with other subversive groups in the city, and, whilst indirectly supporting the Mau Mau campaign up-country, has broken away from direct Mount Kenya control.

Many hundreds of recruits have been sent from Nairobi to the Mount Kenya sphere, not to mention the Aberdares, and Nairobi continues to be the terrorists' chief source of supply, both in material and in finance. China is sure, therefore, that the "210 is still doing a good job."

Note: No. 3 Hika Hika Company is on the Aberdares, controlled by Dedan Kimathi.

The above is the sum total of China's militant forces. One must not count too strongly on the various units being in the areas to which they have been assigned as the militant organisation is extremely flexible, and there is really nothing to prevent a unit commander doing as he pleases *providing higher levels are notified* at the earliest possible moment.

## STRENGTH—PERSONNEL—MOUNT KENYA SPHERE

Simple addition of the strength of the various units, excluding the Hika Hika 210, Nairobi, shows that the grand total of enemy forces on Mount Kenya, and in the area controlled from Mount Kenya, is in the vicinity of 7,500.

It seems, at first glance, difficult to reconcile this figure with our own assessment, based on both information and contact with the enemy. China is, nevertheless, adamant that this figure is, if anything, conservative, saying that his briefcase, which he was wrongly told we had found, would bear him out word for word, and to some extent, name for name.

To a large extent, the differences between our assessment and China's figures is answered by the following:

    a) Depending upon the wishes of company and section commanders, a proportion of the registered militia is permitted to remain as "passive wing" unless and until called up. That proportion, however, knows the units it belongs to and can join such units overnight. This is approximately one-third of the whole command, which reduces the *active* total to about 5,000.

b) The "Special Police," dealt with below, further reduces the total by some 400, leaving a balance of approximately 4,600.

Note:

(1) It must be said that China made no mistakes when re-examined on the personnel and arms strengths of the numerous units mentioned.

(2) If China is to be believed at all, it is perfectly obvious that as a general rule his forces are capable of avoiding contact with security forces.

(3) It is probably true to say that 4,600 terrorists widely dispersed over the vast and largely forested territory of the Mount Kenya enemy command are as difficult to locate as a pair of lost spectacles in Oxford Street [one of London's most crowded shopping areas], particularly when the enemy is endeavouring to avoid contact.

China gives the following reasons for having more than one-third of his forces dormant:

a) There was too much recruiting in 1953 and many had to be returned immediately to their reserves.

b) The grave shortage of ammunition. Without sufficient ammunition, larger forces are worthless.

Basis of Allocation:

As a general rule, the structure of militant Mau Mau on Mount Kenya is as follows:

Battalion: 350 onwards
Company: 160-350
Section: 50-160
*Batuni*: 10-50

# MILITANT WING—GENERAL ORGANISATION

Every unit, at *batuni*, section and company level, has its own committee of four to six persons, usually the most senior. These committees deal solely with the every-day affairs of the unit. As most units are broken down to *batunis*, these committees function primarily at *batuni* level. The following affairs are, for example, left to the committees to deal with:

a)  Discipline
b)  Distribution of food
c)  Collection of money
d)  Discussion with leading members of the Passive Wing
e)  The granting of "leave"

Unlike our system where the unit commander is the head of the force at all times, Mau Mau unit commanders are only in complete authority during battle. At all other times the committee is the authority, though obviously the unit leader is "chairman" and always influential.

## Council of Elders

Prior to August, 1953, a Council of twelve elders sat alongside the Mount Kenya Committee in an advisory capacity. These twelve persons were drawn from the Passive Wing. On the 16th August, 1953, this Council was dissolved for the following reasons:

a)  The Militant Wing became strong enough to direct affairs without the assistance of Passive Wing representatives.
b)  Members of the Council were frightened of the forests.
c)  Members of the Council were repeatedly arrested in the reserves by security forces.
d)  The elders were often regarded as too weak and too slow.

Between the two wings of Mau Mau, there are three Organisations which are neither militant nor passive. They are:

## The Couriers

Each section has two couriers attached to it who are responsible for the conveyance of messages. They do not dress in military or police clothing and seldom sleep in the camps of fighting units.

The couriers work in the reserves and in the forests but are not classed as "soldiers." The number of persons in this courier group in the Mount Kenya sphere does not exceed 250 but each one is regarded as 100% trustworthy and knows the Mount Kenya sphere backwards. They are also well versed on Mau Mau movements and when given a letter it is unnecessary to tell them where to contact the addressee. If the writer and the courier do not know where the addressee is, as is often the case, the latter has his own "informers" who direct him.

## The Scouts

Members of this organisation live in the reserved areas but are neverthe-less, not classed as "passive wing" as, whilst engaged in their duties, they often commit acts of violence. In a sense they are neither "militant" for they do not belong to any unit and are not registered as "fighting men."

The sole task of the scouts, of whom there are two to every *itura* [vil-lage] is to select "sentries" from local supporters whenever fighting units enter their areas, and with the aid of such supporters, to watch and ward over Mau Mau troops. If a unit is suddenly surprised, the scouts remain with the unit until it has left the area. They resort, if necessary, to vio-lence.

## The Special Police

There is a special group known as the Special Police, whose members, although registered as fighting men, are not permitted to enter the forests under any circumstances.

This group is responsible for the collection of intelligence *in the reserve*. There are twelve to each reserve *itura*. Members of the group convey intelligence obtained to the nearest Mau Mau units.

## The Komerera

The definition of *Komerera*, according to China, is the section of Kikuyu which refuses to pay poll tax and which avoids community development work. Many of this type of Kikuyu have grouped together and are frequently shot by security forces "on the score that they are Mau Mau terrorists." China, though against further recruitment, has ordered his forces to capture members of the *Komerera* and take them to the forests as labourers, their activities in the reserve being considered harmful to Mau Mau proper.

## Intentions

China believes that he is winning the "war" but, because of the acute shortage of ammunition, he says he has ordered his forces to "steady up" until more becomes available. (Supported by documentary evidence.)

He had no thought of surrender. He says the Mount Kenya Committee is confident that Mau Mau will win and that, when more ammunition becomes available, "all-out war directed more against the Europeans" is likely to occur, probably towards the end of 1954.

He lists chiefs, headmen, and loyalist Home Guard as Mau Mau's immediate targets, and is particularly against these people "because they are making fortunes out of the Kikuyu people, killing those they do not like and releasing Mau Mau when bribed sufficiently."

Q. Do you really think Mau Mau can beat the British?

A. If Britain beat the Germans who had many arms and cannot, in fifteen months, beat Mau Mau which has few, Mau Mau must win in the end.

Q. Say if 1,000 heavy bombers were used against the Kikuyu people?

A. If you think that would stop Mau Mau, why does Government not use them?

Q. You think you will be able to force the European out of the country?

A. No, but we will get things we were refused before.

Q. Why does Mau Mau concentrate on attacking its own tribe?

A. If you want to go away in a car and you find the back tire is punctured, you have to stop and mend it before you can go on.

Among the documents recovered from the scene of the engagement, there are a number which show that the names of all *thata* i.e. "loyalists" are required to reach Hika Hika HQ by the 2nd February, 1954. Whilst China will not answer in the affirmative, he will not deny that a new campaign is to be launched against loyalists after that date.

*Morale*

China will not have it, and his reasons are somewhat convincing, that Mau Mau morale is low, at least in the Mount Kenya sector.

He says that in early March, 1953, Mau Mau thought it was doomed because young men were reluctant to join, most of the Home Guards were loyal and the militant wing had very little equipment. He says it was uncommon in those days for Mau Mau to move about a reserved area in a party of five without someone giving them away. He now claims that those days have gone, Mau Mau having progressed in every respect, even to the extent of "being able to travel from Ndia to Tumutumu [about four miles] in broad daylight 200 strong, knowing that the people are with you."

He argues that there is now no need to recruit, no need to compel the Kikuyu to do anything—"they volunteer when they hear of their friends being shot and hear firing every five minutes in their home areas."

Money is easy to get, the inhabitants of the reserve willingly giving all they can. They are all, so China says, anti-Tribal Authority "because of what tribal authorities are doing to them."[17]

According to China, every time there is a success for Mau Mau, morale improves, but when there is a reverse the terrorists look upon it as something they were expecting anyway. "When a young man goes to the bush," China says, "he goes there willing to die."

In the Mount Kenya sphere, individual terrorists are allowed to use a proportion of the funds they collect from the inhabitants of the reserve. This practise is enjoyed by the terrorists who see some material gain from being in the militant wing. [This seems to contradict earlier statements.] China considers this is one of Dedan Kimathi's greatest mistakes, for on the Aberdares only "leaders" are entitled to collect funds with the result that the rank and file are frustrated.

China also advances the following reasons for the high degree of morale in both the militant and passive wings of Mau Mau:

a)  "If you want to know one of the reasons why the Kikuyu people help Mau Mau, it is because when we see a woman with a child whose father has been killed by Security Forces, we give her money, say 20/- [shillings], and the whole location knows we are doing good."

b)  "The *Komerera* used to break into people's houses, steal money and rape women. If we catch anyone doing that we kill them. This causes people to like Mau Mau."

c)  "When Government destroys crops and property, the people ask us what we are going to do about it, and morale is improved again."

d)  "Now that the terrorists and people in the reserves can see that we are able to make our own guns, they want to persevere."

e)  "All the people say that God also wants us to win. You clear the plantations at Kabaru, Ngunioa, and Ndathi and evacuate the people, but the rain has caused maize and potatoes to grow in those plantations in greater quantities than ever before, and the elephant and buffalo never touch it now."

f)  "Due to continuous suffering at the hands of Security Forces, even the old people now offer their young men to fight. When young boys grow up seeing Government shooting at their own race, they think it is a life and death struggle and they help their own race."

*Effect of Leaflets*

He says, "The men are fully aware that leaflets are just government propaganda. Many of them do not bother to pick them up. They say that Government is spending such a lot on the Emergency that it sometimes cannot afford bombs, and aeroplanes have to drop paper instead."

*Surrenders*

A number of terrorists wanted to surrender on the Aberdares about four months ago, but when they came out of the forests waving green branches, the Home Guard fired at them killing seven. Mau Mau will never believe again that Government is sincere.

He is emphatic that on the Mount Kenya side there could be *no question of surrender* as determination is stronger than ever.

*Effect of China's Capture*

The people will be angered. It will not have any effect on morale. The people will praise him as a man who has done more than his part.

**Arms**

According to figures given, the strength of arms with the Mau Mau militant wing (Mount Kenya) is, at least, as follows:
Automatic rifles: 14; Rifles/shotguns: 361; Grenades: 4; Bren guns: 1; Revolvers/pistols: 23; Homemade weapons: 1,230.

*Homemade Weapons*

The Engineers' "factory" near Barafu 25 is producing these at the rate of 42 per week. Piping for their manufacture is obtained from:
   a)   European farms, stolen by labour.
   b)   The EAR & H, particularly the type of piping used on 3rd class passenger coaches.
   c)   Hardware shops, particularly Indian-owned, who sell it to Africans without restriction.

China claims that most of the firearms proper held by Mau Mau were stolen from Europeans over the past four years and held individually until the Emergency was proclaimed. Others have been bought from Somalis and Indians and many find their way to the forests from Nairobi. (The fact that only a very small percentage of firearms recovered by security forces are registered tends to support the statement that they were stolen from Europeans.) China has no information that firearms are purchased from the police or from the army. He states his forces "capture" firearms as rapidly as they lose them.

*Training with Arms*

There are no training schools. Terrorist recruits are taught how to use firearms by the old hands.

*Ammunition*

The shortage of this is Mau Mau's greatest problem. The rate of supply of ammunition has not kept pace with the manufacture of "home made" rifles, each of which has to be tested and proved to be capable of firing before issue. As a result of the shortage of ammunition, these "home made" weapons are no longer being tested.

At the same time, the expenditure of ammunition in the last three months has been particularly heavy, and terrorists have used a great deal more than they were able to procure.

There are no main and regular sources of supply of ammunition. Every Mau Mau, passive or militant, does his bit to get what he can, where he can. However, the following "methods" are revealed by China:

a) Sympathetic Home Guard (when as individuals, seven out of every ten according to China) exchange cartridge cases for live ammunition, then produce their "empties" and get the ammunition written off as expended in battle.

b) The "KKB" [see below] at Nanyuki, a "Passive Wing" organisation in that district, is an important source of supply.

c) Police and military *askaris*, "providing a good sum of money is offered."

d) "Houseboys working for Europeans pass over any ammunition they find lying about."

e) Ammunition is sometimes found "dumped" as unfit for further use (not destroyed). When such cases occur, the Engineers are summoned to examine the ammunition. Quite a lot is taken, but on an average only one in eight fires.

It was obvious during the interrogation that China was concealing certain sources of supply. In the present Mau Mau campaign in the Mount Kenya sphere, the accent is on procuring ammunition.

## Dumps

These do not exist, for where there is insufficient to go round, there is none in reserve.

Special weapons are manufactured by the Engineers to take uncommon calibres of ammunition.

## Reliability of Home Made Weapons

a) Rifles: These are considered accurate up to 20 yards, useful up to 100 yards and good for 25 rounds. Users suffered a number of casualties in the early experimental days but the type now turned out, particularly by the Engineers, is considered completely safe.

b) Shotguns: These are not very popular as the barrel is much inclined to split, but as much of the ammunition obtained from Home Guards is of the shotgun type, weapons of this order continue to be produced.

c) Pistols: China ordered that they should *not* be manufactured.

## Issue of Firearms

The names of terrorists are recorded. If a firearm is lost, except in battle, the user is severely punished.

## Care of Weapons

China claims that normally army weapons are not cleaned as well as his is (?). Failure to keep a weapon clean is regarded as a serious disciplinary offence. When terrorists are not employed in committing acts of violence, they have nothing else to do but clean their weapons.

*Bombs*

A number of unexploded bombs have been found. When they are discovered, they are left untouched for *five* days and then removed and hidden. China states that these are valued by the Engineers who are "looking for a way to use them." A very heavy bomb (1,000 lb?) was found in the forest belt above Ruguru location on 2nd January, 1954. Terrorists have tried unsuccessfully to remove it.

*Repairs to Firearms*

Repairs to firearms are carried out by the Engineers. This unit is said to contain a number of experienced armourers. There are a few spare parts with the Engineers but on the whole repairs are made by improvisation, an art in which the terrorists seem to excel themselves.

## Communications

Contact between "gangs" is made almost exclusively by couriers who travel on foot as letter bearers. There are sixteen "special couriers," however, who usually remain with the Hika Hika battalion HQ, who are called the *Hiri Kuora*. These special couriers are used solely for the conveyance of messages to and from the Aberdares and are all men who came over from the Aberdares in November, 1953.

A message to be passed, say, from Kiamachimbi to Meru goes through several links. It remains with the courier who was originally given it but, for security reasons, he is accompanied by two or three terrorists from a given *batuni* as he passes through the area in which such *batuni* is operating. The idea behind this is that, while the couriers know the geography of the country, they may not know of recent Security Force movements.

The Special Police (Intelligence) in reserved areas convey information by foot.

*Wireless*

There are *four* wireless sets in the Mount Kenya sphere, two of which are ex-military. The remaining two are small civilian portable sets. China cannot give details of the sets other than all are battery operated and can only receive.

He states that it is possible to hear the local news and African broadcasts as well as monitor some police stations talking on RT [radio telegraphy—meaning wireless transmitters]. The sets are of certain Intelligence value to Mau Mau.

There is no difficulty in obtaining batteries, or in charging batteries, the ways and means of doing this being obvious.

*Allocation of Wireless Sets*

One ex-WD [War Department[18]]—with Brig. Roriondo, Roriondo Coy, Kaleba Btn. [Battalion], now in Aguthi location.

One ex-WD—with 375 IW Sarema in the Nanyuki area.

Two civilian portable—with General Kassam's battalion in Embu.

*Operators, WT [wireless telegraphy]*

Intelligent English-speaking Africans record notes on news items received and pass these to unit commanders.

*Repairs, WT*

Repairs to sets are carried out by "experts" who were formerly wireless operators in the services. Names of operators are not known.

*General: Communications*

Torches were used in the forests at night for signalling in pre-bombing days. Horns, bugles, whistles, and flags are used during actions or alarms. In attack, the terrorists take their line on the "standard bearer" or on the bugler. Bugles are also used to sound a retreat. Various commanders have their own calls and signs.

In the forests "bird-calls" are used to maintain contact. After an action, a single rifle shot is sometimes used to enable stragglers to re-group with the main party.

## Medical

Every unit obtains medical supplies where and when it can and such supplies accompany the unit at all times. There is no shortage.

Terrorists who have had some form of medical experience are assigned to units in such a way that for every party of ten there is a medical dresser.

There are *no* hospitals, but near the Hika Hika HQ above Muthea there is a large "field station" where badly wounded or seriously ill terrorists are sent.

Penicillin is the most popular item in the medical line.

### Disease

The most prevalent disease among the terrorists is malaria which China claims is easily treated. When no European drugs are readily available, a type of fungus which grows on bamboo is boiled with soup and drunk. During November and December, 1953, units suffered an epidemic of coughs which was thought to have been caused by bombing. In general, China claims that it is particularly healthy living on the mountain.

### Doctors

There are three so-called "qualified" doctors in the Mount Kenya sphere.
> (1) Dr. Kamas, a half-Kikuyu/Masai who belongs to Dagoretti and who worked with an SAS[19] at Nanyuki prior to taking to the forests.
> (2) Dr. Mutheka, a Kamba who was connected with the medical practise for some years in Kabaa, Ukambani.
> (3) Dr. Bisoi, an Aguthi man.

Nos. (1) and (2) are now in Aguthi location. No. (3) is at the Hika Hika HQ. A document from No. 3 to General China dated 19th December, 1953 was recovered at the time of China's capture. It is obvious that No. 3 is a particularly well-educated African. Reserve names of these "doctors" are not known.

## Food

A "Quartermaster General" is based on Muthea and is responsible for the feeding of all terrorists in the forest. His sphere does not, however, extend to the Nanyuki area (including Meru) where the units feed themselves. The "Quartermaster General" is one Bahati (real name ?), of Kariko, north Mathira.

Bahati directs the Wajuda Section of No. 3 Hika Hika Company to places where goods are to be taken, the Wajuda being responsible for the transportation of foodstuffs to "gangs."

Food, according to China, presents absolutely no problem. Terrorists are never short and eating venison is strictly prohibited. Most food is donated by the reserve inhabitants, but items such as *posho* [a maize-based staple] are bought in shops.

Apart from the fact that the indigenous population supplies adequate quantities of food, there is always, according to China, ample food to be got in:

    a)  The "mile strip."[20]
    b)  Evacuated "squatter" plantations in the forest.
    c)  In those areas of the reserve where the inhabitants have been "villagized."[21]

Favorite foods are: meat, dried maize, maize meal, bananas, potatoes.
  No foodstuffs are grown by the terrorists in the forest.

### Rationing

Fighting units and camp followers are given exactly the same rations. All food is pooled, cooked under the supervision of the "committee," and then evenly distributed. "There is no colour bar in our camps," says China.

## Air Attack

China says this of air attack—"We hate the aeroplanes and we have been bombed on many occasions. 46 people have been killed by bombing but we have learnt what to do. We know that no bombing is permitted in the reserve, so we can stay in the reserves without fear. When bombing causes any casualties, the name of the casualty and the place where he was killed is reported to me."

### Warning System

Alarm is sounded by word of mouth and everyone in the camp disperses and lies flat on the ground with his head against a tree.

### Dispersal

Nobody is permitted to move unless the plane is *obviously* coming overhead. Movement when a plane is some distance away is regarded as dangerous in that it will cause observation of the camp. Thus the alarm is only given at the last minute.

### Identification of Aircraft

Aircraft are observed with the aid of binoculars during the hours of daylight. By night the terrorists rely on sound. They know that only Harvards and Lincolns bomb. They take no action on the arrival of other aircraft unless:
  a)  The aircraft circles.
  b)  Marker-smoke is used.
In these cases they abandon the camp and move away fast.

### Night

Camps are never abandoned by night. The drill is to extinguish fires and cigarettes as soon as a plane is heard, then to take cover up to 300 yards from the camp providing the aircraft is approaching.

Although the terrorists have great fear of air attack, China claims that bombing, for the most part, takes place in areas where there are no terrorists. The militant wing would be extremely anxious if hides were bombed frequently for, "when there is a hit there are no survivors." Concussion from heavy bombs is greatly feared and hides are not normally built in valleys for this reason.

There is a rule forbidding terrorists to fire at aircraft as this is regarded as a wastage of ammunition.

## *Return to Hides after Dispersal*

If the leaders feel the hide has been spotted, or if it was actually bombed, the site is abandoned altogether, but not before casualties are buried and useful equipment removed. It is always suspected that ground forces will follow up air attacks.

## *Effects*

The heavier the bomb, the more they dislike it. In the early days of bombing, "big game was often killed but the elephant have now gone to areas which are not bombed." Colobus monkey and Bush-buck are killed frequently, the skins being taken for use as "ground sheets."

## TACTICS: GENERAL

For battle purposes, the forests are preferred to the reserves, but otherwise the reserves are preferred because of the availability of foodstuffs.

Unless a specific attack is regarded as necessary, terrorist units are dissuaded from carrying out major attacks in reserved areas because of communal punishments.[22]

China claims that there is a "standing order" compelling all units to change their positions as soon as a terrorist of or above the rank of "Brigadier" is taken alive. He considers that his arrest will be followed by similar changes. (For obvious reasons, it is not considered that this scheme will be put into practise to any great extent.)

## Dead

Whenever possible, the dead are carried away, stripped of their clothing and buried. If this is not possible, the hands and head are removed in order to prevent identification which might "bring suffering to the people of the dead man's location." In the majority of cases, neither is possible.

Although a hide may be given a definite name i.e. Barafu 25, and be situated in a defined area, it is uncommon to remain in the same spot for more than three days. Moving about within a half-mile radius is considered safest.

When a hide is discovered by ground forces, unless the orders are to fight, the terrorists disperse and travel individually or in small parties to the next nearest hide, the position of which is usually known to all.

a) Reserves: In cases where arms proper are held in some quantity, sentries are posted up to *four* miles from the unit's position. Where few arms are held, sentries are posted up to half a mile.

b) Forests: Sentries are never posted more than quarter of a mile from the camp.

## Camp Signs

China claims that "route signs" (sticks beside path, etc.) now apply to the Aberdares only. In the Mount Kenya sphere most terrorists know the forests well and there are, therefore, a great number of experienced guides.

## Terrorist Activities in the Reserve

According to China, no *large-scale* attacks are carried out in reserved areas unless the *Muhiriga* i.e. the "Clan of the area in question" supports the action. If this is correct, it follows an old and accepted tradition of the Kikuyu that "the *Muhiriga* should decide" and is an extremely cunning tactical move on China's part. It is certainly a move which would capture, for the militant wing, the support and co-operation of the reserve inhabitants. For reasons of security, however, it is doubtful if China practises exactly what he preaches.

## Fires

Wood fires are used in the forests during the hours of darkness. Charcoal fires (the coals of the night fire) are fanned during daylight to cook food. No smoke is thus visible during the hours of daylight.

## Order of March

There is no fixed order of march when units are on the move. The order is decided upon by unit leaders, and varied according to circumstance. The unit leader takes up any position he pleases. Movement in forest areas is usually by day. In reserved areas movement is either by day or by night.

## Indigenous Fruits

These are not normally eaten although plentiful in the Mount Kenya forests.

All terrorists belonging to the Hika Hika are shaved when operating in reserved areas to make identification more difficult.

## Mau Mau Penetration of Government Services

China says, "In the same way as you have CID [Criminal Investigation Department] men in Mau Mau, we have informers in all Government Departments, even in the Army and the Police." He will not enlarge on this save by saying that the Prisons Department is "full of Mau Mau supporters."

It is a serious disciplinary offence to call a man by his proper reserve name. Every terrorist has a bush name and rank must be respected.

Asked why Mau Mau do not try to derail trains, he replied, "For the same reason as you do not bomb the reserves."[23]

China has made another recent change which, he says, tends to retain the support of the masses for Mau Mau. If a man is *suspected* to be siding with Government, he is not killed as was formerly the case but fined in lieu. If the same suspected individual is found to be aiding Government again, he will be killed. Propaganda is then put around to the effect that Government shoot Mau Mau but Mau Mau fine their enemies first and give them the opportunity of "turning a new leaf."

China says he is opposed to the burning down of Kikuyu houses by terrorists.

## Fear of Security Forces

China claims that terrorists are not frightened of the Home Guard which, he says, he could "drive ten miles" if [it was] unsupported [by regular troops]. He states he is not particularly worried about African Police "who panic and hide behind trees when ambushed or counter-attacked." His forces always endeavor to keep out of the way of:
- a) The KAR.
- b) European troops or police.

## Loyalty of Home Guard

Some Home Guard units are totally anti-Mau Mau and because they know the country and the people China considers them dangerous as "Intelligence collectors." Of the organisation as a whole he says, "7 out of 10 Home Guard in Nyeri District are disloyal as individuals and actively support Mau Mau. They are all very frightened people and unless they were supported by other security forces, I would rid them of their arms within a week." He considers the Home Guard in Tetu location (Senior Chief Muhoya) to be particularly good from Government's point of view. In Embu he says 6 of every 10 Home Guard are loyal only to Mau Mau. In Meru the proportion that is loyal to Mau Mau is very small indeed.

## Use of Women

- a) There are no women in the militant wing of Mau Mau in the Mount Kenya sphere.
- b) Women are *not* used as food-carriers. Such practises apply to the Aberdares only. On Mount Kenya the task of food-transportation

is classed as *muritu* i.e. "heavy" and all "heavy" tasks are performed by the militant wing.

c)  Women are used as scouts and play a major part in the role of watch and ward over fighting men in reserved areas.

d)  There are two female couriers to each *Itura* but these are not allowed to leave their own locations.

## China's Favorites (Friendship)

a)  General Rui,
b)  General Gachuma,
c)  General Ndaya—in that order.

## Control and Discipline

It is quite obvious that China, in order to retain the overwhelming support of the reserve masses, has, in the past three months, imposed a number of restrictions on the rank and file of his militant wing, calculated to prevent them doing anything which might cause displeasure to the Kikuyu people as a whole, or, better still, to the large proportion of the tribe which has sympathetic leanings towards Mau Mau.

He has, in fact, made great strides in dividing Mau Mau proper from the purely criminal element which has cashed in on Mau Mau for the sake of protection and personal gain [the *Komerera*—see above].

Orders for Mau Mau offensives need not necessarily come from China. All unit commanders are permitted to raid or attack at their own discretion, but within the guiding policy of the Mount Kenya Committee. Orders from "high-level" are usually of a restrictive nature.

Persons in the militant wing are sentenced to death only if found to be traitors or after they have committed seven minor offences. The Passive Wing is not authorised to kill offenders. It must pass the matter over to the Militant Wing.

As regards rules, etc., there is nothing to add to what we already know.

## Witchdoctors

The prophesies of these continue to influence action. Witchdoctors used by Mau Mau are not always the usual type of elderly *mundu mugo* ["medicine man"] common in peacetime Kikuyu tribal activities. They are often young men who, probably by fortune, have made a number of correct prophesies and who are, in every other respect, active terrorists operating with Mau Mau units. The paramount witchdoctor for the Mount Kenya sphere is, however, an elderly Kikuyu woman named Wachege living in the Keriko area. Her husband was arrested and believed deported for Mau Mau activities on 4th November, 1953.

## Aberdare Affairs

China discloses that:
- a) Stanley Mathenge was alive in September, 1953, and was in Location 14, Fort Hall, which is his favorite stamping ground.
- b) Stanley Mathenge was 2 i/c to Dedan Kimathi but was replaced in August, 1953, as he was "too frightened." Kahiu Itina replaced him.
- c) Dedan Kimathi has lost a lot of prestige as his orders are bad. His troops do not like him. His troops also say he is frightened to leave the forest, and on occasions he has to be forced to move, but "as he was the first leader he must be respected and he cannot be deposed."
- d) The most prominent and favorite leaders on the Aberdares are (under DK [Dedan Kimathi]):
  - (1) Kahiu Itina
  - (2) Ndungu
  - (3) Mungai
  - (4) Ngethe
  - (5) Kimbo

## Long Range Recces

a) On the 17th May, 1953, a *batuni* under Lieut. Gitorga left the Aberdares to recce the Northern Frontier Province (NFP). Gitonga returned and China heard a rumor that the *batuni* was engaged by Police and broke up.

b) On the 12th October, 1953, China dispatched an armed party of 20 under Captain Brukenge, a half Masai/Kikuyu, to the NFP to examine the availability of arms and ammunition in that region. The party has not reported back.

## Agreement between China and Dedan Kimathi

China wants no discord between himself and Dedan Kimathi although he does not consider that Kimathi is a good leader. The two regularly exchange correspondence to ensure that each is prosecuting the war with the same degree of vigor. Personal contact between China and Kimathi is rare as both have to go to considerable risk in order to meet one another so far from the areas they consider "safe."

China last met Kimathi on the 4th January, 1954, at a house in Thegenge location. With Kimathi were Kahiu Itina and Ndungu. China was with Gachuma, Rui and Capt. Faranja. China took a body-guard of ten for the trip.

Kimathi told China that many of his troops had come into the reserves because of the shortage of food on the Aberdares. It was discussed whether Kimathi should come over to Mount Kenya but this was decided against. As most supplies from Nairobi go through the Kinangop, it was felt that Kimathi should remain on the Aberdares. Kimathi intimated that he might split his forces into three groups, one with "Ndungu for the Fort Hall region, one with Kahiu Itina and Kimbo for the 'Lamuria' region, and the third, under him, to transfer to the forests above Meru." Kimathi was persuaded *not* to come over to Meru.

Previous to this occasion they met on the 2nd August, 1953, near Giakanja, on the border of Tetu and Thegenge locations. China claims that Mau Mau forces on the Aberdares are far better equipped than his on Mount Kenya.

## Compartment B—The Passive Wing

China considers that the greater proportion of the Kikuyu people are behind the militant wing of Mau Mau. He divides up the tribe as follows:

a) 60% are willingly active behind Mau Mau and are as determined as the militant wing to persevere "until freedom is achieved."
b) Another 20% are sympathetic with Mau Mau but are too frightened to give active assistance, though they do assist indirectly.
c) Another 10% "are neither pro-Mau Mau nor pro-Government, but because a man will always side with his own nationality, they are bent more towards Mau Mau than against it. They sympathise with the aims of Mau Mau."
d) Another 5% are *against* Mau Mau activities "because they feel that too many Kikuyu are being killed, but they are too frightened to go against the wishes of the population and therefore remain inactive."
e) The remaining 5% are "the absolute enemies of Mau Mau. They side with the European because they see some hope of personal gain. They also side with the European because they can settle old scores with people they do not like."

Of the Embu tribe China says: "About 6 out of 10 support Mau Mau."

Of the Meru China says: "On the reserve-forest borders about 50% are with us and about 50% neither one way nor the other. Further into the reserve the people are *not* pro-Mau Mau because they [are] too stupid to know what it seeks to achieve."

Of the Kamba China says: "I do not know how many are for or against Mau Mau but there are very many Kamba in the Mau Mau. They will, in time, think the same way as the Kikuyu."

# PASSIVE ORGANISATION

In Mathira Division, and possibly further afield, the organisation within the Passive Wing of Mau Mau does not appear to be the same now as it was some months ago when it consisted of a number of committees, each controlling an area. To a large extent, these committees have been dissolved and their functions taken over by individuals who are both influential in the reserve and acceptable to the militant wing of Mau Mau.

Reasons for dissolving Passive Wing committees appear to be:

a) The Militant Wing has grown strong enough to control the affairs of the reserves, thus the need for a committee does not exist. The leaders who have replaced committees need only relay to the population the wishes of the militant wing and theirs will be done.
b) Security Force action repeatedly dislocated the committees.

China contends that every reserve *Itura* now appoints one man to liaise with the Militant Wing. If he is removed his place is occupied by another. China claims he would not know the names of the *Itura* leaders, they would be known only to his sub-commanders who had dealings with them.

The primary functions of the *Itura* leaders are as follows:

a) To comply with the wishes of the Militant Wing (there is usually agreement).
b) To raise funds for the Militant Wing.
c) To keep the Militant Wing posted with the affairs of the *Itura*.
d) To organise, when necessary, oath ceremonies.
e) To encourage individual effort to obtain, by any possible means, supplies that are needed by the Militant Wing.

However, in order that *Itura* leaders can convey to those concerned the wishes of the Militant Wing, they frequently call upon a number of the area "hierarchy" to attend meetings.

In the Nanyuki Native Locations, which are one of the principal collecting-centers for supplies, two Mau Mau sub-organisations operate, evidently in competition. These two sub-organisations are:

a) The KKB, of which the following are leading members:
   (1) Gathoni s/o Ndirango s/o Gatherema (alias) Waitherero
   (2) Kame s/o Kangaita
   (3) Ndoria s/o Karongo
   (4) Kabinga s/o Karanja c/o The Silverbeck Hotel. This man may also be going under the names Kabunga or Kabiunga.
b) The *Kuuga na Gwika* ("To say and to do")—led by one Gitau Kwahire

The above two sub-organisations concern themselves only with the collection and onward transmission of arms and goods needed by Mau Mau. They have supplied a considerable amount of ammunition to China's command, particularly to units operating in the Nanyuki area.

It is perfectly clear that, without the support of the passive wing, which is virtually 80% of the Kikuyu tribe in the region with which we are dealing, the militant wing of Mau Mau would collapse. China was determined to retain the support of the passive wing, and in order to do so he concerned himself closely with:

a) Anti-government propaganda in the reserves, put over in a way fitting to the current outlook of the populace, calculated to excite disaffection against the European and the loyalist, and thus solidify pro-Mau Mau opinion.
b) Operating his forces in a manner unlikely to reverse the present attitude of the masses.
c) Removing those Africans who he considered were likely to preach, to some effect, against his line of propaganda.

It is not possible, on China's information, to go into greater detail on the Passive Wing.

## Asians

China does *not* regard Asians as an enemy of Mau Mau. Without disclosing names, which, in all probability he does not know, he claims that quite a number of Asians assist the passive wing, particularly by way of purchasing for Africans things they would not be able to buy themselves without rousing suspicion, but whether the Asians know they are aiding Mau Mau he dare not say. He hints that most medical supplies are purchased from Asian shops in Kikuyu reserve districts.

He knows nothing of sympathetic Asian lawyers in Nairobi, though in all probability he soon shall.

He does *not* give the impression that there is any "brain," other than Kikuyu, behind Mau Mau activities in his sphere.

## Final Comment

China's information, as a whole, possibly portrays a picture of better organisation than was anticipated, and possibly a more formidable problem to solve than some might have thought, but there is, somewhere in his behavior, a sign that continuous Security Force pressure is causing Mau Mau to seek an outlet. There is some ground for guarded optimism.

The information supplied by China in this paper is not, by any means, all that can be extracted. This interrogation was a preliminary canter and before he is finally dealt with, it is hoped that more information will be forthcoming.

Secret.

# The Trial of Waruhiu Itote (General China)

*General China appeared in front of Judge MacDuff on February 1, 1954, in a trial that lasted three days. He was accused of consorting with "terrorists" and possession of ammunition. MacDuff found China guilty of both offenses, and sentenced him to hang. The transcript of China's trial follows, as well as his rejected appeal of February 13.*

## In Her Majesty's Supreme Court of Kenya at Nyeri Emergency Assize Criminal Case No. 35 of 1954

REGINA[1] . . . . . . . . . . . . . . . . . . . . . . . . . . . . . . . . . PROSECUTRIX
versus
WARUHIU S/O [son of] ITOTE alias "General China" . . . . ACCUSED

Coram [ in the presence of] MacDuff, Judge
1st February 1954.

Accused [China] before Court
Somerhough for Crown.
Somerhough enters *nolle prosequi* for purpose of filing separate informations.
Court: On DPP [Deputy Public Prosecutor, i.e. Somerhough] entering *nolle prosequi* accused is discharged on the present information.[2]

Coram MacDuff, Judge
1st February 1954.
Accused in Chambers.
Accused desires Counsel to be assigned to him; Mr. Cockar assigned [as Defence Counsel].
Accused has no witnesses to be summoned.

Accused before Court.
Somerhough for Crown.
Cockar for Accused.
Information read and interpreted to Accused.

Plea:        (1) [To charge of "consorting"] Not guilty.
             (2) [To charge of possession of ammunition] Not guilty.

Assessors[3]:  (1) Waigwa s/o Waweru.
             (2) Ezekiel Kabora.
             (3) Mateo Makara.

Somerhough Opens

*The prosecution begins its case.*

### First Prosecution Witness—David Murakaru s/o Gichera

Christian sworn[4]: Headman Ichuga sub-location.
In charge Home Guard Post Kiawarigi. Friday 15th January, 1954. I was at post. During morning I heard shots from direction of Kirimukuyu [two miles to the south-west]. Great number of shots. Got men together. European Lieut. [Lieutenant] came along. (Identified as 2[nd]/Lieut. WJ Young). Went with him on patrol to Ichuga School. After short while there saw Mau Mau coming towards us. There was a big group of them— more than 30. They had weapons—rifles. Cannot say how many. Some had *simis* [small Kikuyu swords]. Some of the guns were home-made guns, saw one Sten [submachine] gun. They came through a banana plantation. When they saw us they fired at us, we then fired at them. They were on other side of valley—about 300 yards away. I saw one man stag-

ger. The gang scattered—ran. I saw one man go into a hut. Did not see him come out. The man who staggered was the one who went into the hut. We approached hut slowly. When we got to where gang was we saw blood, on the grass outside the hut. Inside hut we saw much blood on a tin. Tribal Policeman Weru [Prosecution Witness—PW—2] with me. I left Weru inside hut—went outside. None of gang in the hut. Outside I saw blood trail. Followed it for 150 yards. Just outside hut found notebook in the, or near the blood—3 paces from hut. I picked it up and gave it to European Lieut. I identify notebook produced [Exhibit 1] (Draws attention to stamp on page 2). After 150 yards we lost trail. Searched round for it. Then went back to our camp where I was called by European Lieut. He had Accused with him. I identify Accused. I had not seen him before that day. Accused wearing vest and long trousers. He was wounded in chin and throat. The person who ran into hut was wearing long trousers and woollen jacket. Trousers were heavy type—khaki. Accused was wearing trousers of same type.

Cross-Examined:
[I have been a] Headman from 6th January, 1954. Apart from banana palms there was number of black wattle trees. When I first saw gang they were about 300 yards away. Could see all of their bodies and faces. They came out of plantation into an open space. We were on higher ground than the gang. No trees near us. Gang could see us. They opened fire on us. I have made one statement to the Police. Don't know Cpl. [Corporal] Ndiwa of the Police. I could not distinguish who was the leader. I could see the clothes on the members of the gang. I am sure they opened fire on us. I told the police that, they may have missed it out. I told the Police that one man staggered. (Not in statement to police.) This hut was near to where the gang was when I first saw them—about 300 yards away. Saw man stagger while we were still firing. At that time saw the others running. Man who staggered was only in my view a very short time—just a glimpse. I saw him going in direction of huts, I saw him pass the bigger of the two huts—this cut him off from my view. This man, when he started to stagger, was about 10 yards from the huts. We may have wounded others of gang. Action only took a couple of minutes. Then after waiting we advanced. First blood I saw was outside the door of the hut. Saw short

trail of blood—about six yards leading to hut—just drops of blood. I did not notice anything about this man except his jacket and trousers. He had a weapon. Cannot say who had Sten gun. Man who staggered was carrying weapon in same position as a Sten gun. It looked like a Sten gun. *Askaris* [soldiers] found a home-made gun there, but I was not present. About 15 of us followed the blood trail. I am certain I found Exhibit 1 [the notebook] three paces from hut, lying on the grass. There were many round including a military Sergeant Major—Weru was not with me. Book was lying closed. I gave it to Lieut. Young when I got to the Military Camp. I told Lieut. Young that I had picked up notebook near the hut. Lieut. asked me if I knew the African with him, I told him the African was General China. I said he was General China because the rest of our crowd had said he was. I heard a lot of firing about 11am that day on the side of Kirimukuyu. The 11am action was the one in which a policeman was killed.

Re-Examination: Nil.

Assessors: Nil.

Court[5]: 11am firing was about two miles away and came from the right of our post. Action with gang later was about half a mile from post, again to our right. Man who staggered did not have a hat.

### Second Prosecution Witness—Weru s/o Kiuhu

Pagan affirmed: Tribal Policeman Kiawarigi Home Guard Post on 15th January 1954. That morning heard firing; we went towards it. [We were] KAR [King's African Rifles] and Home Guards. KAR under officer (identified as Lieut. Young). Headman PW 1 [Murakaru Gichera] in charge of Home Guard. We went on road near Ichuga School—got there 11.30 to noon. We lay down and heard firing on our right not far. At that time saw people running towards us from the banana plantations—about 30—about 200 yards. They were running and firing. They fired at us. I recognised a shotgun, one with two barrels. I saw four guns in all. We fired at them. They ran away. I did not see anyone hit. They ran down the valley. We followed to where they had been. I saw blood on the ground about 10 paces from a hut. I followed the blood trail into a hut. No one inside. I found belt of ammunition (bandolier), five note books, stamp pad, two rubber stamps, spring for repairing gun. I gave them to a European Sergeant Major. I identify stamp-pad produced. [Exhibit 2] I identify rubber stamp produced. [Exhibit 3] I identify impression taken on paper. [Exhibit 3A] I know a Mathira Division near Karatina. I identify note-books produced—these are three of the five. Black cover. [Exhibit 4A] Red cover. [Exhibit 4B] Paper cover. [Exhibit 4C] (Rubber stamp inside front cover of Exhibit 4A is from impression of Exhibit 3). Middle page of Exhibit 4B—has impression of Exhibit 3. Back cover of Exhibit 4C—has impression of Exhibit 3.

Cross-Examined:
Lots of trees between us and the gang. We could see but not very clearly. PW 1 with me. PW 1 was about 30 yards from me. We were lying in a straight line. Lieut. Young with us, about 30 yards on the other side of me. We all opened fire together. The gang members all had different clothes, some long trousers, black coats, some in great-coats. There were huts near where we saw the gang. We could see these huts: saw blood at entrance to hut in which I found exhibits, others came in after me. PW 1 not there. There were 2 huts in one place, and 3 in another place. I went into the smallest of the three huts. Others of the party went into other huts. No tin or drum in the hut I went into. There was blood—drops, inside hut, also blood on a bed. I went into the other two huts but I saw no blood in them. PW 1 saw blood in one of the two huts. The Headman [PW 1] went to search other huts. The Lieut. went to the camp. There are many huts in the area. First saw blood on hedge. This was close behind where the gang-sters had been. The exhibits I found were on a bed. The hut belonged to one Muguri, employed by Railway. Exhibits were on top of the bed—all in one place, not scattered.

Re-examination: Nil.

Assessors: Nil.

Court: Distance between two huts and the three huts, 25 yards. PW 1 did not find the blood on a tin in the hut in which I found the articles.

## Third Prosecution Witness—Kioki s/o Iseka

Pagan affirmed: Mkamba[6] [ID number] 18114583 Private in 7 [7th battalion] KAR stationed at Kiawarigi.

15th January 1954 I was in camp. About 2.30pm I saw man walking towards camp. I am guessing the time. When I first saw him the man was about 30 paces away. He was walking carrying a khaki shirt in his hand. Identify Accused as man. I told him to stop. Then Lieut. Young came on the scene. Before Young came I told Accused to drop anything he had. I did not ask his name. Accused wearing vest and long trousers, heavy military type.

Cross-examined:

Have not seen anyone come into camp to surrender. When I told Accused to stop—he stopped and raised his hands. When Lieut. Young arrived we went towards him. I told Accused to put his clothes on ground. Then I told him to come near. He did. Lieut. Young and I met him. Accused told Lieut. Young "Mimi China." ["I am China."] Witness statement to police read to him. I made statement to police but it is recorded wrongly. Lieut. Young was there. Lieut. Young did send me to search Accused for a gun. I searched his pockets—found nothing. Then Lieut. and I took him to the tent.

Re-examined:

Mr. Young was with me when I searched Accused. I did not touch Accused myself.[7] Accused produced a book and gave it to Mr. Young. This was outside the camp. Mr. Young did not touch Accused.

Assessors: Nil

Court: Accused was searched by Mr. Young passing his hands over Accused's pockets.

# Fourth Prosecution Witness—Wallace John Young

Christian affirmed: Lieut. 7 KAR in charge detachment Kiawarigi.
In private life Mechanical Engineer, East African Railways. Under
Section 33 Indian Evidence Act—map produced to witness. This is map
prepared by Government showing area in which I was stationed. I had a
platoon of 7 KAR. Near me is Home Guard post. I was in command of
both. Under me was Headman PW 1. Morning 15th January heard firing
from direction of Kiamachimbi, this would be 11.45am. Heard rifle fire
then automatic fire about a mile below us. I sent section in direction of
firing to try and close any line of escape. The firing was coming closer to
us. Sent section under SM Augustino. I remained at camp. Firing continued. PW 1 came rushing up—made report. I then took party of *askaris*
and Home Guard and stopped road at Ichuga School—300 yards from our
camp. I had 20-30 men. I arranged stops facing into valley. Facing N
from I in Ichuga).[8] Placed them 20 to 30 yards apart along road. About
12.15 to 12.30 had stops in position. Few shots came over our heads—
about 10 single shots. They were directed at us. It came from opposite
ridge—300 to 400 yards away. Tree covered. Up to this time had not seen
anyone. We all took cover. I took Bren [a light machine gun, often fired
from a tripod]. I was three-quarters of the way down here. I then saw five
men in black coats—khaki trousers, running down hill—middle length
coats. I fired two bursts at them. They were bunched. One man looked to
have stumbled, he did not fall. They disappeared into dead ground. We
were above them. Then saw what looked like man sitting at edge of
banana plantation—five minutes later. First two bursts—saw movement
after a while—then there was lapse. We waited about half an hour to an
hour. No movement. I decided to sweep area. We went down valley and
up the other side. The valley was bare. On opposite ridge hut on slope.
We searched huts until we came to path overlooking my camp. I returned
to my camp from there. Got to camp about 3pm. I rested for a short while.
I heard that prisoner was coming in. PW 3 called this out. I got off bed
went out of tent. Camp is wired in [surrounded by barbed wire]. I went to
entrance to camp, saw wounded man coming in—still walking towards
me. Identify Accused as man. He had battledress trousers, vest and scarf.
Carrying angora [wool] khaki shirt in hand. He was badly wounded on

chin. Blood on scarf and vest. I waited for him at the entrance. PW 3 was outside coming up behind Accused. Accused came to me and said in English, "I am General China." PW 3 was still behind him. I said, "You are not." Accused replied, "True to God." I placed him in shade of a tent. We did not search him or touch him. We had talk. Accused said he wanted water. After while he wanted soda water. He pulled out 20/- [shilling] note. He had it in a diary type note-book. Sent *askari* to *duka* [shop]. I saw the note-book. I can identify it. At that stage I did not take the book. Identify book produced. [Exhibit 5] (Witness identifies book by stamp impressions on page 2). I asked where Accused had worked in past. He mentioned some Europeans on the Railways, then I recognised him as a person I had known as fireman in East African Railways. No conversation as to why he had come in. He asked me when we would end this war of ours. I said it was up to them. Did not say where he had been or where he had come from. Said he had been wounded across the valley from us. I got transport from Company Headquarters at Kiamachimbi. Within 5 minutes Land Rover with Capt. [Captain] Marshall, Sgt. [Sergeant] Kirkland and 2 *askaris* arrived. We left camp then with Accused. This would be 3.30pm. We went to 7 KAR Command Post Karatina. Medical Officer not in. We got him bottle of soda water and took him to Karatina Police Station where I handed him to Asst. [Assistant] Insp. [Inspector] Arnold. I took Exhibit 5 from Accused while he was in my camp. I asked him for it and he handed it over. From time Accused entered camp until I handed him to Arnold, Accused was not out of my sight. During that time he was not searched. No one could have planted anything on him without my seeing it. No one did.

Cross-examined:
We have had no surrenders.[9] I know of "green branch" surrenders. Accused had no green branch. I think that a condition of surrender is that they should not be wounded. I think PW 1 was on my right. Don't think I could have seen better from right or left sides. I did not see 20 or 30 in gang. No one in my force said they had seen 20 or 30. No one said that any gangster was carrying Sten gun. Positive the one who stumbled was wearing black coat. Can't recollect seeing anything in this man's hand. Did not search Accused because he was so badly wounded. PW 3 did not

search Accused, I would have seen him. PW 3 would not have had this type of ammunition to plant. I saw Accused immediately after he was challenged. I saw Accused lay down his shirt. I did not see PW 3 get behind. Instructions to troops are that no native searches huts or persons unless in presence of European officer. Accused did not say he had come to discuss a few matters. Did not say he wanted to see high official of Government. The gangsters were hiding in trees. Saw them twice, once running down hill, second behind bananas. The first firing that morning was less than half an hour before we saw natives. Long afterwards troops gave me articles they said they had found near hut I had fired last burst of Bren at. PW 1 gave me note-book he had found [Exhibit 1]. Did not see stamps etc. or Exhibits 4A, 4B, 4C. PW 3 is wrong if he says Accused was searched.

Re-examined: Nil.

Assessors: Nil.

Court: Place I fired at gangsters—they would be 200-300 yards from my camp. Trousers of gangsters looked a dark khaki.

### Fifth Prosecution Witness—Harry Kenneth Arnold

Christian sworn: Assistant Inspector of Police.
15th January at Karatina Police Station 3.25pm PW 4 came to Station with prisoner—identified as Accused. He appeared badly wounded on throat and chin. Wearing dirty white vest, battledress trousers, black half boots. Took Accused to MI [Medical Inspection?] tent of 23 KAR. Shortly after prisoner arrived Chief Inspector Woodgate turned up. I stayed in tent with Accused until Doctor arrived. Doctor stitched up Accused's chin and throat. I remained in tent during this time. Accused then wrapped in blanket tightly. I left tent and Chief Inspector Woodgate came into tent. While Accused under my eye no one touched Accused except Doctor and his medical attendant. Accused was not searched.

Cross-examined:
Customary to search prisoners. Accused's throat was bubbling so I did not do it. Took him straight to MI tent. Prisoners are booked into the register and then searched. This Accused was not booked.

Re-examined: Nil.

Assessors: Nil.

### Sixth Prosecution Witness—Norman James Woodgate

Christian sworn: Chief Inspector of Police, Karatina.
15th January 1954 I arrived at Karatina Police Station 3.30pm. There I saw a prisoner—identified as Accused. He was then at entrance of Police Station in custody of PW 5. I went with them to MI tent. Either I or PW 5 with Accused all the time. I saw Accused wrapped tightly in blanket and put on stretcher. He was then taken outside and put in ambulance. I remained with him until he was driven away. He was not searched by myself or anyone. Accused wearing clothes as before. No one could have planted anything on him.

Cross-examined: I thought Accused in semi-coma.

Re-examined: Nil.

Assessors: Nil.

### Seventh Prosecution Witness—Desmond Walker

Christian sworn: Lieut. RAMC [Royal Army Medical Corps] Karatina. Qualified Doctor. B/Medical B/Surgery [medical degrees]
15th January, 1954 attached 23 KAR at Karatina. Had First Aid Station there in compound of Police Station. Afternoon I went to MI tent where I saw patient who said through interpreter he was General China. Identifies Accused. Accused wearing neck scarf, singlet, long trousers, boots, and stockings. I removed scarf only. He had two wounds.

(1) Diagonal wound—lower on right on front of neck. Lower would be entry.
(2) Second wound just under and on left of under side of jaw. This was a laceration which had chipped off small part of edge of jaw.
(1) Had cut through tissues and laid bare the wind-pipe. There was a hole through which bubbles of air came if he coughed or breathed deeply. In my opinion the wounds caused by one bullet—fired at angle of 45 degrees lower than Accused. Rendered first aid and sent Accused to Nyeri. He was still in same clothes except the neck scarf.

Cross-examined: Accused's condition much improved when he left. He had all his faculties. He was weak from loss of blood.

Re-examination: Nil.

Assessors: Nil.

## Eighth Prosecution Witness—Raburu s/o Charles

Pagan, affirmed: Private RAMC Karatina on 15th January 1954.
That afternoon about 3pm I saw Land Rover coming. I went there. Saw injured man—the Accused identified. He was carried to Police Station. I went to MI tent to get it ready. European Police Officers brought Accused to tent. Placed him on bed. Doctor attended him—PW 7 [and] I assisted. They then took him out and after 5 minutes he was put in ambulance. I went with him. I got in ambulance and travelled with Accused to Nyeri. We talked on way in Kikuyu. At Nyeri Accused taken from ambulance, we carried him into hospital and put him on a bed. He was wearing vest and battledress trousers. I left as his vest was cut and thrown away.

Cross-examined: Nobody searched Accused while I was present. At Nyeri I saw a European in civilian clothes take Accused's pants off. Did not see European put hands in Accused's pocket.

## Ninth Prosecution Witness—Wachera s/o Kimaro

Pagan affirmed: Tribal Policeman No. 25 Karatina.

15th January, 1954 I was at Karatina when prisoner brought in. Identified Accused. I saw Accused put in ambulance and driven off to Nyeri. I was escort of DO [District Officer] Richardson. We were behind ambulance on way. At Native Civil Hospital in Nyeri I assisted to carry Accused's stretcher into hospital. Accused put on bed. We took his clothes off him. Inspector CID [Criminal Investigation Department] (identified as Chief Inspector Collins) instructed us to do so. I took off Accused's trousers— battledress. Inspector Collins helped. We stood on opposite sides of bed. As I pulled them off I put hand in pocket on my side. Collins put his hand in hip pocket. I put hand in left hand pocket. Found some papers and under that two rounds of ammunition which I handed to Collins, who marked them with a pair of scissors.

Cross-examined:

There were 4 European officers present as well as Chief Inspector Collins. One on left and three on other side of bed. Accused said, "There is some money in the pockets." Accused did not look alarmed. He looked as if he was feeling pain. Accused not shown ammunition but he could see it being shown to European officers. Inspector Collins waiting for us at hospital. We went into hospital together. There were other *askaris* but not CID. I cannot say if rounds shown to Accused or not. Accused could see us search his trousers. He was not lying fully on the bed, had he been he could have seen.

Re-examined:

Recognise trousers produced. [Exhibit 6] (Witness indicates left hand pocket) First time I put hand in pocket only felt papers. Second time I got the two rounds. Only felt the papers the first time. They were near top of pocket.

## Tenth Prosecution Witness—Cyril Augustine Collins

Sworn: Chief Inspector CID Nyeri.
15th January, 1954 at Nyeri Civil Hospital 5.30pm. Military ambulance arrived. Wounded man—identified as Accused taken from it on stretcher. He was put on bed. I gave instructions for his clothing to be removed. Pair of battledress pants removed, one vest, one underpants, booties, and socks. I was on one side of bed and PW 9 was at foot of bed, another Tribal Policeman on other side. As we took pants off Accused I took them and put them at foot of bed. As we took them off the Accused said in English--"there's my money." Someone said how much, Accused said 160/-. I picked trousers up. I searched hip pocket. Recognise Exhibit 6. In pocket I found 1954 diary produced. This is as I got it. (Stamp on 1st page) [Exhibit 7] PW 9 was holding pants on the other side. I saw him put his left hand into left-hand pocket of trousers. He first took out some scraps of dirty paper. He put his hand in again. I saw him pull hand out and in it were 2 rounds of ammunition. I took the rounds from his hand. I drew attention of Supt. [Superintendent] Spencer, Assistant Inspector of Police McCann to this. I held the ammunition out to accused, said in Swahili "Whose is this?" He replied saying, "This is mine.' (Counsel makes no objection) I said where did you get this?

Court:
At this stage I propose to disallow both this and the previous question. In view of the fact that prosecuting Counsel offered Defence Counsel on three occasions the opportunity to object I formed the opinion that Defence wanted this question and answer in evidence. Having now heard the answer I am doubtful if this is so. I propose to adjourn now to enable Defence Counsel to ascertain from Accused if the answers to these questions are part of the defence. If he so assures me I will let them in. If he cannot I will disallow the reply to this witness and will instruct the assessors to ignore it.

Somerhough: Do not press for answers to go in, [I] offered Defence] Counsel every opportunity to object.

Cockar: Would be grateful for adjournment. Asks sus. [?] to General Erskine to produce surrender pamphlet.

Somerhough: To avoid inconvenience will agree to copy to be put in by defence.

Court: At this stage Court will be adjourned. Accused remanded in custody to 2nd February 9am.

\* \* \*

2nd February, 1954.
Appearances as before.

Cockar: Will now take objection under Rule 3 Judges' Rules.

Court: Answers to questions as marked are deleted from record. [The last three sentences of Collins' testimony from 1st February are struck from the record.] Assessors instructed.

### Tenth Prosecution Witness—Cyril Augustine Collins [continued]

Resworn. When I asked Accused questions in respect of the ammunition he replied to me. I then marked the bullets—identified, produced. 9mm— three scratches on tip. This fits Sten, Patchett, or Lanchester [submachine guns]. .38 I marked with scratch on cartridge case. I fired this to test it. It exploded. I recovered bullet.[10] Bullet. [Exhibit 9A] Case. [Exhibit 9B]. This only fits .38 revolver. Up to this stage Accused had not been charged or cautioned. I noted contents of diary, etc. then Mr. Little, Notary Public, arrived. Mr. Little asked me to act as interpreter for him. I spoke to Accused in Swahili and told him I was going to ask him questions but he need not answer them. This was 6pm. I did not charge him. Questions were put to him and he answered them. I then left.

Cockar: Object to answer—caution not full.

Court: Answers not admissible.[11]

Cross-examined: I learnt of this case on afternoon of 15th January. I was not detailed in charge of case. I was in Nyeri. Part of my duty to strip and search Accused. I did not make enquiries as to whether he had been searched. I knew nothing about how he came into police hands at that stage. Both Exhibits 8 and 9 can be in possession of officials. Accused lying on back—head on pillow. I was standing right up against foot of bed. Accused had his head slightly stretched back. He could see us searching his trousers. If last witness says Accused could not have seen us searching—(NB this is not correct statement of previous witness' evidence). Accused's shoulders were propped up. I am not certain but I think PW 9 was there when I asked Accused questions. I did have conversation with Accused over bullets. I did not look at Accused as I was searching. Cannot say if he was alarmed. These bullets were found in trousers of Accused.

Re-examined: Accused mentioned his money just as we commenced to pull his trousers off. It was two or three minutes later when we found bullets.

Assessors: Nil.

Somerhough: Does not propose to call: Capt. Marshall
                                       Sgt. Kirkland
                                       M'tongori
                                       L/Cpl. [Lance Corporal] Fluester
But will tender for Cross-examination.

Cockar: Do not require them.

### Eleventh Prosecution Witness—Patrick McCann

Christian Sworn: ASoP [Assistant Superintendent of Police] CID Nyeri. PW 10 is under me in my Department. 15th January 1954 went Nyeri Civil Hospital 5pm. While there prisoner, identified as Accused, brought in. He was taken to ward. PW 10 and I went with him. He was put on bed. PW 10 and someone else—African Tribal Policeman—removed clothing.

I was present during whole time. Identify Exhibit 6 as trousers. One undresser on each side of bed—removed trousers by pulling them down. Few seconds after PW 10 said in English something and same time showed me 2 rounds ammunition. I did not see where they came from. Rounds similar to Exhibits 8 and 9. PW 10 spoke to Accused and showed ammunition to him. He spoke in Swahili saying "To whom does this ammunition belong"—Accused made a reply.

Cross-examined: I can only remember one question being asked of Accused. I did not watch search.

Re-examined: Nil.

Assessors: Nil.

### Twelfth Prosecution Witness—Thomas Patterson McBrierley

Christian, Sworn: Supt. Of Police, CID Headquarters, Nairobi.
Midday 23rd January, 1954 I went to cell in Nairobi Prison. Accused—identified—was in cell. Mr. Barlow[12], of African Information Services with me. He is fluent in Kikuyu. Dr. Bali, prison Doctor showed me into cell. He left Barlow and self in cell. Spoke to Accused—greeting in Swahili, introduced Barlow—enquired how wound getting on, he replied wound improving. Appeared, apart from wound, perfectly normal cheerful and rational. I charged Accused with being in unlawful possession of 2 rounds ammunition in Swahili—speak Swahili fluently. Accused's Swahili very good. After charging Accused he spoke to Barlow in Kikuyu—I do not understand it. As a result of what Barlow said to me, I again read charge, Mr. Barlow interpreted it into Kikuyu. (Witness reads from Exhibit 10 what he said to Accused) Mr. Barlow interpreted this to Accused. Accused replied to Barlow in Kikuyu. Mr. Barlow translated this to me in English. As a result I read over three other charges.

Cockar: No objection to statements on two present counts. These charges included one of consorting. (Witness reads from Exhibit 11 what he read to Accused.) This was interpreted by Mr. Barlow into Kikuyu. Accused then addressed me in Swahili that he understood and was prepared to answer any questions. I told Accused I could not do this and it was up to Accused whether he wanted to say anything or not. Accused then said he wanted to make statement. I again charged and cautioned Accused in respect of possession of ammunition. He understood. I repeatedly asked him if he understood, he said yes. I recorded in English what Accused said in Swahili. I read it back and he said it was correct and signed it. (Statement read to court.) [Exhibit 10] I produce statement. Few minutes later charged him again with consorting and after caution he made statement which I wrote down etc. and produce. (Statement read to court.) [Exhibit 11]

Cross-examined: Know Ian Henderson—Supt. of Police Special Branch. I understand he saw Accused on a number of occasions. When I took statements he asked for Mr. Henderson to come and see him again. His reason was that he, the Accused wanted to see an African and a European member of Legislative Council,[13] and wanted Mr. Henderson's assistance to do so.

Re-examined: Nil.

Assessors: Nil.

**Thirteenth Prosecution Witness—Arthur Ruffell Barlow**

Christian Sworn: Officer in charge Translation Bureau. African Information Services.
East Africa since 1903. Missionary in Kikuyu until 1941. Author of standard work on Kikuyu 1914 and 1950. Speak and understand fluently. 23rd January, 1954 with PW 12 at Nairobi Prison, taken to cell by him and Dr. Bali. Prisoner in cell—identified as Accused. PW 12 read charges in Swahili to Accused. 1st charge related to possession of ammunition—2 rounds. Identify Exhibit 10 as charge read to Accused. Accused first said he had not understood—in Swahili then to me in Kikuyu. I then interpreted charge and caution to Accused in Kikuyu. Other charge read and accused answered them all in Swahili quite composed, appeared to understand everything.

Cross-examined: Nil.

### Fourteenth Prosecution Witness—Madan Mohan Bali

Hindu Sworn: Medical Officer Prison Nairobi.
Recognise Accused. Patient of mine since 18th January 1954. Treated for wound in throat. Examined him 8.30am 23rd January, 1954. I removed half of stitches. Normal physical condition, good health. Later same day took PW 12 and 13 to cell. Later I examined Accused again—1pm. Accused then normal physically and mentally. Later evening 8.30-9pm— normal.

Cross-examined: Nil.

*Deputy Public Prosecutor Anthony Somerhough has now finished his side of the case. China's lawyer Saeed Cockar now opens the defense.*

Accused elects to give evidence on oath.

Cockar: Accused's defence is that after being elected a general of gangsters on his own conditions he was looking for opportunity to get in touch with security forces. 15th January he was going to military [camp] at Kiawarigi. Unarmed, no ammunition. On way he was involved in exchange of fire from which he received wound, but still proceeded to camp. He intended to surrender in accordance with offer of surrender. He hoped to arrange surrender terms for followers.

### First Defence Witness—Harold Leslie Stringer

Christian, Sworn: I am African Information Officer Central Province. August 1953 surrender terms offered to terrorists. I received copies. Produce copy of English translation, as supplied by my Head Office. [Exhibit A] As far as I know the offer is still open.

Cross-examined: Nil.

## Second Defence Witness—Waruhiu s/o Itote

Pagan, Affirmed: I am Kikuyu. In private life I worked in Railway as fire-man. After that I collected money for Mau Mau. I left Railway in 19;1 and went home to Reserve[14] at Karatina in Mathira Division. I am married. When I returned to reserve I found wife arrested for taking oath I left home because I thought I would also be arrested. I went into hiding and started to work for Mau Mau. I collected money from Reserve and took it to Nairobi. This was in 1952. As I understood I was a wanted person I did this up to beginning of Emergency. When leaders were arrested I went into forest. I stayed there until January 1953 in hiding. I did not try to come out of forest. On 20th January, 1953 there was a meeting of leaders. I was elected General because I was collecting money. I was in charge of funds. Stayed in the forest because we were afraid to be beaten, killed or imprisoned, not because we wanted to fight. Stayed until August 1953. On 2nd August 1953, a group from Mount Kenya had meeting. We decided that the leader in the Aberdares [Dedan Kimathi] had bad rules because when people from forest came out for food, the people cried. We decided to have a leader from Mount Kenya. I was elected as leader. I told then I would agree to be leader if they did what I told them and the people in the reserve should not cry out when they saw us coming.

(1) I do not want them to kill European or African women or young children, because women and children do not know anything.

(2) Not to burn houses of people they said were bad.

(3) Not to beat people in the reserve who demanded poll tax.

(4) Not to keep children from going to Mission Schools, although Independent Schools were closed.

If they agreed to follow these rules I would lead them. I thought I would one day meet the Government and talk to them, but before this would go around in the forest and see their aims, then go round the reserve and see the cause of trouble on the estates. After learning all these things I would surrender to Government according to what the Governor and General Erskine had said. I wanted to go round because I knew the Government would ask me many questions and I would be able to tell all about the

troubles in the Reserve and forest. 28th December, 1953 I invited the
leaders to a meeting, I told them now is the time for me to surrender, and
I want to tell them all our troubles. From 28th December, I departed from
the forest and came to investigate the Reserve. I stayed in the Reserve
until the morning of 15th January, 1954. I came with a man who carries
my bag. I was coming from Gichuthiriu. Gichuthiriu is on left, Kiawarigi
is on the right. I was going to Kiawarigi. About 300 yards from Kiawarigi
I told my orderly to go back. He said he did not know the way and for me
to take him back to Ichuga School. We crossed the valley and came up
the hill. I had no arms or ammunition. I had a bag only. I was wearing a
leather jacket and black jersey and a hat and trousers and a warm shirt.
As we came up the hill there is another valley where there is a banana
plantation. I heard shots being fired. I saw two men going up-hill running. When I turned I was shot by a man on my right. I think he shot me
with a Sten gun. I turned back with my orderly. We met one Gouri (forest name). I told him to take my orderly to help him to carry the bag. I
took off leather jacket and jersey and gave them to my orderly. Leaving
me shirt and trousers and 3 books—one contains 1954 calendar and a
small and a larger book—the small one had records of money; the other
one contained sections I had not completed yet. I also had 190/-. One
100/- [shilling note], 4 20/-, 1 10/- note. I came across valley facing
Kiawarigi Military Camp. I wanted to go without being seen. I decided
to go along the valley. Before that I had gone into a hut. I got some water
there, the water was in a pot. After resting I walked to the military camp.
15 or 20 paces I was told to halt and raise my hands—I did so. He told
me to take off all my clothes. I took off my shirt and put it on ground.
There were other *askaris*. They called a European who told them to let
me in. I asked for water. They gave it to me. I asked for soda and produced 20/- note. Soda not available, money was returned. I was searched
first by a Mkamba [PW 3] at the place. I stopped where he asked me if I
had a pistol or a grenade. He found nothing. The European told me to
give him what I had. I handed him a book and told him I had some
money. I gave him two books—one long, one short—the money one and
the sections one. I retained the calendar one in my hip pocket. I had nothing else. We talked about Railways. He asked me what I wanted in his
camp. I told him I wanted to surrender and to know when this fight will

be over. He kept silent. He said, "It's over to you." After that I was taken to Karatina Police Station. There many people surrounded me, women and men. Then some Europeans came and took my wrist-watch. I was standing by door handcuffed. African put his hands in my pocket asking if I had a pistol or a grenade. European officer dispersed the people. The people were all putting their hands in my pockets. I was taken to hospital, where they stitched my wounds. I was taken out and photographed. There were many people round. I was brought to Nyeri in ambulance. I was in much pain. I did not know I arrived in Nyeri. Came to when my vest was cut—my trousers were taken off. I did not know who did it. I could not see them. I said my money in hip-pocket. Did not say or hear anything else. I did not know where I was until I reached Nairobi. I felt conscious about 10pm when I asked European on guard. Later I saw Mr. Henderson who asked me all about the forest people, and he asked me if I knew certain names. I assisted Mr. Henderson. I saw him many times. I don't want Mr. Henderson called. I made statements to Mr. McBrierley. When I told him about going with terrorists I meant this to relate to before the 15th January, not the 15th January.

Cross-examined: Born 1922. Went to Church Missionary School at Ichuga.[15] I was Church of Scotland. Army 1942, went to Ceylon [modern-day Sri Lanka]—Cpl. in Intelligence Section HQ [Headquarters] Coy [Company] 36 KAR. Returned to Kenya 1944, after being in India and Burma. Received exemplary discharge in 1944. Joined Mau Mau in 1951 by taking oath, started working for them 1952. I was leader of Mount Kenya group. Before going into forest not member of KA [Kenya African] Union. I thought up "Chaina"[16] out of my own head. In forest people take a special name. The Committee gave me title of General. The Mau Mau leaders who were arrested at start of Emergency, I cannot now remember who was arrested. I had more than 15 in my group. There were 7 leaders below me. I would not know the full number of our forces—more than 4,000 fighting troops. These would be armed forces I consorted with up to 15th January. Leader of Embu, Meru, part of South Nyeri Reserves, the settled area including Nanyuki was under me. Dedan Kimathi is above me. He is the only one above me. Troops I commanded from January 1953 were hiding in the forest and fighting with

Government and other Kikuyu. People were killed on both sides. Knew surrender offer included murder.[17] I had copy of pamphlet, had one on me when arrested. I left it with my books in the bag my orderly carried. Orders for operations in areas were given by junior leaders. The committee decides the rules, that is the operations. All 1953 the committee of which I was the leader brought in ammunition and arms. I had nothing to do with this myself. Exhibit 1 is mine, also Exhibit 2 and Exhibit 3. Exhibit 2 and 3 carried by my clerk. I left them with him on 28th December. When I wrote letters I put my stamp. I had second stamp like a shield. Exhibit 4A is not mine—stamp on it is mine. Exhibit 4B is not mine—stamp on it is mine. Contents are method of telling future. Exhibit 4C is not mine—has my stamp on it. Exhibit 5 is mine. I always put my initial with the stamp—as on this book. Gave this to Young. The writing in this is mine. Exhibit 6 are mine—ones I wore 15th January. Exhibit 7 is my diary—one I kept my money in—taken from my hip-pocket. Writing on Exhibit 1 is mine. I gave this book to the Military Officer. Decided to surrender at meeting of 27th October 1953. I told committee I was going to and I told them the reason. They did not agree. My committee agreed in December to my coming to see the Government—28th December. Up to then I was still in charge of my troops. Letter produced to me bears my stamp and is dated 28th December. Charcoal is code name for ammunition. (Letter put to witness.) The signature is mine. I dictated it.

(NB This letter was amongst leaves of Exhibit 7 and was taken in with it.) Letter produced to me [Exhibit 7B]—I wrote it, but I did not send it. It is dated 7th January 1954. I wanted a rest and I wanted someone else to be the leader.

Letter produced to me [Exhibit 7C]—I wrote but I did not send it. Witness referred to Exhibit 5—these are entries of things in my writing. Witness referred to entry under date 13th December, 1954. This is in my handwriting. I wasn't sure about some about it. This was not so. I was given this news at the time. This was at Tumutumu. We were caught in a hut. I did not kill myself. The *askaris* had lots of arms and ammunition. They were for fighting. December 1953 I record receiving amounts of .303 and Sten gun ammunition.[18]

(Witness referred to letter dated 4th December 1953.) [Exhibit 12]

This is signed by me. In this I do not say killed—I have said given an oath i.e. their troubles to be finished.

*The Court Interpreter now reads a section of China's letter, Exhibit 12:*

Court Interpreter: "9 barren women should be finished because they are causing people to be finished."[19]

*China continues:*

This letter was in my book. It is just a report which I intended to investigate. I was in the Reserve from 28th December to 15th January. I did not write and say I would surrender at a certain time and place. On 28th December I decided to surrender. On 14th January I decided to surrender on the 15th. I did not have green branches[20] because I knew if a man raised his hands he would not be shot. I do not know why I did not tell Supt. McBrierley I had no ammunition. He said it had been found. The Mkamba took everything out of my pockets and put them all back again. He touched my two front trouser pockets, not the back one; he was called by a European. I don't know who put the ammunition in my pockets.[21] At Karatina my pockets were searched again. At Karatina I was handcuffed as soon as I got there—hands in front. I now say I was handcuffed by my left hand only. I admit that Mr. McBrierley referred to midday, on the 15th. I did not say anything to him about referring to before the 15th. I now say that I told him I was not with terrorists on the 15th. I now say this is a mistake, I meant to tell him but I forgot. Spent night 14th-15th at Itiati. I was shot about 10.30am near Kiawarigi. I am guessing the time. I was shot on a slope—at the bottom by bananas. Lieut. Young and men were at top of road firing down. I do not know who were firing at the Government troops.[22] I saw them running on another hill. I was shot after some shots had been fired. When I got near Kiawarigi the firing had not started. Firing lasted a short time. I was shot at the end. I was about 300 yards from the terrorists I saw running. I was at the bottom of the hill— they were at the top of the same hill. I was not leading large gang that day. It was in my operational forces. I was not with gang that fired on security forces. I did not know who they were. I know the group which operates in that area. I was shot in throat but not in that battle. I saw Home Guard coming down hill into valley. I did not want to surrender to Home Guard. I went some distance before I hid in a hut. I walked. After I left the hut I went to the military. I did not think I was going to die, I told Mr. McBrierley that I wanted two Government leaders. I did not tell him I had wanted to surrender.

Re-examination: Nil.

Assessors: Nil.

Court: Did not lie on bed.

*Cockar has now finished his defense. What follows are Cockar and Somerhough's final submissions to the court about their arguments. The shorthand makes for difficult reading, but the "Judgment" (below) fully explains the evidence and reasoning of the court.*

Cockar:
"A" Both offences excused if terrorist surrenders to forces. Admit that surrender does not pardon murders. But have Crown proved murders [?].[23] Submits that on these two counts Accused entitled to acquittal.
"B" Evidence for prosecution insufficient—beyond reasonable doubt.
   (1) Evidence of Headman [PW 1]—not to be believed—disagrees with Young over numbers. Not proved Accused was with gangsters.
   (2) Would person in Accused's position walk into military camp with ammunition on him [?].

List of prosecution witnesses not fool proof against plant[ing of ammunition].
Doubt.
Kioki [PW 3]—Accused was searched—must also raise a doubt.

Somerhough: No law.[24]

A. [response to Cockar's point A] Surrender offer is stat. [a statement]
   and legal defence to charges—no authority for this statement.
This can not affect the law of the land.
Only indication of exercise of prerogative.

B. [response to Cockar's point B] Relevance is to credibility of Accused
   only.
Common ground.
Accused wounded and afraid of Home Guard. Two rounds found in
   pocket.
Accused admitted 1st Count ["consorting"]
Question of plant—see his statement to police.
Accused under observation of someone responsible all the time from
   capture.
When charged with consorting, Accused admitted it—every element
   clear.

Facts: in own operational area. Firing started 11.15-12.15. Accused on
   own admission wounded towards end. Accused went into hut, admitted being badly wounded and had note-book Exhibit 1 on him. Where
   Headman thought he saw him. Finding of book—corroborating evidence.
Accused was with gang—only reasonable inference.
Correspondence is against his own story as to when he decided to surrender.
Damaging to credit.

*At this stage, Judge MacDuff sums up the evidence and gives instructions
to the three assessors, who will determine whether they believe China is
guilty (though their opinions carry no legal weight).*

## 1st Count

Read section 8C(1)[25] [of the colony's Emergency Regulations
This accused consorted with persons carrying firearms contravention of
Regulation 8C(1) circumstances raising reasonable presumption that
accused had recently acted with such persons in manner prejudicial to
public safety.

[The] real dispute [is] on [points] 1, 2 and 3 [below]:

(1) Accused's story that he was not with these persons [the gang, and was] shot while on way to surrender—[but] surrender not mentioned by Young.

Assessors entitled to say whether they believe or not. If believe, or sufficiently believable to raise reasonable doubt as to whether he was with persons carrying firearms, or whether they had firearms, advise "Not Guilty."

Some corroboration in his attempt about 7th January 1954 to resign. Again entitled to test his story by admissions in cross-examination and against evidence of Young on books. Impress not being tried for being General Chaina but on two counts before court.

(2) If the Accused's evidence of itself not sufficient—remember burden still lies on prosecution to prove beyond reasonable doubt each element of offence.

Was he consorting? He was not actually seen and identified as one of gang. Crown asked to draw inference from circumstances.

[You must use these facts to make your determination:]

(a) Firing in area Kiamachimbi.

(b) Gang sighted by Ichuga School and someone fired at guard. Discrepancies between Home Guards, and Police and Lieut. Young as to numbers—more apparent than real. Ignore evidence of Headman and Lieut. Young as to wounding—not sufficiently clear, but all agree as to approximate position of gang by huts.

(c) Someone wounded either earlier or then.

(d) Blood in huts.

(e) Books of Accused in hut—some with blood on them.

(f) Bleeding badly—300 yards from action.

(g) Accused's admission in evidence—letters.

(h) Accused's full admission—after reference to midday 15th January. Main point—gang in area of huts—Chaina in same area same time.

If from evidence [you] consider [that the] only reasonable conclusion is that he was with them—entitled to find consorting. If any other reasonable conclusion to be drawn from same facts, including his own story, no consorting.

(3) Were these persons carrying firearms?
Evidence of witnesses who saw them—may be open to doubt, but again main evidence is firing of shots from area at security forces and came from those two points. If satisfied that the persons seen in the area of huts had firearms and fired, [you must] find persons unknown were carrying firearms.[26]

(4) Regulation 8C utilise Reg. 8C(3) presumption.

(5) Circumstances.
If hold consorting then circumstances can lead to conclusion:
Firing at security forces.
Carrying of arms under present circumstances.

## 2nd Count

Read Regulation 8A[27] [of the colony's Emergency Regulations]:
Any person having in possession ammunition without lawful authority or excuse.

(1) No question of identity. Evidence of Tribal Police and CI [Chief Inspector] Collins

(2) Possession: Accused denies knowledge. Suggestion is plant— again not necessary [to] believe but [if] sufficient to raise reasonable doubt—benefit to Accused. Plant is possible at any time but who planted?
— Evidence of succeeding witnesses from Young [PW 4] onwards covers possibility.
— Still leaves Tribal Policeman Wachera [PW 9] who found it—would he have this type of ammunition? Collins—would he do it—denies.

— Question of plant not referred to witnesses.

— Refer evidence of Private Kioki [PW 3], Young [PW 4]

— Suggest that Kioki unreliable and appeared to be in a state when he would answer anything "yes." 3 different versions. Can accept Lieut. Young alone if consider reliable and he saw Accused from time he dropped shirt—says was not searched. If can completely exclude plant then can accept evidence of prosecution.

(3) Accused's knowledge from circumstances.

(4) Ammunition—evidence of CI Collins

(5) [The question of a] lawful [surrender] etc., [does] not arise. Satisfy beyond reasonable doubt.

## Surrender

1st Count: Must hold that proclamation cannot change law. Where would one get to. [If surrender terms held as valid,] unsuccessful or badly wounded can escape consequence of an action by surrendering.

2nd Count: No mention to Young. No mention to McBrierley. Decide whether surrender consequent on offer or not.

## Opinions of Assessors, Count 1

 (1) Waigwa s/o Waweru — Guilty. He was with those people.
 (2) Ezekiel Kabora  — Guilty.
 (3) Mateo Makara  — Guilty.

## Opinions of Assessors, Count 2

 (1) Waigwa s/o Waweru — Not Guilty. He was not searched at the camp. He was searched at the Hospital, therefore I do not know if he had them [rounds of ammunition] or not.

(2) Ezekiel Kabora          — Guilty.
(3) Mateo Makara           — Guilty.

Judgment reserved.
Accused remanded in custody to 3rd February, 1954, at 10am.

*MacDuff's judgment follows.*

# JUDGMENT

The Accused is charged on two counts, the first being that on 15th January, 1954, near Kiawarigi, he consorted with persons carrying firearms in contravention of Regulation 8C(1) of the Emergency Regulations, 1952, in circumstances which raise a reasonable presumption that he had recently acted with such other persons in a manner prejudicial to public safety.

*MacDuff now explains the reasoning behind his decision about Count 1.*

The Accused admits that he is one "General Chaina" a member of the Mau Mau which he joined in 1951, and for which he commenced active work in 1952, prior to the declaration of the present Emergency. He also admits that in January 1953, he was elected a "general" and that on 2nd August, 1953, he was elected to command of the Mount Kenya area, comprising Meru Reserve, in which areas he says he had a force of 4,000 active terrorists. He has said that he accepted the appointments on certain terms in respect of which it will suffice to say that if the terms he laid down are true, he has failed singularly to abide by them since.

The Crown alleges that the accused was in company with a terrorist gang in the area of the Ichuga School about 1pm on 15th January. In an action with the security forces this Accused was wounded as a result of which, fearing that it was a serious wound, he gave himself up to the military post at Kiawarigi.

The Accused, on the other hand, denies that he was in the company of the terrorist band. He admits being in the area at the time of the action between the terrorist and security forces, during the course of which action he was wounded. He says, however, that he first formed the intention of surrendering in August, 1953, when he obtained a copy of the pamphlet issued by HE [His Excellency] The Governor and General Erskine calling upon the Mau Mau to surrender. Subsequently he notified his committee on 27th October, 1953, that he had decided to surrender but the committee did not agree. Finally on 28th December he again told his committee that he was going to surrender and on this occasion they agreed. He there-upon left his forces and returned to the reserve. On 15th January, he was proceeding in company with his orderly, towards the Kiawarigi Army Post to give effect to his intention to surrender. Some 300 yards short of the post he turned back to show his orderly the way back, presumably to the forest, when he became involved in the action in which he was wounded. After that he made his way to the Kiawarigi Post and surrendered.

There is this to be said in favor of the truth of the Accused's story. Counsel for the Crown has put to the Accused two letters which were found in his diary, dated the 7th January 1954—eight days before the date to which this present charge relates—although both letters were obviously not despatched—both letters reading:

> "To all leaders of war *askaris*—I first of all beseech you, with all the *askaris*, to allow me to rest. I shall be working because I cannot get a place to rest. I also ask earnestly to give my seat to someone else. The reason is that I don't want to die."

These letters would indicate that the Accused wanted to leave, at least for a period, the organisation to which he belonged because he feared to die. From one point of view, this may be said to indicate a state of mind consistent with an intent to surrender. There is also the fact that Accused did eventually approach the Kiawarigi military post and give himself up.

Despite these points, however, the Accused's story of itself is almost impossible of belief as is the coincidence of his becoming involved with his own terrorists at the one moment he was innocently making his way to Kiawarigi Army Post. To add to that impossibility is the fact that subsequent to Accused's original intentions to surrender in August and October, as expressed so eloquently by himself, nevertheless on the 4th

December, 1953, he admittedly wrote instructing that "9 barren women should be finished because they were causing people to be finished." On the 13th December, 1953, he admittedly entered in his diary "China visited the village of Ngurumo with the Embu leader General Ndaya and [they] were met by the Government at the village of Kahuro, there was happiness because ten *askaris* and Home Guards, as well as whites 6 were killed" and as late as 28th December, 1953, admittedly he wrote one Njogo s/o Kisugo *inter alia* [amongst other things] as follows

> "I inform you to send all the things—charcoals (a code name for ammunition) and other things. Give to that young man Gikaria Ngi."

These are not the letters or actions of a person who had formed an intention of surrendering in pursuance of the authority's offer. There was ample opportunity, if the Accused's story that he left his gangs on 28th December, 1953, were correct, between that date and the 15th January, 1954, for the Accused to surrender and for him to make proper arrangements to surrender. His explanation as to why he did not do so is unconvincing in the extreme. There are other reasons, and a number of them, all evident in the Accused's own evidence, why I should consider him incapable of belief. I am quite satisfied that the Accused had formed no intention of surrendering prior to his being wounded and that his own evidence of being on his way to surrender when he was wounded cannot be believed

What then are the facts proved by the Crown? Lieut. Young [PW 4]'s evidence shows that the action that morning commenced somewhere round Kamachimbi about 11.45am. The firing continued and came closer to his post at Kiawarigi until he eventually took a combined force of his own men and Home Guard to stop the valley along the road by the Ichuga School. Here, between 12.15 and 12.30pm he and his men came under fire from the ridge on the other side of the valley. He then saw some men, five in number, who from their dress would appear to have been terrorists, run down the hill. At the same time, Headman Murakaru [PW 1] and Tribal Policeman Weru [PW 2], who were both in Lieut. Young's force, also saw a number of natives, whom they estimated as about 30 in number, break from the cover of a banana plantation. These natives were seen to scatter, some disappearing behind some huts in the vicinity of the plantation. Some point has been made of the discrepancy in the numbers seen, and the type of clothing worn, as evidenced by Lieut. Young on the one hand and the two Home Guards on the other. To my mind, this is no more than the different parts of the same scene as observed by witnesses separated by thirty or more yards and observing a scene that was not clear of trees and growth. I am satisfied that all these witnesses observed members of a gang, which could only have consisted of terrorists, and the members of the gang were observed by all three witnesses in the same close vicinity—variously described as being "by the banana plantation," "by a hedge," and some "10 yards from the huts."

Some time, 30 minutes or more, after the disappearance of the gang, the security force approached the area where they had seen and fired on the gang. Here traces of blood were found. Tribal Policeman Weru found traces of blood leading him to one hut where he found blood, a bandolier of ammunition, some books stamped with General China's headquarters stamps and the stamp itself. At another hut Headman Murakaru found traces of blood outside, and inside blood on a tin. On coming outside the hut he discovered a trail of blood leading away from the hut and beside the trail a note book [Exhibit 1], obviously the property of the Accused and ownership of which he admits. Accused says he did not lose his notebook at this spot. I prefer, however, to accept the evidence of Headman Murakaru that he found the book by the trail of blood, and the evidence of Lieut. Young that he did not receive this book from Accused.

The Accused, of course, admits in his sworn evidence that it was in this area that he was wounded, that he went into a hut where he had a drink of water, and that it was right at the end of the shooting that he was hit.

There is, then, no doubt about two facts, first that there was a gang within a very small area, and that the accused was also in the same area, at the same time as the gang when the gang was fired on by the security forces. To that I should add at least two other facts. The Accused admits that this was in his operational area, and that he was General Chaina. Were he there for no lawful purpose it is a fair inference that he would be accompanied by some of his terrorists. I have not accepted the Accused's reason as to what he was doing in this vicinity. This then leaves as the only reasonable and in fact the irresistible inference to be drawn from the facts, that the Accused was in company of the gang of terrorists seen and fired on by Lieut. Young's security force.

I now come to the question as to whether this gang was carrying firearms. On this point there is the evidence of Headman Murakaru that he saw some guns, he cannot say how many, except that he saw some home made guns, and a Sten gun. His evidence might ordinarily be open to doubt in view of the distance at which he saw these firearms. Tribal Policeman Weru, however, was much more definite, and in my opinion a much more accurate witness. He says he actually identified a double-barrelled shotgun, and three other guns. Again his evidence may ordinarily be open to the same objection of the distance at which he identified these firearms. There is, however, no doubt from the evidence of both of these witnesses, and from the evidence of Lieut. Young, that the security force was fired on by this gang. The total of this evidence satisfies me that some members of the gang were armed with firearms and such firearms were in fact discharged.

If firearms were in the possession of this gang they must be held to have been in possession contrary to Regulation 8A of the Emergency Regulations, 1952.

I next come to such presumption as may reasonably be raised by the circumstances. The fact that this band of terrorists fired on the security forces certainly raises the presumption that at the time they were acting in concert in a manner prejudicial to public safety, [and] the fact that what may be described as a running action had taken place over a period of an hour before the Accused was wounded, obviously raises the reasonable presumption that the accused in concert with the gang had recently so acted. Apart however from the overt acts of this band, at this stage of the present Emergency it must be considered almost an irrefutable presumption that a gang of what can only be described as obvious terrorists has, or will, act in a manner detrimental to public safety.

I do not propose to consider whether the Accused has knowledge of the fact that he was in company with armed persons further than to say that with his position in this organisation and his presence with the gang his knowledge must have been obvious.

On the facts as I have outlined them, and as I have found them to be proved, I am satisfied beyond a reasonable doubt that all the elements required by the definition of the offence charged on this account have been proved.

I may say I am somewhat fortified in that decision by the statement made by the Accused in reply to Supt. McBrierley, when after being cautioned and charged with the offence of consorting with persons in possession of arms and ammunition about midday on 15th January, 1954, near Kiawarigi, the Accused said—*inter alia*:

> "You write I wish to admit this entirely and every day I go like this. But I want to be asked why I go with these people."

Before I leave this count, I should refer to a defence raised by Accused that this offence is excused if a terrorist surrenders to the authorities in accordance with the pamphlet to which I have already referred. Apart altogether from the reasons which in my opinion actuated the Accused in his surrender at Kiawarigi Army Post this pamphlet has no legal effect in respect of the present count. I refer particularly to the words:

> "Come in and surrender yourself. If you do, Government will understand your position and will not execute you for having carried arms or consorted with the Mau Mau terrorists."

They are no more and no less than an indication that under certain circumstances His Excellency the Governor will be inclined to exercise his prerogative of mercy. It may even go so far as to suggest that in certain circumstances no prosecution will be taken against the person surrendering. It can, however, have no effect on the finding of or in a case such as this, the sentence to be passed by this Court once an information has been laid.

In the result the Accused is found Guilty on the first count charged.

*MacDuff now explains the reasoning behind his decision about Count 2.*

The Accused is further charged on a second count that on the 15th January, 1954, at Nyeri, he had in his possession two rounds of ammunition, without lawful authority or excuse.

This count arises out of an event slightly later in the day than the ones to which I have already referred. The Crown alleges that on the Accused being brought to Nyeri Civil Hospital his clothing was there removed and searched when the two rounds of ammunition, the subject of this charge, one round of .38 calibre revolver ammunition and one round of 9 millimetre ammunition, were found in and removed from the pocket of his trousers by Tribal Policeman Wachera [PW 9].

It will be remembered that the accused surrendered to the Kiawarigi Army Post somewhere about 3pm on the 15th January. The Accused says he did not have these rounds in his possession then. He further says that he was searched there by the Mkamba private, Kioki[28] [PW 3], who took everything out of his pockets and then put the articles back again. According to the accused he was again searched at the Karatina Police Station, again by an African. The Accused also says that his recollection of the search at Nyeri Civil Hospital was hazy on account of his wound, that he did not see the ammunition found, nor was he shown it at the time. Accordingly he claims, in effect, that if these rounds were found in his clothing they must have been placed there without his knowledge.

I have already said that I consider the Accused, on the previous part of his evidence, to be impossible of belief. There are at least two points in this part of his evidence that I also do not believe. The first is the search by Private Kioki. Kioki, in his evidence, gave a most amazing account of the surrender of this accused at Kiawarigi, he went on to give three different accounts of how the Accused was searched, together with a denial that he was ever searched. I formed the opinion that this native had the unfortunate mentality that when he was before this Court, whether from nervousness or some other reason, he did not know, or did not care, what he was saying, and that he was prepared to agree to any suggestion put to him. In my opinion not one word of his evidence can be accepted. Fortunately, Lieut. Young, who gave a clear and believable account of the same events, first saw the Accused while he was still walking towards the Kiawarigi Military Camp. At that stage Kioki was behind the Accused but Lieut. Young says that he also saw the Accused lay down his shirt. In other words Lieut. Young was watching the Accused over the whole of the period when he could have been searched and that Officer is definite that the Accused was not searched. Lieut. Young I believe, and I find as a fact that the accused was not searched on his arrival at Kiawarigi camp. The second point of conflict between the evidence of Accused and that of the prosecution witnesses relates to the finding and demonstration to the Accused of the two rounds of ammunition. Chief Inspector Collins [PW 10] says that when Wachera took the rounds from Accused's trouser pocket he took them from Wachera, showed them to some Police Officers in the room, then showed them to Accused and asked him questions about these rounds to which the Accused replied. I have no hesitation in accepting CI Collins as a truthful witness, and on this point I believe his version as against that of the Accused. Accordingly I am again compelled to hold that I can believe no part of the Accused's own evidence as to the events subsequent to his arrival at the Kiawarigi Post insofar as it disagrees with other evidence.

I am satisfied that the two rounds were found in Accused's trouser pocket at Nyeri Civil Hospital. There is, of course, always the possibility of ammunition being planted on an accused. In most instances it must be almost impossible to disprove that possibility. In the present instance the Crown have produced a number of witnesses to cover the period between Accused's arrival at Kiawarigi Post and the search at Nyeri Civil Hospital, a period of some two to two and a half hours. Lieut. Young was with, or had the Accused under observation from his arrival at that post, during his stay at the post, and during his removal first to the 7 KAR Command Post and then to Karatina Police Station, where he handed the Accused to Asst. Insp. Arnold [PW 5]. During the period Accused was at Karatina Police Station, in the First Aid Tent, and until his removal from that point by ambulance the Accused was under the close observation of Asst. Insp. Arnold or Chief Inspector Woodgate [PW 6]. All of these officers are certain that no one, during those periods, could have planted ammunition on the Accused's person. During the drive from Karatina to Nyeri, Medical Orderly Raburu [PW 8] was in attendance on the Accused, until he was delivered at Nyeri Hospital, from which time he came under the eye of Chief Inspector Collins. In view of this evidence the chances of anyone planting ammunition in the Accused's pocket are remote. One should also take into account the type of ammunition, a type not on issue to Home Guard or Tribal Policemen, but to the Army and Police Officers. One should also take into account the fact that this type of ammunition is utilised by the terrorist forces, and that the Accused admits having dealt with ammunition while he was with the terrorist forces. One must take into account also the inherent improbability of anyone worrying to plant ammunition on a person so notorious as General Chaina. To the native, in any case, the manufacture of evidence would not be necessary.

In my opinion, the proper conclusion to be drawn is that these two rounds were not planted on the person of the Accused, that they were found in his clothing at Nyeri Hospital, and that they were in his clothing when he approached Kiawarigi Post.

That this is ammunition within the definition of that term in the Arms and Ammunition Ordinance is evident from the evidence of Chief Inspector Collins. From the circumstances it must also be inferred that the Accused knew that he had this ammunition.

I then come to the final requirement in respect of this offence, that is that such possession should be without lawful authority or excuse. On this point it can be argued, and probably with some merit, that a terrorist, who surrenders pursuant to what may be termed the surrender offer and who brings his ammunition in with him, does so with lawful excuse. In this present instance it is unnecessary for me so to decide, and that for two reasons. The first is that the burden of establishing such lawful excuse lies on the Accused. Here he has not done so in that he has denied possession of the ammunition altogether. The second reason is that I do not believe that the Accused gave himself up pursuant to that surrender offer. The evidence shows that he was badly wounded and apparently separated from his men. He, in all probability, thought he was more seriously wounded than he was. He did not conform to one of the conditions of the offer, that is he did not utilise the distinguishing sign of a green branch From the time he approached Kiawarigi Army Post he had many opportunities to indicate his surrender, pursuant to the surrender offer. He says he told Lieut. Young he had surrendered which Lieut. Young denies. As late as 23rd January when charged with these two offences by Supt. McBrierley he again did not mention either the surrender or the surrender offer. I am quite satisfied that at the time he approached the military post there was no thought of Government's surrender offer in his mind—he approached that post as a deserted terrorist *in extremis* looking for medical assistance, and he has utilised the terms of that offer for the first time in this court as a Defence. In my opinion Accused had no lawful authority or excuse for the possession of the ammunition charged.

The Crown has proved the elements required by this offence. Accused will be found Guilty on the second count.

J. MacDuff, Judge.

3rd February, 1954.

## Conviction

> (1) On the first count Accused is convicted of: "Consorting with persons carrying firearms contrary to Regulation 8C(1) of the Emergency Regulations, 1952."
> (2) On the second count Accused is convicted of: "Unlawfully being in possession of ammunition contrary to Regulation 8A(1) of the Emergency Regulations, 1952."

J. MacDuff, Judge.

3rd February, 1954.

## Allocutus[29]

Somerhough.

Accused when asked if he has anything to say why sentence according to law should not be passed upon him says: "I would like to appeal."

## Sentence

1st Count: "Consorting etc. cont.[rary] to Reg. 8C(1) Emergency Regulations, 1952."

The Accused is sentenced to be hanged by the neck until he is dead.

2nd Count: "Possession of ammunition cont. to Reg. 8A(1) of Emergency Regulations, 1952."

In view of sentence on the first count at this stage I pass no sentence in respect of the conviction on this count.

J. MacDuff, Judge.

3rd February 1954.

Right of appeal advised.

Certificate under Section 378 (1)(b) refused.

    J. MacDuff, Judge.

3rd February, 1954.

*China filed the paperwork for his appeal on February 13, 1954.*

## Memorandum of Appeal
## In Her Majesty's Court of Appeal
## for Eastern Africa at Nairobi
## Criminal Appeal No. 122 of 1954

From the original Criminal Case No. 35/54 tried by the Supreme Court of Kenya (Emergency Assize) held at Nyeri.

WARUHIU S/O ITOTE ............................. Appellant

Versus

REGINA ..................................... Respondent

I, the undersigned, do most humbly beg leave to appeal against the conviction and sentence of death passed upon me by the Supreme Court of Kenya (Emergency Assize) held at Nyeri, in the above Criminal Case, on the 3rd February, 1954, on the following grounds:

(1) That the learned Judge erred in law in holding that the surrender pamphlet issued by and under the hand of His Excellency the Governor of Kenya and the Commander-in-Chief had no effect in law and that it did not constitute a legal defence.

(2) That the learned Judge also erred in the interpretation of the surrender pamphlet in coming to the conclusion that it did not apply to the Appellant [China] as it is clear in the pamphlet that the offence of being in possession of ammunition and consorting with terrorists are pardoned.

(3) That the learned Judge failed to take into account that the Appellant had ammunition in his possession under a lawful excuse which is that surrender offers urge terrorists to surrender with their arms and ammunition.

I wish to be present at the hearing of this appeal.

Convict No. 1611/J WARUHIU s/o ITOTE

*China signed his appeal with his left thumbprint.*

## Ruling of the Court of Appeal
## In Her Majesty's Court of Appeal
## for Eastern Africa at Nairobi
## Criminal Appeal No. 122 of 1954
## (From Emergency Assize Criminal Case No. 35
## of 1954 of HM [Her Majesty's] Supreme Court
## of Kenya at Nyeri)

WARUHIU S/O ITOTE alias "General China" . . . . . . . . . . . . Appellant
Versus
REGINA . . . . . . . . . . . . . . . . . . . . . . . . . . . . . . . . . . . . . . . Respondent

ORDER UNDER RULE 4(1) OF THE EASTERN AFRICAN COURT OF APPEAL (KENYA EMERGENCY ASSIZES) RULES, 1953

I have perused the record of this case and am satisfied that it does not disclose any matter, either of law or of fact, sufficient to raise a reasonable doubt as to the correctness of the conviction.

The trial Judge having refused, in exercise of his discretion under section 378(1)(b) of the Criminal Procedure Code of Kenya, as amended by the Emergency (Amendment of Laws) (No. 17) Regulations, 1953, to certify the case as fit for appeal on questions of fact or mixed law and fact, an appeal lies on questions of law alone. The memorandum of appeal puts forward three points involving consideration of the meaning and effect of a surrender pamphlet issued by the Governor of Kenya and the Commander-in-Chief, East Africa. These may be points of law, but they do not arise out of the findings of fact by the trial Court.

These findings were—
  (a) that the appellant was consorting with persons carrying fire-arms in contravention of Regulation 8C of the Emergency Regulations 1952 in circumstances as charged;

  (b) that he was in possession of ammunition without lawful authority or excuse contrary to Regulation 8A of the same Regulations;

  (c) that he gave himself up to the Military as a deserted and wounded terrorist *in extremis* and that he had not, prior to being wounded, formed any intention of surrendering, as the appellant alleged in his defence, and that at the time he did surrender he had in his mind no thought of the Governor's surrender offer.

No appeal has been lodged or can be lodged against these findings of fact. In view of those findings it was, strictly, unnecessary for the trial Judge to consider the meaning and effect of the surrender offer and anything that he did say on that question was *obiter*.[30] If this appeal were admitted to hearing on the grounds raised in the memorandum [China's appeal], nothing that this Court might say on that question could have any effect on the issue, for whether this Court agreed or did not agree with the learned Judge's remarks on the surrender offer, the position would in either case still be that the conviction must follow from the unchallenged findings of fact.[31]

I am satisfied therefore that this appeal has been lodged without any sufficient ground for complaint and I therefore summarily reject it.

N.A. WORLEY
VICE-PRESIDENT.

NAIROBI,
20th February, 1954

# Letter from Waruhiu Itote to the Chief Mechanical Engineer, East African Railways and Harbours, October 16, 1953*

*This letter is likely the only one written by China from the forests that is still in existence. It seems to be part of a short series of letters exchanged between China and the Chief Mechanical Engineer of the East African Railways and Harbours (EARH), who was probably Wallace Young, the man who later arrested him. China had asked his former employer for money, probably to assist in the promulgation of the war. Though China knew a few words of English, it is unlikely that he knew enough to write this letter; probably, it was dictated to a scribe.*

*In the letter China provides a possible answer to the age-old question of why Mau Mau never tried to sabotage the railway line.[1] The line—running between Mombasa and Lake Victoria—was an essential resource for the colonial administration, which could move large quantities of troops and supplies along it. Here, China reminds his former employer that he knows the "secrets" of the train; but that he believes the management of the railways has little in common with the colonial government, and his never made any "mistake." It seems that China's affection for his former boss may have played into his decision to avoid damaging the line.*

*This letter is from the Bodleian Library of Commonwealth and African Studies at Rhodes House, Mss. Afr. s. 235, Papers of George Gibson. I am grateful for permission to reprint t here.

*The contents of this letter are reproduced precisely as they were written.*

General China
P.O. Box
Mount Kenya
16th Oct. 1953

Office of the Chief Mechanical Engineer
Nairobi
Kenya Colony

Dear Sir,

First of all I have to request your letter that I received on the 7th Oct. 1953 together with another copy of 24th Oct. 1953.

I had been very glad for the Government of EARH. I have then a question to ask and the question is that I want to [know] whether the government of EAR has got difference from the other government [the colonial government]. Has it got difference? The reason is that I am seeing as the government of EAR as it is good as much than the the other government.

How do you think about me? From 1951 this is the time to remember kindness and obidience? I think that you don't know more about me well and I want to advice you a little bit and then you notice the news. I want you to tell me clearly whether the money you mentioned will come or not.

PLEASE LISTEN TO ME.

Do you remember that I have worked in the EAR for a long time without any mistakes. From the time that I left business of yours I got much troubles and the troubles let enter into the Forest till this time we are speaking with you.

If I speak or tell the truth, I am the man who leads the fight in these districts, Nyeri, Meru, Embu, Nanyuki and now I have got more power to round all around the Kenya. Therefore I think that perhaps you don't know more about me and how I stay and perhaps you don't want to things of my own by force. Again note that I know all secrets and more about the loco-motive or train and I have never think any thing to destroy the business of yours. I have never see any mistake of the government of EAR.

Now I have adviced you all about myself and how I do stay, and therefore think yourself clearly whether you will send the money so that I have to show you where I am and you send the money at the place where I am. If that will not be clearly completed, I have to come there myself because even I do come there.

When I saw your letter I saw as if it was a dream. My addresses are as follows:

WARUHIU S/O ITOTE
ID, NYI [Nyeri] 449541/1
C/O CHIEF MUHINDI
IC[H]UGA
P.O. KARATINA

Please if you write these addresses clearly the letter will reach alright without any difficulties.

If there is any question you want to ask me ask then and I shall answer it. Then if you are telling the truth let me get your early reply please I praise you all.

Please I beg you to tell me how you do think about me.

I wish you good-bye and GOD will let us meet and speak together again.

YOURS OBIDIENCE SERVANT
SO & SO
[Signed and stamped by China]

# Eulogy: Waruhiu Itote

BY JOHN NOTTINGHAM

The Late
WARUHIU ITOTE, EBS[1]
(General China)
Born 1922—Died 27th April, 1993
Gichigirira Farm, Ol-Kalou
Friday, 7th May 1993

Few men have the chance to fundamentally change the history of their country and fewer still take it. Waruhiu Itote, a legend in his own lifetime as General China, was one such man. At the beginning of the active phase of Kenya's struggle for freedom he was unanimously chosen as the overall commander (*Karangaita*) of the patriotic forces in the Mount Kenya sector. It was a task he performed brilliantly in the face of the awesome strength of a full British Army Division with its sophisticated and powerful weaponry, backed up by a massively reinforced colonial police force and a squadron of RAF [Royal Air Force] Lincoln bombers.

In 1951 the looming threat of a White Settler take-over in Kenya forced the leaders of the Kenya African Union (KAU) to establish a strategy to internationalize their rapidly deteriorating political situation. A vital tactical part of this plan was to raise their own military force. In 1952 China became responsible for recruiting and training in the forest sanctuaries a dedicated band of young patriots. Over the next five years they were to initiate a sustained and unique guerrilla campaign whose sheer courage, ingenuity and ferocity forced Kenya into newspaper headlines throughout the world and brought the colonial government to its knees.

The odds against them were immense. They were isolated and existing in conditions of extreme hardship and danger. There was no help from friendly outside countries. Guns, grenades, and ammunition had to be captured or stolen or fashioned out of bicycle frames and door handles. There was very little money and supplies of food and medicine were scarce and uncertain. There was, however, a profound and indomitable determination to free this land and its suffering people once and for all from the shackles of foreign oppression. Waruhiu Itote single-handedly trained his band of brave young men into a most effective fighting force whose successful exploits inspired the freedom fighters throughout Africa. Nelson Mandela, President of the African National Congress in South Africa, emphasized on his 1990 visit to Kenya how much he and other leaders had been "influenced by the life and example of General China."

Waruhiu was born in 1922 at Kaheti in Mukurweini in Nyeri District. His mother, Wamuyu, came from the Anjiru clan. Her father, Matindira, had been a famous doctor. His father, Itote, was a Muicakamuyu, of the *Mbari ya Thairu* [Thairu's lineage group]. Itote's father, Kibira, died while Itote was still of an age to herd goats. Itote's elder brother, Njuho, left Kaheti and found new land at Gachuiro. When he died in 1934 he had no sons and Itote took over both the land at Gachuiro and Njuho's stock-trading business. In 1929 Waruhiu, backed by his aunt Bertha Wangui, went to the CSM [Church of Scotland Mission] school at Kiangurue. Here he learnt to write Kikuyu and do basic arithmetic. He also became a keen Christian. In 1933 he was transferred to Mihuti School. Over the next six years the young Waruhiu led a roving and adventurous life but somehow managed to continue his schooling at Ichuga, Mahiga and Nyeri township CSM schools.

In 1939 at the age of 17 he left home for Nairobi, taking a job with Unga Ltd looking after a grinding machine at a wage of eighteen shillings a month. At the end of 1939, he started a vegetable business in Pumwani with two partners, Gachihi and Gakunga, which had a turnover of some three hundred shillings a month. In December 1940 Waruhiu married Leah Wambura, Gakunga's sister, at Gachuiro. Later he married two other wi /es, Grace Nduta and Margaret Wanjiru. In 1941 Gac ihi join d the army, Gakunga went to Kisumu and the business closed down. On 2nd Janu ary 1942, Waruhiu himself enlisted in the King's Afr can Rifl s and after basic training he was posted to the 36 [th battalion of the] KA R at Moshi. His regiment was soon drafted to Ceylon [mode n-day S ri Lanka], whence, by this time a full corporal, he quickly found himself in action against the Japanese in Burma.

His experiences there were of profound importance to his la er care r. Not only did he learn much about military organisation, tra ning, and morale. He also grew up politically and began vigorously t question what he was fighting for and to see the need for radical change in his own country which was so riddled with political, economic and ocial dis-criminat on on racial grounds. In late 1944, his unit returned to Nairobi where his troop-train was met by Eliud Mathu, the first Africa Member of the Legislative Council. In 1945 he was posted to the 3 KAR depot at Jinja wh re there was some political unrest. By now Waruhiu and his fel-low Kikuyu soldiers were increasingly questioning their role and dreai n-ing of the day Jomo Kenyatta would return from England to lea d them on the road to freedom.

After demobilization, his first ventures were into a family charcc al operation at Nanyuki and a firewood business at Mathira. In 1 46, wh le looking for further outlets in Nairobi, Waruhiu decided to jo n the East African Railways and Harbours as a fireman, earning Shs. [shillings] 60 per month. In 1946 China joined the KAU and in 1947 he beca e a mem-ber of a society known as *Anake a 40* ("Forty Group") which had been started by Mwangi Macharia and included many ex-soldiers. He was also a member of the Transport and Allied Workers' Union, led by John Mungai. These were the groups that were organizing the growi g body of dissent and which felt that the settler government's increasing ly oppres-sive measures and brutalities could only be countered by force, which seemed o be the only thing they could understand. He stayed with the Railways until 1951, being a fireman by day and a revolutionary by nigl t. The situation in the country worsened and in August 1952 Ch na had his last momentous meeting with Kenyatta before the Emergency Kenyatta told him that they might have to buy their freedom with their bl od. Sor e would be killed and many would be imprisoned in the service f the people. A few days later Waruhiu received his orders to go to Karatina to take the first 40 recruits into the forest to become the nucleus of an Army of Liberation, in which he worked closely with Generals Kassam Njogu, Bahati, Mwariama, Kariba, Tanganyika, Kamwamba, Kimbo, Ndungu Gicheru and many others. Simultaneously, Dedan Kimathi was establishing his base in the Aberdares and China was in continual touch with him.

In his two published books, *"Mau Mau" General* and *Mau Mau in Action*, and in a third recently completed but as yet unpublished manuscript, Waruhiu has vividly and eloquently described the events of the war that followed. It is an astonishing and unforgettable story of heroism, self-sacrifice, courage, and perseverance. These were men and women that should hold the most honoured and respected place in our history and in all ours hearts and minds, not just today but for all time.

On 15th January 1954, at 9.00am, General China was shot in battle in the chin and neck. Nearly forty years later one of the bullets with which he had lived all those years had to be removed by surgery. In the ensuing trial, China was inevitably sentenced to death but his astute lawyer, later to become Judge Cockar, had this sentence commuted to life imprisonment. On 14th April, he was flown to Lokitaung Prison where a fellow-inmate was Jomo Kenyatta. One of the more extraordinary stories of his time in prison was that of Kenyatta giving him English lessons and Mzee insisting, even when extremely ill, that China must do his nightly homework. In November 1959, his life-imprisonment was commuted to "indefinite detention" and on 14th June 1962 China was finally freed to be greeted by a tumultuous reception of thousands in Nyeri on what he called "the happiest day of my life."

China's life in independent Kenya became, as one would expect, a continuing story of selfless service to his country and his people. After further military training both in Kenya and Israel, he found another major task confronting him when on 14th August, 1964 he was posted to the National Youth Service (NYS) with the rank of captain. Waruhiu saw the newly created National Youth Service as both a formidable challenge and a great opportunity. He had taken up arms so that future generations of Kenyans would be free to develop the enormous potential of the human and natural resources of the country. The time had come to turn the swords into ploughshares and, as determined as ever, he vowed to dedicate the rest of his life to the young people of Kenya. His long years in various prisons in remote parts had convinced him that the arid areas of the country could and indeed must be made to help feed the growing population, a view confirmed by his training and observations in Israel. He also passionately believed that the NYS could become the fulcrum for transforming the nation's young people into a productive force imbued with disciplined patriotism, high ideals and strong moral values.

Waruhiu was also a very practical man and he immediately began to translate his vision into practice with his usual enthusiasm and efficiency. Vocational schools were established, experimental agricultural and horticultural units were set up and the potential of irrigation was systematically explored. Meanwhile the NYS rapidly became a byword in industrial and commercial circles for the diligence, courtesy and zeal of its members. China's services to the NYS, from which he retired in November, 1984, were recognized by the Presidential award of the EBS in 1967 and by his appointment as Deputy Director of the Service in 1970.

On 27th April, 1993, Waruhiu Itote—General China—died on his way to Ol-Kalou Hospital after a sudden attack of asthma. He is survived by his three widows, Leah Nyambura, Grace Nduta and Margaret Wanjiru, 15 children, 37 grandchildren and two great grandchildren.

He had no fear of death—he had escaped it many times already in a long and memorable life of achievement. But none of us gathered here today should be in any doubt that we are witnessing the funeral of a very great man, a true son of Kenya, whose high place in the pantheon of Kenya's heroes is permanent and irreplaceable. Those who worked with him during the formation of the NYS and the subsequent years up to the time he retired, consider General China as one of those who contributed most significantly to its growth and development, and the undoubted success it has become today.

# Study Questions

## General

(1) How does China's account of his experiences published in *"Mau Mau" General* differ from evidence that appears in the other sources? How do you explain the discrepancies?

(2) Dedan Kimathi, the leader of Mau Mau, labeled China a "collaborator" for working with the British in 1954, and his acts at that time as "treacherous." Do you agree with Kimathi? Why or why not?

(3) You have read a variety of sources about General China. Is it possible to put yourself in his shoes, and understand his motivations for acting the way he did during the mid-1950s?

(4) How were Mau Mau forces able to hold out against the might of the British Army and its allies for several years?

(5) What sort of challenges faced African peoples as they formed movements to contest colonial rule during the last days of the British Empire?

## "Mau Mau" General

(1) China's memoir was published by East African Publishing House in Nairobi in 1967, more than two decades after some of the events it describes. What effect might this delay have had on China's depiction of the Mau Mau conflict?

(2) How does China characterize Mau Mau? Was it a nationalist movement, ethnic uprising, crime wave, or perhaps some combination of the above?

(3) As John Lonsdale wonders in his Foreword to this collection: "Why does China write of 'Mau Mau' only in quotation marks?"

# Interrogation

(1) Why did China give up information to Ian Henderson of the Special Branch during his interrogation?

(2) What does China's interrogation reveal about the way Mau Mau forces operated—and were organized—in the forests?

# Trial

(1) Why was the judicial system—and the very public exercise of its authority—so important for the colonial administration during the 1950s?

(2) What approach did China take to defend himself during his trial? Why did he not use the public forum to expound upon Mau Mau's merits and justify the conflict?

(3) How would you characterize China's testimony during his trial compared to the text of his interrogation—or indeed his memoir?

(4) Consider the evidence used to condemn China at trial. Do you find the prosecution's case convincing? Why or why not?

# Letter from Waruhiu Itote to Chief Mechanical Engineer

(1) Published on October 16, 1953, this letter provides a first-hand window into China's state of mind while in the forests. What does a close reading of the letter reveal? What does it show us about China's personality?

# The Historiography of Mau Mau

## BY MYLES OSBORNE

Though it is difficult to produce an accurate estimate of the numbers of books and articles written about Mau Mau, the movement has likely inspired more scholarly production than almost any other topic in the history of sub-Saharan Africa.[1] Primary sources, too, abound: they range from government reports produced during the 1950s, to accounts by British policemen involved in the conflict, to a wealth of memoirs written by Africans. As a result, this short essay is only a point of entry into the literature.

As Mau Mau began during the 1950s, the world was instantly fascinated. The term "Mau Mau" itself quickly became a household word: parents in Britain told their children to eat their vegetables otherwise Mau Mau would come and "get them," and the term soon entered the Oxford English Dictionary meaning "to intimidate, harass; to terrorize."[2] Because Mau Mau leaders faced tremendous difficulties portraying their version of the conflict to the world's press, British efforts to depict the movement as an irrational, semi-religious cult—whose members were violent, bestial savages—were highly successful. The two official government publications on Mau Mau were, of course, less sensationalist, though not by much. John Carothers, a psychologist, wrote a report in the midst of the conflict (at the behest of the Government of Kenya) in which he explained Mau Mau as appearing as a result of the breakdown of "tribe" caused by the modern world. This produced "anxiety.... [Which] often takes forms ... of unconstraint and violence," Carothers noted, though he also suggested that the Kikuyu deserved a more active role in the colony's political system.[3] Frank Corfield authored the second report in 1960, at the end of the conflict. It was a far more extensive work and laid the blame for Mau Mau firmly at the feet of Jomo Kenyatta, in a broad attempt to discredit Mau Mau as lacking any legitimate political grievances.[4]

For many, the most authoritative European voice was that belonging to Louis Leakey, the "white Kikuyu" and consultant of sorts for the Kenya Government on all things "Mau Mau." In *Mau Mau and the Kikuyu* (1952), Leakey provided a glowing account of Kikuyu traditions and customs. These institutions, he argued, had come under tension from the implementation of the colonial system. Irresponsible ("semi-educated") Kikuyu intellectuals had egged on their people to view themselves as the recipients of tremendous wrongs at the hands of the British, resulting in the outbreak of violence.[5]

A series of memoirs written by Europeans—and one American, William Baldwin—provided more simplistic and less sympathetic accounts of the conflict. Baldwin—a University of Colorado graduate— found himself fighting on the British side in central Kenya after several years of global wandering had led him to Mombasa in April 1954. He wrote a deeply racist account in which he justified his frequent executions of Mau Mau because they were sub-human.[6] Others, like Ian Henderson—who interrogated China in 1954, and captured Kimathi in 1957—and Fred Majdalany provided toned down but nevertheless strong attacks on the character and morals of Mau Mau fighters, who appeared as primitive and backward in their accounts.[7]

These portrayals were arguably more widely spread, however, through popular culture. In the United States and Britain, Mau Mau was—and to some extent, rather extraordinarily, still is—defined by Robert Ruark's novel, *Something of Value*.[8] Published in 1955—and made into a feature film in 1957, starring Rock Hudson and Sidney Poitier—Ruark told the story of Peter, the son of a European settler, who was raised with a Kikuyu boy, Kimani.[9] Though Peter and Kimani are initially friends in the fictional account, they grow apart: Kimani joins Mau Mau, and at the end of the book, Peter executes him (though in the film version, he falls into a spiked pit). The novel was a bestseller, and—as one scholar describes—"gory ... with graphic descriptions of killings and mutilations." Both novel and film were blockbusters, and came to constitute the dominant narrative of Mau Mau in the United States. Ruark received $300,000 for the rights to the film from Metro-Goldwyn-Mayer, which was possibly the highest such advance paid at that point in history.[10]

When Kenya became independent, Jomo Kenyatta—certainly no sup-porter of Mau Mau, despite British beliefs—did not even mention the organization in his celebratory speech on that landmark evening of December 12, 1963. Over the following years, he avoided rescinding a colonial-era ban on Mau Mau. Kenyatta expressed his view that Kenyans should "forgive and forget" (though he later occasionally associated him-self with the memory of Mau Mau for political gains).[11] This official amnesia—combined with British policies during the 1950s—meant that the colonial and popular portrayals of Mau Mau were not seriously chal-lenged until the 1960s. Few Mau Mau veterans ever won high positions in government (with notable exceptions including Itote and J.M. Kariuki), meaning that any attempt to rehabilitate Mau Mau's memory had to come largely from outside official channels. Kariuki's autobiography—pub-lished in 1963—was the first such effort, which recounted his experiences in the colony's detention camps. He depicted Mau Mau as an entirely rational response to the harsh colonial regime.[12]

Two works published in 1966 expanded the scope of Kariuki's efforts. The first—*The Myth of "Mau Mau"*—was co-authored by University of California, Berkeley scholar Carl Rosberg, already an established author-ity on Kenya, and the former British district officer, John Nottingham. In what quickly became a foundational text, Rosberg and Nottingham con-ceived of Mau Mau as a nationalist movement. They viewed it as follow-ing in a long line of African-led protest movements against colonial rule in Kenya from the 1920s onward.[13] The second was the first memoir authored by a forest fighter, Karari Njama.[14] Njama was Dedan Kimathi's secretary, and together with Donald Barnett, produced a lengthy account of the forest war. (This was the first of four memoirs co-authored by Barnett and former Mau Mau.[15]) Since the early 1950s, Njama had been occupied with recording the movement's history in the forests, desiring to give it legitimacy and ensure it was remembered in the decades that fol-lowed. The account powerfully rejected British depictions of disorgan-ized "terrorists" by demonstrating how Mau Mau forces employed formal systems of military rank, and organized themselves according to British standards of battalion, company, and section.

The following year, Itote wrote *"Mau Mau" General*, a book which needs little introduction to readers of this collection—and over the following decade, Nottingham's East African Publishing House (later Transafrica) became further engaged in the business of recording Mau Mau accounts. During the 1970s, it produced five: three were forest memoirs;[16] one a somewhat scattered series of remembrances by Itote;[17] and the last the memoirs of Bildad Kaggia. The latter was of immense value: an account by a Mau Mau luminary who had enjoyed political power until his socialist ideas in government led to his fall from grace. The book contained a strong exhortation that the Kenya Government address its failings in honoring those who had sacrificed much to secure the country's freedom.[18]

By the 1970s, more scholars had turned their attention to Mau Mau. Reflecting a popular approach to historical method at the time, Dutch historian Robert Buijtenhuijs depicted Mau Mau as a peasant uprising,[19] something later expanded upon by Wunyabari Maloba.[20] In Kenya, the country's senior historian Bethwell Ogot challenged scholars to begin asking difficult questions about Mau Mau, especially given that the "loyalists"—who had sided with the colonial government during the conflict—had profited in the postcolonial era. "What was the anatomy of the Loyalist crowd?" he asked in his presidential address at the Historical Association of Kenya Annual Conference in 1971, "[They] won the military war, lost their argument, but still dominate in Kenya."[21]

In Kenya, Mau Mau was even more significant for the disenfranchised than for scholars. In the 1970s, it formed part of a political struggle between Kenyan activists—representing the poor and jobless—and the government of Jomo Kenyatta. The most prominent intellectual at the time was Ngugi wa Thiong'o, who became one of Africa's most famous novelists and playwrights over the following decades. In 1976, Ngugi's play *Ngaahika Ndeenda (I Will Marry When I Want)* led to his arrest and detention because of its political themes: the play suggested that Mau Mau had not fought for freedom from British colonialists to have them simply replaced with African elites who behaved in the same manner.[22] The play was followed by the better known *The Trial of Dedan Kimathi*—co-authored with Micere Mugo—that lauded Dedan Kimathi as a Kenyan hero and attacked neo-colonialism.[23]

Outside Kenya, Ogot's challenge to think more deeply about the conflict inspired scholars in the 1980s and early 1990s to provide a wealth of information on the involvement of women (though Kathy Santilli had first broached the issue a decade earlier).[24] Cora Ann Presley, Tabitha Kanogo, and Luise White all explored how women participated in the conflict, and revealed how it was impossible to understand Mau Mau without addressing its gendered aspects.[25] Books by Kanogo, Frank Furedi, and David Throup published at the same time provided a never-before-seen level of detail in reconstructing precisely *why* Mau Mau appeared.[26] All paid close attention to the "squatters," landless Kikuyu who labored on European farms, who were evicted during the mid- to late 1940s. Throup and Furedi particularly tried to understand why a combination of economic, social, and governmental factors provoked the uprising of the early 1950s.

The study of Mau Mau—and indeed the African continent—was transformed by John Lonsdale's book-length essay, "The Moral Economy of Mau Mau" in 1992. It reflected a career of deep thought on the nature of ethnicity, and engagement with Kikuyu society. Lonsdale suggested that trauma in the Kikuyu "moral economy" sat at the core of understanding Mau Mau. Mau Mau was a crisis of gender and generation: the previous thirty years of colonial rule had caused deep fissures in the ordered functioning of society that had exploded in the early 1950s. Lonsdale's argument, moreover, provided a new way to understand ethnicity in sub-Saharan Africa: it separated the virtues and values that members of a group believed constituted their core cultural material from the distinct external manifestations of ethnicity that he labeled "political tribalism."[27] Lonsdale's work was inspired in part by knowledge derived from Greet Kershaw's careful fieldwork in central Kenya during the late 1950s and early 1960s, which appeared in a monograph in 1997.[28]

Just as it seemed that scholarship on Mau Mau had quieted, it experienced a resurgence during the early years of the twenty-first century. This began with an important edited volume by E.S. Atieno Odhiambo and Lonsdale. *Mau Mau and Nationhood* collected essays by twelve of the world's foremost scholars on the subject to push forward the frontiers of research. Lonsdale further developed his ideas about gender and generational authority among the Kikuyu; Joanna Lewis looked at Mau Mau and the popular press in Britain; Marshall Clough wrote about memory;

Kennell Jackson and David Anderson did the "real military history" of Mau Mau; and Derek Peterson demonstrated how Mau Mau participants utilized writing and records to "imagine a sovereign state" that transcended potential divisions in the Kikuyu population, and provided an alternative to the British system of rule.[29]

But it was two monographs—published in 2005—that were chiefly responsible for driving Mau Mau back into the public eye in a way reminiscent of the 1950s: David Anderson's *Histories of the Hanged* and Caroline Elkins' Pulitzer Prize-winning *Imperial Reckoning*.[30] Anderson used the criminal cases of the 1,090 hanged Mau Mau fighters as a lens through which to view the conflict, producing its first "informed and candid general history."[31] His marshaling of the trial transcripts permitted an extraordinary glimpse into the minds and social lives of Mau Mau activists. Elkins explored the world of the "detention and rehabilitation" camps into which the British thrust over 80,000 Kikuyu.

Elkins' work, in particular, was controversial.[32] Some Kenyanist scholars believed that it simplified the complex intra-Kikuyu relationships that Lonsdale had highlighted, and minimized the abilities that Kikuyu Mau Mau possessed to negotiate against the colonial state, and maintain control of their social lives.[33] John Blacker took issue with Elkins' casualty figures, though he accepted that it was practically impossible to estimate the number of deaths and "unaccounted for" persons with much accuracy.[34] The book was received with great fanfare in Kenya, and provided a catalyst to the legal case brought against Britain by former Mau Mau.

The case pitted the Kenya Human Rights Commission and Mau Mau War Veterans' Association against the British Government. The two groups argued that Mau Mau veterans were the victims of systematic, government-sanctioned torture in Kenya's detention camps. The case dragged on until 2013, when—against all odds—the veterans won in a landmark decision. Academics Anderson, Elkins, and Huw Bennett gave expert testimonies during the case, drawing their evidence in part from a vast number of documents discovered at a government-owned country estate in 2011. Bennett's book *Fighting the Mau Mau*—the first to use material from these documents—appeared in 2013. In it, Bennett demonstrated how despite the best efforts of their higher-ups, British troops and their loyalist allies were able to torture and beat suspects with something approaching impunity.[35]

In the intervening period, a variety of new approaches to Mau Mau had appeared. Daniel Branch added a further layer of complexity to the movement by revealing the flexibility of the categories "loyalist" and "Mau Mau." People moved between the two as best suited their circumstances, often alternating several times between the ostensibly different camps.[36] Others extended scholarly analysis beyond the Kikuyu: Sana Aiyar, Julie MacArthur, and Myles Osborne analyzed how several of Kenya's other groups (Indians, Luyia, and Kamba respectively) negotiated the conflict.[37] And Lotte Hughes showed how Kenyans have debated the memorialization of Mau Mau in recent years. Mau Mau veterans and other non-state groups have tried to "rewrite" history (in part through museum exhibits), sometimes situating Mau Mau as an episode in a longer trend of multi-ethnic anti-colonial protest.[38]

In a book review published in the *Journal of African History* in 1988, Frederick Cooper wrote: "As the frontiers of research into archives and oral traditions push into the era of decolonization, Mau Mau seems more elusive than ever. The people who were involved spoke with many voices, and so now do the historians." Cooper's statement evoke the complexity and variety of research on Mau Mau, which is further complicated year after year by the repeated political uses of its memory for contemporary ends.[39] On several occasions, it has seemed that there is surely nothing more to be written on the movement; yet such moments of potential satisfaction are inevitably ruined by outbursts of new and original research that reveals more about not just Mau Mau, but the history of sub-Saharan Africa.

# Notes

## Foreword

1. Christopher Cheney, *Medieval Texts and Studies* (Oxford: Clarendon Press, 1973), 8.

2. Do the records before us here, for instance, give any support to the view that, later in his career, Henderson would become the alleged "butcher of Bahrain"? John Nottingham was a junior British administrative officer during the Emergency, regarded as "soft" by many of his colleagues but as "the good district officer" by many Kikuyu. Since independence he has lived in Kenya as a Kenyan citizen.

## Introduction

1. John Nottingham, Eulogy: Waruhiu Itote, May 7, 1993.
2. Kimathi to Kago, March 2, 1954, in Maina wa Kinyatti, ed., *Kenya's Freedom Struggle: The Dedan Kimathi Papers* (London: Zed Books, 1987), 77. Kimathi's sentiments were certainly not unique (see below), but it is important to note that Kinyatti's reproductions of Kimathi's letters are problematic. Cristiana Pugliese, in particular, has questioned the fidelity of his translations from Kikuyu into English, and few except Kinyatti have ever had access to the original letters. Cristiana Pugliese, "The Organic Vernacular Intellectual in Kenya: Gakaara wa Wanjau," *Research in African Literatures* 25 (1994): 177-97.
3. The Kikuyu numbered 1,026,431 out of an African population of 5,251,120 (19.5 percent). Colony and Protectorate of Kenya, *African Population of Kenya Colony and Protectorate: Geographical and Tribal Studies* (Nairobi: East African Statistical Department, 1950), 6.
4. Cege wa Kibiru—nicknamed Mugo—lived between c. 1850 and 1908. Godfrey Muriuki, "Cege wa Kibiru," in *Dictionary of African Biography*, Vol. III, eds. Emmanuel Akyeampong and Henry Louis Gates (New York: Oxford University Press, 2012), 49-50.
5. On the early years of British administration in East Africa see Marie de

263

Kiewiet Hemphill, "The British Sphere, 1884-94," in *History of East Africa*, Vol. I, eds. Roland Oliver and Gervase Mathew (Oxford: Clarendon Press, 1963), 390-432, and in Kenya, Gordon Mungeam, *British Rule in Kenya, 1895-1912: The Establishment of Administration in the East Africa Protectorate* (Oxford: Clarendon Press, 1966).

6. In King Leopold's words. Adam Hochschild, *King Leopold's Ghost: A Story of Greed, Terror, and Heroism in Central Africa* (Boston, MA: Houghton Mifflin, 1998), 58.

7. Alice Conklin, *A Mission to Civilize: The Republican Idea of Empire in France and West Africa, 1895-1930* (Stanford, CA: Stanford University Press, 1997).

8. Sir Charles Eliot, *The East Africa Protectorate* (London: E. Arnold, 1905), 178-79.

9. Frederick Lugard, *The Dual Mandate in British Tropical Africa* (London: W. Blackwood and Sons, 1922).

10. David Anderson, *Histories of the Hanged: The Dirty War in Kenya and the End of Empire* (New York: W.W. Norton, 2005), 345.

11. Richard Wolff, *The Economics of Colonialism: Britain and Kenya, 1870-1930* (New Haven, CT: Yale University Press, 1974), 47-67; Tiyambe Zeleza, "The Establishment of Colonial Rule, 1905-1920," in *A Modern History of Kenya, 1895-1980*, ed. William Ochieng' (Nairobi: Evans Brothers, 1989), 35-70.

12. Rita Headrick, "African Soldiers in World War II," *Armed Forces & Society* 4 (1978): 503-4.

13. For a useful overview see David Killingray and Richard Rathbone, eds., *Africa and the Second World War* (New York: St. Martin's Press, 1986).

14. *The Atlantic Charter*, 1941, accessed February 25, 2014. http://www.nato.int/cps/en/natolive/official_texts_16912.htm.

15. Fay Gadsden, "The African Press in Kenya, 1945-1952," *Journal of African History* 21 (1980): 515.

16. John Spencer, *The Kenya African Union* (London: KPI, 1985), 182.

17. Reserves were areas of land designated for habitation by Africans. They were often overpopulated.

18. Frank Furedi, *The Mau Mau War in Perspective* (London: James Currey, 1989), 52-54.

19. For more on the lead-up to Mau Mau see Tabitha Kanogo, *Squatters and the Roots of Mau Mau, 1905-63* (London: James Currey, 1987), and David Throup, *Economic and Social Origins of Mau Mau, 1945-53* (London: James Currey, 1988).

20. John Lonsdale's seminal essay on Kikuyu society demonstrates how a crisis in the "moral economy" contributed to the outbreak of Mau Mau. See John Lonsdale, "The Moral Economy of Mau Mau: Wealth, Poverty & Civic

Virtue in Kikuyu Political Thought," in *Unhappy Valley: Conflict in Kenya and Africa*, Book II: *Violence and Ethnicity*, eds. Bruce Berman and John Lonsdale (London: James Currey, 1992), 315-504.

21. There are many theories: some argue that the Mau Escarpment serves as its inspiration, others that Mau Mau was a name assigned by British administrators who mistranslated "Uma Uma" (get out, get out) as "Mau Mau." Perhaps the most likely explanation, though, is "greedy-eaters," which relates to the generational tensions in the insecure Kikuyu world that existed at the time. See John Lonsdale, "Authority, Gender and Violence: The War within Mau Mau's Fight for Land and Freedom," in *Mau Mau and Nationhood: Arms, Authority & Narration*, eds. E.S. Atieno Odhiambo and John Lonsdale (Oxford: James Currey, 2003), 59-60.

22. Lonsdale, "Moral Economy," 446.

23. For more on Waruhiu see Evanson Wamagatta, "African Collaborators and Their Quest for Power in Colonial Kenya: Senior Chief Waruhiu wa Kung'u's Rise from Obscurity to Prominence, 1890-1922," *International Journal of African Historical Studies* 41 (2008): 295-314.

24. Opuku Agyeman, *Nkrumah's Ghana and East Africa: Pan-Africanism and African Interstate Relations* (Cranbury, NJ: Associated University Presses, 1992), 58-67.

25. On the international aspect of Mau Mau see A.S. Cleary, "The Myth of Mau Mau in Its International Context," *African Affairs* 89 (1990): 227-45, and Dane Kennedy, "Constructing the Colonial Myth of Mau Mau," *International Journal of African Historical Studies* 25 (1992): 241-60.

26. Gerald Horne, *Mau Mau in Harlem? The U.S. and the Liberation of Kenya* (New York: Palgrave Macmillan, 2009).

27. Lonsdale, "Moral Economy" and "Authority, Gender and Violence."

28. See the work of Maina wa Kinyatti in this regard. Kinyatti, ed., *Kenya's Freedom Struggle,* and Maina wa Kinyatti, ed., *Thunder from the Mountains: Mau Mau Patriotic Songs* (London: Zed Press, 1980).

29. Wunyabari Maloba, *Mau Mau and Kenya: An Analysis of a Peasant Revolt* (Bloomington: Indiana University Press, 1993).

30. Waruhiu Itote, *"Mau Mau" General* (Nairobi: East African Publishing House, 1967), 16-22.

31. Itote, *General*, 23-29; Hubert Moyse-Bartlett, *The King's African Rifles: A Study in the Military History of East and Central Africa, 1890-1945* (Aldershot, UK: Gale & Polden, 1956), 610-62. On the experiences of African soldiers during the Second World War see David Killingray's work, most recently David Killingray with Martin Plaut, *Fighting for Britain: African Soldiers in the Second World War* (Woodbridge, UK: James Currey, 2010).

32. Itote, *General*, 9-15.

33. Itote, *General*, 30-37.

34. Throup, *Origins*, 173.
35. Anderson, *Histories*, 36-37; Timothy Parsons, *The African Rank-and-File: Social Implications of Colonial Military Service in the King's African Rifles, 1902-1964* (Portsmouth, NH: Heinemann, 1999), 230-60. For more on the Olenguruone squatters see Kanogo, *Squatters*, 96-124.
36. For an introduction to the Mau Mau oath see Marshall Clough, *Mau Mau Memoirs: History, Memory, and Politics* (Boulder, CO: Lynne Rienner, 1998), 85-125.
37. For a representative "European" perspective (although he was an American), see William Baldwin, *Mau Mau Man-Hunt: The Adventures of the Only American Who Has Fought the Terrorists in Kenya* (New York: Dutton, 1957), 94, or Louis Leakey, *Defeating Mau Mau* (London: Methuen, 1954), 84-85.
38. Itote, *General*, 40; H.K. Wachanga, *The Swords of Kirinyaga: The Fight for Land and Freedom* (Kampala: East African Literature Bureau, 1975), 35; Joram Wamweya, *Freedom Fighter* (Kampala: East African Literature Bureau, 1971), 52.
39. Itote, *General*, 40-49.
40. Richard Frost, "Sir Philip Mitchell, Governor of Kenya," *African Affairs* 78 (1979): 552.
41. It is unclear how Itote chose his forest name. Ali Mazrui suggests that it was perhaps related to Mau Mau's admiration for Chinese fighters serving in the Korean War or in Malaya. Ali Mazrui, "Mau Mau: The Men, the Myth and the Moment: A Foreword," in Robert Buijtenhuijs, *Mau Mau Twenty Years On: The Myth and the Survivors* (The Hague: Mouton, 1973), 11.
42. Anderson, *Histories*, 232.
43. Itote, *General*, 88.
44. General Kaleba's name is spelled "Kareba" in some sources and documents. "Kaleba" is used throughout this volume.
45. Gomery—sometimes spelt Ngomery—was a Mau Mau leader whose forest name was inspired by Field Marshal Bernard Montgomery. Montgomery was titled the 1st Viscount Montgomery of Alamein, in honor of his North African victory there in 1942 over combined German and Italian forces.
46. Wachanga, *Swords*, 68-72.
47. Kenya National Archives [hereafter KNA], BB/1/210, Interrogation of Waruhiu Itote ("General China"), January 26, 1954.
48. Clough, *Memoirs*, 10-11.
49. Itote, *General*, 70-74. For more on "forest-craft" see Kennell Jackson, "'Impossible to Ignore Their Greatness': Survival Craft in the Mau Mau Forest Movement," in *Mau Mau and Nationhood*, 176-90.
50. Itote, *General*, 285-91.
51. Men and women in the forests struggled with questions of appropriate gen-

der relations. Lonsdale, "Authority, Gender and Violence," especially 60-(9.

52. Itote *General*, 139-41, 285-91; Lonsdale, "Authority, Gender and Violence," 61.

53. Itote *General*, 56-57.

54. Itote *General*, 147-54.

55. Anderson, *Histories*, 249-50.

56. KNA, AC/3684, Regina vs. Waruhiu Itote ("General China"), Testimony of Desmond Walker, February 1, 1954. Fred Majdalany dismissed the wound as "not severe." Fred Majdalany, *State of Emergency: The Full Story of Mau Mau* (London: Longmans, 1962), 193.

57. Itote *General*, 161-64. On several occasions, China describes Mau Mau receiving assistance from the KAR, although there is little supporting proof for such assertions. During this engagement, it is difficult to believe that KAR soldiers would have helped him, given their roles and the potential penalties for aiding a Mau Mau general. None of the men in this battalion were Kikuyu, in any case, and it is doubtful whether they would have recognized China.

58. Ian Henderson with Philip Goodhart, *The Hunt for Kimathi* (London: H. Hamilton, 1958), 28.

59. An extensive literature exists on interrogation techniques, confession, and the psychology of interrogation, although these topics fall outside the scope of this introduction. See, for instance, Saul Kassin, "The Psychology of Confessions," *Annual Review of Law and Social Science* 4 (2008): 193-217.

60. Information presented here from Henderson's interrogation of Itote is taken from KNA, BB/1/210, Interrogation of Waruhiu Itote ("General China"), January 26, 1954.

61. Henderson died on April 13, 2013. "Ian Henderson," *Telegraph*, April 22, 2013, accessed September 17, 2013. http://www.telegraph.co.uk/news/obituaries/10011292/Ian-Henderson.html.

62. Amnesty International, "Bahrain: A Human Rights Crisis," MDE 11/016/1995, September 25, 1995, accessed December 10, 2011. http://www.amnesty.org/en/library/info/MDE11/016/1995/en. Amnesty International, "Amnesty International Welcomes Investigation into Henderson's Role in Torture in Bahrain," EUR 45/003/2000, January 7, 2000, accessed December 10, 2011. http://www.amnesty.org/en/library/info/EUR45/003/2000/en. See also Rob Cobridge, "Britain's Klaus Barbie Still Walks Free," *New Statesman*, November 29, 1999, 66-67.

63. Caroline Elkins, *Imperial Reckoning: The Untold Story of Britain's Gulag in Kenya* (New York: Henry Holt, 2005).

64. Wambui Otieno, *Mau Mau's Daughter: A Life History* (Boulder, CO: Lynne Rienner, 1998), 64.

65. Itote *General*, 188; Paul Maina, *Six Mau Mau Generals* (Nairobi: Gazelle

Books, 1997), 86; Wachanga, *Swords*, 161-62.

66. As revealed in David Anderson's pioneering work. In his words: "In no other place, and at no other time in the history of British imperialism, was state execution used on such a scale." Anderson, *Histories*, 7.

67. The Kamba comprised a large proportion of the army and police and were considered a "martial race" by the British. See Myles Osborne, *Ethnicity and Empire in Kenya: Loyalty and Martial Race among the Kamba, c. 1800 to the Present* (New York: Cambridge University Press, 2014).

68. Itote, *General*, 164.

69. Itote, *General*, 104, 147-60. See also Waruhiu Itote, *Mau Mau in Action* (Nairobi: Transafrica, 1979), 8-9, 34-40.

70. Itote, *General*, 285-91.

71. Older men, in particular, proved adept at manipulating customary law to suit their own interests, especially with regard to restricting the freedoms of women and the youth. The foundational work on customary law in Britain's colonies is Martin Chanock, *Law, Custom and Social Order: The Colonial Experience in Malawi and Zambia* (Cambridge: Cambridge University Press, 1985). See also Mahmood Mamdani, *Citizen and Subject: Contemporary Africa and the Legacy of Late Colonialism* (Princeton, NJ: Princeton University Press, 1996).

72. The New Emergency Regulations of May 1953 were even more rigid: "It is now an offence, punishable by death, to do, attempt or conspire to do any act likely to endanger life, assist terrorists or impede the operations of the security forces.... The death penalty will also be imposed on anyone who gives, sells, lends, lets out or hires or delivers possession of firearms, ammunition or explosives." KNA, DC/MKS/26/2, "Press Office Handout No. 139: New Emergency Regulations," May 18, 1953.

73. The National Archives of the United Kingdom [hereafter TNA], CAB 21/2906, Baring to Lyttelton (telegram), February 8, 1954.

74. Testimony from the proceedings of Itote's trial is from KNA, AC/3684, Regina vs. Waruhiu Itote ("General China"), February 1-3, 1954.

75. Anderson summarizes their role: "Assessors sat in each trial, drawn from the same ethnic group as the accused. Although they had no powers over the outcome of a case, the judge was required to ask them for their verdicts and to take these views into account." Due to press coverage of the trials—and open courtrooms—assessors' "pronouncements" were known to the public, and many were attacked. Anderson, *Histories*, 198.

76. TNA, CAB 21/2906, Lyttelton to Baring (telegram), February 5, 1954.

77. TNA, CAB 21/2906, Baring to Lyttelton (telegram), February 9, 1954.

78. TNA, WO 32/21902, Report by the Director of Intelligence and Security, "General China—Appreciation," February 11, 1954.

79. TNA, CAB 21/2906, Baring to Lyttelton (telegram), February 9, 1954.

80. TNA, WO 32/21902, Report by the Director of Intelligence and Security, "Future Possible Use of China," February 5, 1954.

81. See, for instance, Parliamentary Debates, House of Commons, vol. 186, cols. 70-71, March 3, 1954.

82. TNA, PREM 11/696, Baring to Lyttelton (telegram), March 1, 1954; Lyttelton to Churchill (telegram), March 7, 1954.

83. KNA, MAC/KEN/34/1, Press Extracts, March 4, 1954.

84. Itote to Kimathi, February 16, 1954, in Kinyatti, ed., *Kenya's Freedom Struggle*, 66-67. Itote signed the letter "Goodbye," still under the assumption that he would be hanged.

85. Presumably a reference to the world-famous china-producing company started by Josiah Wedgwood in 1759. Like Wedgwood china, General China was valuable and required careful handling!

86. Itote, *General*, 188-91.

87. Kimathi to Government, February 16, 1954, in Kinyatti, ed., *Kenya's Freedom Struggle*, 67-68.

88. Statement of Kimathi, April 3, 1954, in Kinyatti, ed., *Kenya's Freedom Struggle*, 68-69.

89. "Kenya Land Freedom Army Charter," in Kinyatti, ed., *Kenya's Freedom Struggle*, 16-17.

90. Anderson, *Histories*, 273-76. A remarkably similar scene appears in the film version of Robert Ruark's *Something of Value* (1957).

91. KNA, DC/TURK/1/10, Lokitaung Sub-District Annual Report, 1953; Elizabeth Watkins, *Jomo's Jailor: Grand Warrior of Kenya: The Life of Leslie Whitehouse* (Watlington, UK: Britwell Books, 1996), 183-89.

92. Itote, *General*, 192-96; Jeremy Murray-Brown, *Kenyatta* (London: G. Allen & Unwin, 1972), 284.

93. Itote, *General*, 212-15.

94. KNA, PC/NFD/8/3, Turkana District Annual Report, 1953; "Letter from Prison," *Observer*, June 8, 1958; Murray-Brown, *Kenyatta*, 294-95; Watkins, *Jomo's Jailor*, 187. For more on the *Observer* letter—and a second that followed it, as well as the inquiries into the allegations in the letters—see correspondence in TNA, FCO 141/6334, 1958.

95. In his second book, Itote describes his detention with Kenyatta but again makes no mention of Chotara's attack. Itote, *Mau Mau in Action*, 113-20.

96. Itote, *General*, 215-17.

97. KNA, AC/3684, Criminal Appeal No. 122 of 1954, February 20, 1954; KNA, AC/3684, Waruhiu Itote: Memorandum of Appeal, February 11, 1954.

98. TNA, WO 216/967, Erskine to War Office, February 27, 1954.

99. Baldwin, *Mau Mau Man-Hunt*, 220.

100. Majdalany, *State of Emergency*, 193; "KENYA: General China and Friends," *Time*, March 15, 1954.

101. Peter Hewitt, *Kenya Cowboy: A Police Officer's Account of the Mau Mau Emergency*, 3d ed. (Johannesburg: 30° South Publishers, 2008 [1999]), 111, 211.
102. Anderson, *Histories*, 266.
103. Kimathi to Kago, March 2, 1954, in Kinyatti, ed., *Kenya's Freedom Struggle*, 77-78. Kinyatti dedicated his book to fifteen Mau Mau generals, not including China.
104. Donald Barnett and Karari Njama, *Mau Mau from Within: Autobiography and Analysis of Kenya's Peasant Revolt* (New York: Monthly Review Press, 1966), 331-32, 357.
105. Richard Coe, *The Kenya National Youth Service: A Governmental Response to Young Political Activists* (Athens: Ohio University Center for International Studies, Africa Program, 1973).
106. Usually, though, Kenyatta preferred to "forgive and forget," the last word in particular his usual watchword for Mau Mau. In the words of two scholars, "a new political culture of orderly amnesia emerged." John Lonsdale and E.S. Atieno Odhiambo, "Introduction," in *Mau Mau and Nationhood*, 4.
107. Anderson, *Histories*, 230; Marshall Clough, "Mau Mau & the Contest for Memory," in *Mau Mau and Nationhood*, 251-67.
108. Ngugi Kabiro and Donald Barnett, *Man in the Middle: The Story of Ngugi Kabiro* (Richmond, BC: Liberation Support Movement, 1973); Mohamed Mathu and Donald Barnett, *The Urban Guerrilla: The Story of Mohamed Mathu* (Richmond, BC: Liberation Support Movement, 1974); Karigo Muchai and Donald Barnett, *The Hardcore: The Story of Karigo Muchai* (Richmond, BC: Liberation Support Movement, 1973).
109. Gucu Gikoyo, *We Fought for Freedom/Tulipigania Uhuru* (Nairobi: East African Publishing House, 1979); Kiboi Muriithi with Peter Ndoria, *War in the Forest* (Nairobi: East African Publishing House, 1971); Wachanga, *Swords*.
110. Mathu, *Urban Guerrilla*, 67. Ngugi wa Thiong'o and Micere Mugo seem to offer a similar criticism of China in their play *The Trial of Dedan Kimathi*. In the play, Henderson calls China a "collaborator," and there is nothing in the text to contradict his assertion. At the end of the play, when two British soldiers and a KAR *askari* are being tried by Kimathi and his leading generals, there is no mention of China. Ngugi wa Thiong'o and Micere Mugo, *The Trial of Dedan Kimathi* (London: Heinemann, 1977), 34, 63.
111. Bildad Kaggia, *Roots of Freedom, 1921-1963: The Autobiography of Bildad Kaggia* (Nairobi: East African Publishing House, 1975); Maina, *Six Mau Mau Generals*.
112. Kariuki dedicated his 1963 account of the Mau Mau struggle to Itote, among many others including Kimathi and Mathenge. J.M. Kariuki, *"Mau Mau" Detainee: The Account by a Kenya African of His Experiences in*

*Detention Camps, 1953-1960* (London: Oxford University Press, 1963).

113. The best account for putting these murders in historical context is Daniel Branch, *Kenya: Between Hope and Despair, 1963-2011* (New Haven, CT: Yale University Press, 2011).
114. Buijtenhuijs, *Twenty Years On*, 48; Clough, *Memoirs*, 75.
115. The classic work that depicts Mau Mau as a nationalist struggle is Carl Rosberg and John Nottingham, *The Myth of "Mau Mau": Nationalism in Kenya* (New York: Meridian, 1970 [1966]).
116. Itote, *General*, 210-11.
117. Majdalany, *State of Emergency*, 195.
118. Itote, *General*, 180.
119. Itote, *General*, 176, 179.
120. Lonsdale, "Moral Economy."
121. TNA, WO 32/21902, Report by the Director of Intelligence and Security, "Future Possible Use of China," February 5, 1954; TNA, WO 32/21902, Report by the Director of Intelligence and Security, "General China—Appreciation," February 11, 1954.
122. Itote, *General*, 137-38.
123. TNA, WO 32/21902, Report by the Director of Intelligence and Security, "Future Possible Use of China," February 5, 1954; TNA, WO 32/21902, Report by the Director of Intelligence and Security, "General China—Appreciation," February 11, 1954.
124. Bodleian Library of Commonwealth and African Studies at Rhodes House, Mss. Afr. s. 235, Papers of George Gibson, Itote to Chief Mechanical Engineer, East African Railways and Harbours, October 16, 1953.
125. Clough, *Memoirs*, 230-32; Itote, *General*, 260, 270-72.
126. "He Lived with a Bullet for 34 Years," *Daily Nation*, April 15, 1988.

# "Mau Mau" General

1. See Introduction, footnote 17, page 264 for an explanation of the "reserve" system.
2. D.F. Malan was prime minister of South Africa between 1948 and 1954. The foundations of the apartheid system were laid down during his premiership.
3. Kenyatta's nickname. A respectful Swahili term literally meaning "old man."
4. China is referring to Toussaint L'Ouverture, who led the successful slave rebellion against the French in St. Domingue (later Haiti) from 1791 until 1802.
5. The "villagization" process was a British effort to isolate Mau Mau, by preventing them from communicating with—or receiving assistance from—the

reserve inhabitants. Much of the civilian Kikuyu population was forced to live in enclosed villages under curfew. Abuses were common.

6. A collective punishment imposed to try to dissuade people from harboring sympathies with Mau Mau. It reflected the British inability to separate civilians from Mau Mau fighters.

7. See Introduction, footnote 75, page 268 for a fuller explanation of the assessors' role.

8. See footnotes 5 and 6 above for an explanation about these villages and the "special tax."

9. According to Kikuyu lore, Gikuyu and his wife Mumbi were the original couple from whom all other Kikuyu are descended.

# Interrogation

1. Circumcision was an important rite of passage that marked the transition between childhood and adulthood.

2. In China's autobiography—as well as Nottingham's eulogy—it is stated that China attended Church of Scotland schools. "CMS"—an abbreviation often used to refer to the Church Missionary Society—is likely a misprint in both instances here.

3. The East African Military Labour Service employed men to work as drivers, road-builders, and so forth. They did not serve as soldiers like the men of the King's African Rifles.

4. See Introduction, footnote 17, page 264.

5. See Introduction, pages 7-8.

6. British officials believed that someone who had taken the Mau Mau oath could be "cleansed" of its hold by Kikuyu elders. These elders were occasionally known as "Her Majesty's Witchdoctors."

7. The colony's highest representative political body. Though multiracial, the first African only entered the Council in 1944, and it was dominated by Europeans.

8. *Barafu* means "ice" in Swahili, presumably a reference to the high altitude and cold of the headquarters.

9. See *"Mau Mau" General*, pages 70-73 for details on the Naivasha Raid.

10. The terminology here is significant. From the perspective of the colonial government, the Mau Mau conflict was an "Emergency" and "crime wave." If it was termed a "war," a series of international treaties to which Britain was a signatory would have come into force, including the Geneva Convention of 1949 that governed the treatment of prisoners of war.

11. Also spelled "Ngomery"—see Introduction, footnote 45, page 266.

12. His Excellency—the governor of the colony, Evelyn Baring.

13. Presumably named after Kabaka Mutesa II of Buganda. "Kabaka" is an honorific title given to the King of Buganda, one of Uganda's oldest kingdoms. During the 1950s, Mutesa II was exiled from the British protectorate of Uganda for opposing a potential East African Federation of Uganda, Kenya, and Tanganyika (under British rule). He became something of an African hero as a result of his actions.

14. A mile-wide section of cleared land at the edge of the forest, designed to make it difficult for Mau Mau or their supporters to communicate or transfer supplies.

15. Presumably named after Emperor Hirohito of Japan whose countrymen fought against the Allies during the Second World War.

16. The battalion presumably gained its name from the infamous Colonial Paper 210, which Africans called "Haraka Two Ten." The paper—published in February 1947—"repudiated the principle of racial equality" that was promised by Colonial Paper 191 of December 1945. Bethwell Ogot, "Mau Mau and Nationhood: The Untold Story," in *Mau Mau and Nationhood: Arms, Authority & Narration*, eds. E.S. Atieno Odhiambo and John Lonsdale (Athens: Ohio University Press, 2003), 18. Atieno Odhiambo goes further and refers to the period between 1945 and 1955 as the "Age of 210," characterized by urban poverty, fear, and a reassertion of colonial control, amongst other things. E.S. Atieno Odhiambo, "The Formative Years, 1945-1955," in *Decolonization and Independence in Kenya*, eds. Bethwell Ogot and William Ochieng' (Oxford: James Currey, 1995), 25-27. Coincidentally—perhaps?—employees at the Kenya National Archives filed China's interrogation under the reference BB/1/210.

17. China is referring to government-appointed chiefs and headmen, the most visible faces of the colonial system in the villages, and notorious for abuses of power.

18. The War Department was renamed the War Office in 1857, but the old term was still in common usage. The War Office was the department of the British Government responsible for the army.

19. This is probably nothing to do with the Special Air Service, the elite force of the British Army. More likely, it refers to a Salvation Army Superintendent or Station—or perhaps Settled Area Surgery—hence explaining the medical connection. I am grateful to John Lonsdale for his thoughts on this acronym.

20. See footnote 14 above.

21. See *"Mau Mau" General*, footnote 5, page 272.

22. See *"Mau Mau" General*, footnote 6, page 272.

23. Compare China's response here to Letter, pages 243-45.

# Trial

1. Queen Elizabeth II, represented here by the colonial government and more directly by the deputy public prosecutor, Somerhough.
2. Here, Somerhough informs the court that he will not seek to prosecute China on the original four charges (see Introduction). Consequently, China is temporarily free, at which point Somerhough refiles to charge China with the two counts that constitute the content of this case.
3. See Introduction, footnote 75, page 268 for a fuller explanation of the assessors' role.
4. Africans took different oaths in court depending on whether they were Christian or not.
5. Sections labeled "Court" contain either responses to MacDuff's clarificatory questions, or the judge's summaries.
6. For more information on the Kamba see Introduction, footnote 67, page 268.
7. Judge MacDuff comments on this confusing evidence below.
8. Young is presumably explaining that he faced west from a location on the map where the "I" in the word "Ichuga" appears.
9. See Introduction, pages 27-28 for details on the surrender offers.
10. This serves to prove that the bullets were—from a technical, legal perspective—"ammunition." See Trial, page 237.
11. MacDuff determines that Collins did not properly caution China about his rights.
12. Arthur Barlow—the thirteenth prosecution witness (see below)—was a Scotsman, and one of Kenya's best-known missionaries. He had spent much of the past half-century living in the colony, and was one of the foremost experts on the Kikuyu language. For more on Barlow see Robert Macpherson, *The Presbyterian Church in Kenya: An Account of the Origins and Growth of the Presbyterian Church of East Africa* (Nairobi: Presbyterian Church of East Africa, 1970) and Derek Peterson, *Creative Writing: Translation, Bookkeeping, and the Work of Imagination in Colonial Kenya* (Athens: Ohio University Press, 2004).
13. See Interrogation, footnote 7, page 272.
14. See Introduction, footnote 17, page 264.
15. This was most likely a Church of Scotland mission school. See Interrogation, footnote 2, page 272.
16. This spelling was commonly used by China and appears sporadically throughout the trial transcript.
17. Either China is mistaken, or the original typescript contains an error. The surrender offer did not excuse murder.
18. This section is somewhat confusing. China seems to be responding to

Cockar's questions about a series of letters he authored that had been entered into evidence.

19. The prosecution contends that "finished" means "killed." China rejects this meaning (above).
20. People who surrendered were meant to hold green branches to show their intentions.
21. Here China vocalizes his defense to Count 2 of the indictment: the ammunition discovered in his pocket was planted.
22. Here China tries to separate himself from the Mau Mau "gang" in the engagement on January 15 to defend himself against the charge of "consorting" (Count 1).
23. A rhetorical question: the Crown has not charged China with murder.
24. That is to say, the surrender offer has no basis in the colony's laws.
25. References to Emergency Regulations 8A and 8C are mixed up in parts of the original transcript. They are corrected here. Regulation 8C relates to "consorting"—Count 1 of the indictment. It variously appears as "8C" and "8C(1)" in the trial transcript. Section 8C of the Emergency Regulations, 1952 states: "Any person who … consorts with or is found in the company of another person who is carrying any firearm, ammunition, explosive substance or arms, in circumstances which raise a reasonable presumption that he intends to or is about to act with, or has recently acted with such other person in a manner prejudicial to the public safety, or the preservation of the peace, shall be guilty of an offence against these Regulations." "Emergency Regulations, 1952," in the *Kenya Official Gazette Supplement No. 50*, October 21, 1952. Cited in Colony and Protectorate of Kenya, *Proclamations, Rules and Regulations*, Vol. 31 (Nairobi: Government Printer, 1953), 491-502.
26. If the gang members were carrying guns, then China could be found "consorting" with "persons carrying firearms."
27. Regulation 8A relates to the possession of ammunition—Count 2 of the indictment. It variously appears as "8A" and "8A(1)" in the trial transcript. Section 8A of the Emergency Regulations, 1952 states: "The Governor may … prohibit, either absolutely or subject to such exception as he may prescribe, the buying, selling or otherwise dealing in any arms, parts of arms, ammunition or explosive substance … if any person contravenes such an order or direction he shall be guilty of an offence against these Regulations." "Emergency Regulations, 1952," in the *Kenya Official Gazette Supplement No. 50*, October 21, 1952. Cited in Kenya, *Proclamations*, 491-502.
28. MacDuff mistakenly refers to Kioki as "Kioto" throughout his judgment. The text has been corrected.
29. The court is obliged to offer a convicted person the chance to make a statement before sentencing.

30. A shortening of the legal term *obiter dictum*. The term refers to part of a judge's decision which is "beside the point" and irrelevant to issues of legal determination.
31. In short: the surrender offer is irrelevant because Judge MacDuff did not believe that China was in the process of surrendering on January 15, 1954.

## Letter from Waruhiu Itote to Chief Mechanical Engineer

1. See also Interrogation, page 191.

## Eulogy

1. Elder of the Order of the Burning Spear, a high-level state commendation in independent Kenya.

## The Historiography of Mau Mau

1. Marshall Clough, Kennell Jackson, and Thomas Ofcansky have published useful bibliographies on Mau Mau, though they are by now extremely dated. Ofcansky's contains a particularly valuable series of references to articles on Mau Mau published in various newspapers in Africa during the 1950s. Marshall Clough and Kennell Jackson, *Mau Mau Syllabus*, Vol. II: *A Bibliography on Mau Mau* (Stanford, CA: Stanford University Press, 1975); Thomas Ofcansky, "The Mau Mau Revolt in Kenya, 1952-1960: A Preliminary Bibliography," *Africana Journal* 15 (1990): 97-126.
2. Joanna Lewis, "'Daddy Wouldn't Buy Me a Mau Mau': The British Popular Press and the Demoralisation of Empire," in *Mau Mau and Nationhood: Arms, Authority & Narration*, eds. E.S. Atieno Odhiambo and John Lonsdale (Athens: Ohio University Press, 2003), 227-50; *Oxford English Dictionary*, v. "mau-mau," accessed October 4, 2013. http://www.oed.com.
3. J.C. Carothers, *The Psychology of Mau Mau* (Nairobi: Government Printer, 1954), 3.
4. F.D. Corfield, *Historical Survey of the Origins and Growth of Mau Mau* (London: H.M.S.O., 1960).
5. Louis Leakey, *Mau Mau and the Kikuyu* (London: Methuen, 1952). See also Louis Leakey, *Defeating Mau Mau* (London: Methuen, 1954).
6. William Baldwin, *Mau Mau Man-Hunt: The Adventures of the Only American Who Has Fought the Terrorists in Kenya* (New York: Dutton, 1957).

7. Ian Henderson with Philip Goodhart, *The Hunt for Kimathi* (London: H. Hamilton, 1958); Fred Majdalany, *State of Emergency: The Full Story of Mau Mau* (Boston, MA: Houghton Mifflin, 1963).

8. Robert Ruark, *Something of Value* (Garden City, NJ: Doubleday, 1955).

9. Several films about Mau Mau—or Kenya more broadly—appeared during the conflict, including *Mogambo*, which starred Clark Gable, Grace Kelly, and Ava Gardner. See David Anderson, "Mau Mau at the Movies: Contemporary Recollections of an Anti-Colonial War," *South African Historical Journal* 48 (2003): 71-89.

10. Gerald Horne, *Mau Mau in Harlem? The U.S. and the Liberation of Kenya* (New York: Palgrave Macmillan, 2009), 121-28. Horne's work provides a deep analysis of the links between the United States and Kenya during the 1950s.

11. On the political use of Mau Mau's memory see Marshall Clough, "Mau Mau and the Contest for Memory," in *Mau Mau and Nationhood*, 251-67, and Caroline Elkins and John Lonsdale, "Memories of Mau Mau in Kenya: Public Crises and Private Shame," in *Memoria e Violenza*, ed. Alessandro Triulzi (Napoli: L'Ancora del Mediterraneo, 2005), 42-71.

12. J.M. Kariuki, *"Mau Mau" Detainee: The Account by a Kenya African of his Experiences in Detention Camps, 1953-1960* (London: Oxford University Press, 1963).

13. Carl Rosberg and John Nottingham, *The Myth of "Mau Mau": Nationalism in Kenya* (New York: Meridian, 1970 [1966]).

14. Karari Njama and Donald Barnett, *Mau Mau from Within: Autobiography and Analysis of Kenya's Peasant Revolt* (London: Macgibbon and Kee, 1966).

15. Ngugi Kabiro and Donald Barnett, *Man in the Middle: The Story of Ngugi Kabiro* (Richmond, BC: Liberation Support Movement, 1973); Mohamed Mathu and Donald Barnett, *The Urban Guerrilla: The Story of Mohamed Mathu* (Richmond, BC: Liberation Support Movement, 1974); Karigo Muchai and Donald Barnett, *The Hardcore: The Story of Karigo Muchai* (Richmond, BC: Liberation Support Movement, 1973).

16. Gucu Gikoyo, *We Fought for Freedom/Tulipigania Uhuru* (Nairobi: East African Publishing House, 1979); Kiboi Muriithi with Peter Ndoria, *War in the Forest* (Nairobi: East African Publishing House, 1971); Joram Wamweya, *Freedom Fighter* (Nairobi: East African Publishing House, 1971).

17. Waruhiu Itote, *Mau Mau in Action* (Nairobi: Transafrica, 1979).

18. Bildad Kaggia, *Roots of Freedom, 1921-1963: The Autobiography of Bildad Kaggia* (Nairobi: East African Publishing House, 1975). See also H.K. Wachanga, *The Swords of Kirinyaga: The Fight for Land and Freedom* (Kampala: East African Literature Bureau, 1975). Marshall Clough's monograph about the "Mau Mau Memoirs" is an important resource when reading these sources. Marshall Clough, *Mau Mau Memoirs: History, Memory,*

*and Politics* (Boulder, CO: Lynne Rienner, 1998).

19. Robert Buijtenhuijs, *Le mouvement "Mau-Mau": Une révolte paysanne et anticoloniale en Afrique Noire* (The Hague: Mouton, 1971). See also Robert Buijtenhuijs, *Mau Mau Twenty Years On: The Myth and the Survivors* (The Hague: Mouton, 1973).

20. Wunyabari Maloba, *Mau Mau and Kenya: An Analysis of a Peasant Revolt* (Bloomington: Indiana University Press, 1993).

21. Bethwell Ogot, ed., *Politics and Nationalism in Colonial Kenya* (Nairobi: East African Publishing House, 1972), 134-48.

22. Ngugi wa Thiong'o, *Ngaahika Ndeenda (I Will Marry When I Want)* (London: Heinemann, 1982 [1976]).

23. Ngugi wa Thiong'o and Micere Mugo, *The Trial of Dedan Kimathi* (London: Heinemann Educational Books, 1976). Ngugi also treated Mau Mau extensively in his novels, though in slightly less politically overt fashion. Ngugi wa Thiong'o, *Weep Not, Child* (London: Heinemann, 1964); Ngugi wa Thiong'o, *The River Between* (London: Heinemann, 1965); Ngugi wa Thiong'o, *A Grain of Wheat* (London: Heinemann, 1967); Ngugi wa Thiong'o, *Petals of Blood* (London: Heinemann, 1977).

24. Kathy Santilli, "Kikuyu Women in the Mau Mau Revolt: A Closer Look," *Ufahamu* 8 (1977): 143-59. Women have authored two memoirs about the conflict, but unfortunately both possess difficulties. Charity Waciuma's *Daughter of Mumbi* is written from a child's perspective, and Wambui Otieno's *Mau Mau's Daughter* is factually problematic. Wambui Otieno, *Mau Mau's Daughter: A Life History* (Boulder, CO: Lynne Rienner, 1998); Charity Waciuma, *Daughter of Mumbi* (Nairobi: East African Publishing House, 1969).

25. Tabitha Kanogo, "Kikuyu Women and the Politics of Protest: Mau Mau," in *Images of Women in Peace and War: Cross-Cultural and Historical Perspectives*, eds. Sharon MacDonald, Pat Holden, and Shirley Ardener (Madison: University of Wisconsin Press, 1987), 78-99; Cora Ann Presley, *Kikuyu Women, the Mau Mau Rebellion, and Social Change in Kenya* (Boulder, CO: Westview Press, 1992); Cora Ann Presley, "The Mau Mau Rebellion, Kikuyu Women and Social Change," *Canadian Journal of African Studies* 22 (1988): 502-27; Luise White, "Separating the Men from the Boys: Constructions of Gender, Sexuality, and Terrorism in Central Kenya," *International Journal of African Historical Studies* 23 (1990): 1-25. See also the fictional account, Muthoni Likimani, *Passbook Number F.47927: Women and Mau Mau in Kenya* (New York: Praeger Publishers, 1985), and the useful interviews on Kikuyu life in Jean Davison, *Voices from Mutira: Lives of Rural Gikuyu Women* (Boulder, CO: Lynne Rienner, 1989).

26. Frank Furedi, *The Mau Mau War in Perspective* (London: James Currey, 1989); Tabitha Kanogo, *Squatters and the Roots of Mau Mau, 1905-63* (Athens: Ohio University Press, 1987); David Throup, *Economic & Social*

*Orig ns of Mau Mau* (Athens: Ohio University Press, 1988).

27. John Lonsdale, "The Moral Economy of Mau Mau: Wealth, Pove rty & Civ ic Virtue in Kikuyu Political Thought," in *Unhappy Valley: Confli t in Ken ya and Africa, Book II: Violence and Ethnicity*, eds. Bruce Berma n and Jo in Lons dale (London: James Currey, 1992), 315-504.

28. Gree Kershaw, *Mau Mau from Below* (Athens: Ohio Unive sity Pre s, 1997).

29. Odhi ambo and Lonsdale, eds., *Mau Mau and Nationhood*, 6, 6. See al o Dere Peterson, *Creative Writing: Translation, Bookkeeping, a l the Wo rk of Im agination in Colonial Kenya* (Portsmouth, NH: Heineman , 2004).

30. Davi l Anderson, *Histories of the Hanged: The Dirty War in Ke ya and t e End f Empire* (New York: W.W. Norton, 2005); Caroline Elki , *Imper al Reck ning: The Untold Story of Britain's Gulag in Kenya* (New ' rk: Hen ry Holt, 2005).

31. And rson, *Histories*, 395. Though Robert Edgerton's quite pr blematic — but u nfairly forgotten—work provides some little known, usefu insights in a br ad account of the conflict. Robert Edgerton, *Mau Mau: n Afric n Cruc ible* (New York: The Free Press, 1989).

32. See, for instance, Susan Carruthers, "Being Beastly to the lau Mau," *Twen tieth Century British History* 16 (2005): 489-96.

33. Dere Peterson, "The Intellectual Lives of Mau Mau Detainees, *Journal of Afric n History* 49 (2008): 73-91.

34. John Blacker, "The Demography of Mau Mau: Fertility and I ortality in Ken a in the 1950s: A Demographer's Viewpoint," *African ffairs* 1 )6 (200 ): 205-27.

35. Huw Bennett, *Fighting the Mau Mau: The British Army and Co nter-Insi r-genc in the Kenya Emergency* (Cambridge: Cambridge Unive sity Pre s, 2013).

36. Dani l Branch, *Defeating Mau Mau, Creating Kenya: Countei nsurgen y, Civil War, and Decolonization* (Cambridge: Cambridge Unive sity Pre s, 2009).

37. Sana Aiyar, *Out of India: Diasporic Politics and Colonialis in Ken a* (Can bridge, MA: Harvard University Press, forthcoming 2015) Chapter 4; Julie MacArthur, "Between Loyalism and Dissent: Ethnic Imagi ing duri g the Mau Mau Rebellion" (paper presented at the 54th Annual M ting of t e Afric an Studies Association, Washington, DC, November 18, 2 1); Myl s Osbc rne, *Ethnicity and Empire in Kenya: Loyalty and Martial I ce amo g the K amba, c. 1800 to the Present* (New York: Cambridge Univ sity Pre s, 2014), 192-224.

38. Lott Hughes, "'Truth Be Told': Some Problems with Historic l Revisic n-ism i n Kenya," *African Studies* 70 (2011): 182-201.

39. Fred rick Cooper, "Review Article: Mau Mau and the Di courses of Decc lonization," *Journal of African History* 29 (1988): 313.

# Select Bibliography

## Primary Sources

Baldwin, William. *Mau Mau Man-Hunt: The Adventures of the Only American Who Has Fought the Terrorists in Kenya*. New York: Dutton, 1957.

Barnett, Donald, and Karari Njama. *Mau Mau from Within: Autobiography and Analysis of Kenya's Peasant Revolt*. London: Macgibbon and Kee, 1966.

Carothers, J.C. *The Psychology of Mau Mau*. Nairobi: Government Printer, 1954.

Corfield, F.D. *Historical Survey of the Origins and Growth of Mau Mau*. London: H.M.S.O., 1960.

Itote, Waruhiu. *"Mau Mau" General*. Nairobi: East African Publishing House, 1967.

Kariuki, J.M. *"Mau Mau" Detainee: The Account by a Kenya African of His Experiences in Detention Camps, 1953-1960*. London: Oxford University Press, 1963.

Kinyatti, Maina wa, ed. *Kenya's Freedom Struggle: The Dedan Kimathi Papers*. London: Zed Books, 1987.

Leakey, Louis. *Mau Mau and the Kikuyu*. London: Methuen, 1952.

Otieno, Wambui. *Mau Mau's Daughter: A Life History*. Boulder, CO: Lynne Rienner, 1998.

Ruark, Robert. *Something of Value*. Garden City, NJ: Doubleday, 1955.

Wachanga, H.K. *The Swords of Kirinyaga: The Fight for Land and Freedom*. Kampala: East African Literature Bureau, 1975.

## Secondary Sources

Anderson, David. *Histories of the Hanged: The Dirty War in Kenya and the End of Empire*. New York: W.W. Norton, 2005.

Atieno Odhiambo, E.S., and John Lonsdale, eds. *Mau Mau and Nationhood: Arms, Authority & Narration*. Oxford: James Currey, 2003.

Bennett, Huw. *Fighting the Mau Mau: The British Army and Counter-Insurgency in the Kenya Emergency*. Cambridge: Cambridge University Press, 2013.

Branch, Daniel. *Defeating Mau Mau, Creating Kenya: Counterinsurgency, Civil War, and Decolonization*. Cambridge: Cambridge University Press, 2009.

Clough, Marshall. *Mau Mau Memoirs: History, Memory, and Politics*. Boulder, CO: Lynne Rienner, 1998.

Elkins, Caroline. *Imperial Reckoning: The Untold Story of Britain's Gulag in Kenya*. New York: Henry Holt, 2005.

Hughes, Lotte. "'Truth Be Told': Some Problems with Historical Revisionism in Kenya." *African Studies* 70 (2011): 182-201.

Kanogo, Tabitha. *Squatters and the Roots of Mau Mau, 1905-1963*. London: James Currey, 1987.

Lonsdale, John. "The Moral Economy of Mau Mau: Wealth, Poverty & Civic Virtue in Kikuyu Political Thought." In *Unhappy Valley: Conflict in Kenya and Africa*, Book II: *Violence and Ethnicity*, edited by Bruce Berman and John Lonsdale, 315-504. London: James Currey, 1992.

_____. "Mau Maus of the Mind: Making Mau Mau and Remaking Kenya." *Journal of African History* 31 (1990): 393-421.

Maloba, Wunyabari. *Mau Mau and Kenya: An Analysis of a Peasant Revolt*. Bloomington: Indiana University Press, 1993.

Osborne, Myles. "The Kamba and Mau Mau: Ethnicity, Development, and Chiefship, 1952-1960." *International Journal of African Historical Studies* 43 (2010): 63-87.

Peterson, Derek. "The Intellectual Lives of Mau Mau Detainees." *Journal of African History* 49 (2008): 73-91.

Presley, Cora Ann. *Kikuyu Women, the Mau Mau Rebellion, and Social Change in Kenya*. Boulder, CO: Westview Press, 1992.

White, Luise. "Separating the Men from the Boys: Constructions of Gender, Sexuality, and Terrorism in Central Kenya." *International Journal of African Historical Studies* 23 (1990): 1-25.

CPSIA information can be obtained
at www.ICGtesting.com
Printed in the USA
FSHW011353051218
54264FS